SOE AND THE RESISTANCE

SOE and The Resistance
As told in *The Times*
Obituaries

EDITED BY
MICHAEL TILLOTSON

FOREWORD BY PROFESSOR
MICHAEL FOOT, CBE

continuum

Continuum International Publishing Group

The Tower Building	80 Maiden Lane
11 York Road	Suite 704
London	New York
SE1 7NX	NY 10038

www.continuumbooks.com

First published 2011
Reprinted 2011

British Library Cataloguing-in-Publication Data
A catalogue record for this book is available from the British Library.

ISBN: HB: 978-1-4411-1971-1

Typeset by Fakenham Prepress Solutions, Fakenham, Norfolk NR21 8NN
Printed and bound in Great Britain

Contents

List of Plates

Plates between pages 174 and 175

with a Montenegrin guerilla.

Page 6: Jedburgh Association sixtieth anniversary reunion at
Milton Hall on June 12/13, 2004: David Stern, Bob Keloe
(USA), Ron Brierley, Ken Brown, Dick Rubinstein, Don
Gibbs, Frank Bailey, Jack Grinham, Paul Aussaresses
(France), Arthur Brown, Bob Rogers, Jack Singlaub
(USA), Glyn Loosmore, Oswin Craster, Tom Carew, John
Sharp, Harry Verlander.

Lisa de Baissac.
Colonel John Davis.

Page 7: 'Troff' Trofimov with Karen fighters in Burma.
Peter Dobrée with Lieutenant Mohamed Nor bin Rani in
Malaya in 1945.

Page 8: George Fielding.
John Coates.
Andrew Croft.
Peter Kemp.

Foreword

Professor M. R. D. Foot, CBE

SOE was never a popular department in Whitehall. It was formed in a tearing hurry during the summer crisis of 1940, under Churchill's direct prompting, and many ministries were glad when Attlee wound it up early in 1946. It managed all the same to exercise a notable impact on the conduct of the war against the Axis, and has enriched the nation's stock of heroic legends, many of them true.

Public memory has taken in that it worked in France, in Holland (very badly) and in Yugoslavia; in fact, as the pages below help to show, it worked pretty well the world over, except in Soviet Russia and in Japan. What it did in Latin America, standing-by to counter pro-Axis sympathies, still remains largely unknown, but much of the rest of its story has become known in outline, and practically all its surviving papers are now in the National Archive at Kew.

Major-General Tillotson assembles here a selection of obituaries of former members of SOE; excluding of course those who died in action during the war, of whom there were too many, at a time when the mere existence of the service was forbidden to be mentioned on an unscrambled telephone. His book shows, among much else, the extraordinary social diversity of the agents and staff, some of them from very grand families, some from the proletariat. There was a young Polish countess, for instance, who used her friendship with the local skiing instructors to bring Polish officers out of Poland into Hungary in the autumn of 1939, with such success that the Polish authorities in exile assumed she must be working with German support; she survived to act as courier to Francis Cammaerts in south-eastern France in 1944 and to buy him out from the Germans who had captured him, There was a seventeen-year-old Breton railway clerk who provided for the RAF the timings of munition trains, so that they could be bombed; he went on to provide liaison between SOE and the SAS who organized Breton village resistance in June and July 1944.

All these agents were volunteers, and all were brave: it was no task for a coward to precipitate oneself, usually by parachute and therefore quite alone, into territory held not only by a hostile army but also by one of the most barbarous police forces known to history. Too many agents went straight to their deaths, received on their dropping zones by forewarned Gestapo who had broken the simple ciphers used to arrange the drops; no *Times* obituaries for them.

That SOE was active in the Far East as well as in Europe is not as widely remembered as it deserves to be. A great many agents who had already done a stint in occupied territory in Europe volunteered to endanger themselves yet again, in Burma or Malaya or Siam, as Thailand was then known. Sydney Hudson, for instance, who was arrested within a fortnight of reaching Vichy France in 1942, escaped in January 1944, parachuted back into France in May with a girl courier (who is still with us) to earn a DSO running a circuit round Le Mans, and volunteered for a third sortie, this time into Burma, before the first two nuclear weapons used in anger brought the war to an abrupt end.

Like half the war cabinet, SOE was not privy to ultra-secret intelligence. Being outside the ultra loop did it little harm. From inside the loop, it was clear that SOE had been pursuing a misguided policy in Yugoslavia, and on Churchill's order it dropped Mihailovic and supported Tito, thus further exasperating the Germans and killing more of them. Had it not been for SOE's support, Tito's struggle to seize power would have been much more difficult; his intention to set up a communist regime after the war did not deflect SOE from helping him to drive out the Germans. Across the frontier in Greece, SOE was supporting right-wing guerillas against the communist-backed guerillas of ELAS, thus helping to save Greece from communist domination in the late nineteen-forties. Such political complications were seldom visible to the agents 'in the field', dealing with the day-to-day exasperations of life in totalitarian states; but they weighed on the senior staff officers, several of whom also get attention below: above all, Colin Gubbins, hailed by Gladwyn Jebb when he left SOE early in 1942 to go back to the

Foreign Office as already the organization's lynch-pin. Gubbins steered SOE through to help secure victory over the axis – to find his whole organization closed down, by bureaucratic fiat, and his own military prospects sharply diminished due to being so long outside the strictly military swim.

One at least of SOE's operations earns it a place in the history of the war. Codenamed *Gunnerside*, it was carried out by nine Norwegians who between them scuppered Hitler's effort to make an atomic bomb. One of the lives below is that of Knut Haukelid, who followed up SOE's successful attack on a heavy water plant west of Oslo that had baffled the RAF, the commandos and the USAAF. Haukelid sank in a lake a hundredweight of heavy water that had escaped SOE's attention. Heisenberg, the scientist in charge of the German project, told his chiefs of staff that it would take him three more years at least to build a bomb. In that case, they said, forget it; the Fuehrer would rather that you worked on jet engines; so Hitler had no devastating bomb.

These obituaries speak clearly enough for themselves. In Michael Tillotson they have found an editor who can place them, with a general's overseeing eye, in their places in the strategy of the war; and their reader can at once satisfy the desire for knowledge and enjoy the spectacle of great secret feats of arms.

M. R. D. Foot

Introduction

The capitulation of France in June 1940 left Britain bereft of allies, other than the Commonwealth countries and the valiant Poles who had escaped the dual violation of their country by Hitler and Stalin. The coastline of continental Europe lay under German control from the North Cape to the Pyrenees; the victorious enemy was concentrating across the Channel and the Luftwaffe attacks on our airfields and ports were daily more frequent. The army evacuated from Dunkirk had little more than their personal weapons to repulse the threatened invasion. Only the Royal Navy and RAF Fighter Command stood between Britain and disaster.

On seizing the helm as the new Premier on 10 May 1940, Winston Churchill gave an order to Dr Hugh Dalton, the Minister for Economic Warfare, to 'Set Europe ablaze'. The idea was not entirely new. Thought had already been given by the earlier administration, as the fall of France appeared increasingly likely, for a structure to be devised 'to co-ordinate all action, by way of subversion and sabotage, against the enemy overseas.'

Conscious perhaps even more than the citizens of the countries under Nazi domination of the dangers and ignominy facing them, Churchill assumed that they would be simmering with resentment and determination to attack and harass their tormentors. In that expectation he ordered SOE into immediate action. Neither he nor the series of Ministers he appointed to drive this project forward anticipated how long it would take to achieve any worthwhile results, nor the obstacles their efforts would encounter. In occupied Europe his call to arms met with mixed reactions.

The German invasions of Poland, Denmark, Norway, Belgium, Holland and northern France had been conducted with terrifying efficiency, coining the term *Blitzkrieg* – lightning war – leaving their civilian populations disorientated and leaderless. Even so, some defiant patriots, perceiving the British Isles as the only bastion against Nazi tyranny, made their way there, providing an invaluable indigenous manpower source; but the instinct of the majority was self-preservation. In France, inland from the Atlantic coast and south of the Loire – the region unoccupied under the armistice agreement – it was generally accepted that the war was over, France had been defeated and Britain must soon seek terms.

This general antipathy to new risks in the countries of occupied Europe was not immediately apparent to those responsible for recruiting, training and motivating volunteers for SOE 'duties of a hazardous nature'. The basic requirements were fluency in a European language and, ideally, some familiarity with the country concerned. To this was added the self-confidence to act alone in a hostile environment and the self-discipline to adhere to security rules protecting operational plans, one's SOE comrades and local Resistance workers and – vitally – the communications back to SOE's main headquarters in London's Baker Street.

Following practice of the Security Service MI 5 and Secret Intelligence Service MI 6, the more senior recruits, including those to the headquarters staff, were often individuals known to and trusted by those already working for SOE. The agents, of which there were eventually thousands, were recruited either by systematic trawls through enlistment entries of servicemen or the MI 5 reception centre at the Royal Victoria Patriotic School at Wandsworth, where all escapees from occupied Europe were screened. Agents were commissioned into their own regiment if they had one, otherwise into the General Service Corps. Radio operators recruited from the Royal Armoured Corps or the Royal Signals were granted the rank of sergeant and the women, required chiefly as radio operators or couriers – although many rose well above that role in a crisis – were commissioned into their own service or enlisted into the First Aid Nursing Yeomanry (FANY), with officer status.

Training was intensive and monitored throughout so that recruits who lacked initiative, talked or drank too freely or revealed inadequate moral fibre could be weeded out before they became liabilities. They were first subjected to careful scrutiny in one of several requisitioned country houses in England, one for each country in which SOE planned to inspire subversion and sabotage. Those who survived this process went on to Arisaig, in the western highlands of Scotland, where they were taught to live off the countryside, handle small boats, rock climbing, sabotage using plastic explosives, the use of small arms and methods of silent killing. The comfortable accommodation in what had been a luxury hotel and a convivial atmosphere were intended to build a sense of camaraderie.

Graduates from what was known as Group A training at Arisaig moved to Altrincham near Manchester for parachute training at Ringway airport. From there, it was to Beaulieu in the New Forest for their enlightenment: they were to become secret agents. Induction to the world of passwords, cut-outs and security rules essential for success in clandestine missions began. Subsequently the successful were tested individually by a rigorous three-day exercise in the form of a notional attack on a real target in some nearby town. This stage also covered the organization of the German armed forces. Those destined to be radio operators then went to Thame Park in Oxfordshire for intensive training on the equipment they would operate using Morse code for transmissions. The would-be saboteurs went to Brickendonbury in Hertfordshire to be taught industrial sabotage.

While at Beaulieu, it was made clear to all trainees that their activities in enemy occupied territory had no place in the established tenets of war and, if captured, they had no protection under the Geneva Conventions. They could expect interrogation under torture and execution, under Hitler's order that anyone caught working against his interests behind the battlefronts, even in uniform, would 'receive the severest treatment'.

Despite the enthusiasm of the small SOE staff and the majority of the volunteer agents, it took a long time before any concrete results became apparent. Always eager to see the results from initiatives he had ordered, Churchill pressed the SOE leadership so hard that a few hastily planned and riskily executed operations against Continental coastal installations were made, usually with an outcome scarcely commensurate with the casualties sustained. As may be imagined, there were stresses and strains within the Baker Street headquarters. The organization had no established structure or proven working practices as had MI 5 and MI 6 which, although still non-attributable so far as the press and public were concerned, had been formed on the eve of the First World War with the experiences of that conflict on which to draw.

Relations between SOE and other secret organizations operating in enemy occupied territory were a constant source of concern.

Relations with MI 5 were good, as were those with MI 9 – the staff responsible for communication with prisoners of war and aiding escape attempts, each SOE country section having a sub-section dealing specifically with MI 9. In contrast, MI 6 was apprehensive that SOE – enthusiastic amateurs with a mission to create havoc in the areas its own agents were establishing systematic sources of intelligence – would be operating against its interests. This led to SOE having to receive communications from its own agents in the field through an MI 6 filter, a mechanism that imposed delay and fostered mistrust until it was abandoned in 1942.

The national intelligence agencies of the occupied countries, which formed Governments in exile in London, also posed difficulties for SOE and in some instances for MI 6 as well. Defeated yet proudly defiant, their leaders understandably demanded a say in what was to be attempted in their occupied territories. While arguably right in principle, this carried a risk to the security of operations. The French and Belgians in particular were concerned that the wholesale delivery of arms to resistance groups could lead to civil war between rival adherents of the political right and left when the Allies eventually liberated their countries from Nazi control.

Before any SOE agents reached occupied Europe, a number of *ad hoc* escape lines had been set up in the autumn of 1940 to facilitate the escape of soldiers left behind after the evacuation of the British Expeditionary Force, airmen shot down while on operations and local patriots who wished to continue the struggle against Nazism. Some were run by Belgians, others by Poles but predominantly by Frenchmen and -women. Most led to Marseilles or the Pyrenees, but in the early stages a few ran through Brittany and the shortest available sea crossing to England.

Success in forming circuits in France encouraged the practice in Norway and Denmark and in the Low Countries, with starkly varied results. Aside from the mountainous region of Norway, the geography and population density of these countries restricted clandestine operations. Security of intentions proved difficult, as in such small populations everyone knew almost everyone else in their social milieu – and their business. SOE achieved a striking success against the German atomic bomb programme heavy water project in Norway, but only qualified success elsewhere.

The German invasions of Yugoslavia and Greece in April 1941 opened up the Balkans for SOE. The Allied invasion of French

North Africa in November 1942 made available Italy and the western Mediterranean for operations controlled from the SOE *Massingham* headquarters in Algiers, later moved forward to Bari in Italy. All these operations, and in Yugoslavia most significantly, encountered political factionalism among the resistance fighters with consequent difficult choices to make.

An initiative taken to limit either factionalism or overenthusiasm from interfering with the Allied invasion of Normandy in June 1944 involved the insertion of agents in uniform. This was done using three-man teams codenamed 'Jedburghs', usually comprising an American or British leader, a French speaker familiar with the country and a radio operator. They were dropped by parachute into selected areas of France with the specific aim of making contact with the local Resistance leaders. Once the *bona fides* of the latter had been assured and there appeared to be little chance that their followers would use any weapons provided for activities against the legitimate French authorities, the Jedburgh team would call for an air drop of arms and explosives, train the Resistance fighters in their use and embark on a programme of industrial and railway network sabotage as directed by Baker Street.

Some Jedburgh teams joined already established SOE circuits or relied upon them to put them in contact with Resistance groups. In the main, they were to prove successful in their missions although some met with disaster. They wore uniform to emphasize that they were not 'spies', although this did not necessarily provide any protection if captured.

When making his report on the campaign for the liberation of France, the Allied Supreme Commander, General Dwight D Eisenhower, equated the contribution of the French Resistance movements, despite their political diversity, to the equivalent of six divisions. While SOE provided aid or guidance to only a proportion of them, significant credit for that is due.

Throughout this period and until the defeat of the Japanese in August 1945, the SOE arm in South East Asia – Force 136 – with its headquarters in India and later in Ceylon maintained contacts with agents in Burma, Indo-China, Malaya, Sumatra, Thailand and elsewhere in the region. The geography of the region imposed difficulties for the insertion and recovery of agents far beyond those encountered in Europe, resulting, for example, in the uncertainty of submarine rendezvous on isolated beaches. Radio communications were also much less reliable than in Europe, due in part to the

mountainous terrain and the difficulties in maintaining the radios
and charging the batteries under jungle conditions.

Successes were achieved in Burma and Malaya, especially by
some Jedburgh teams on their redeployment to the Far East on
completion of their missions in France. Partisan groups were raised
and armed and operated under SOE leadership against Japanese
lines of communication. Those in Burma in particular fought
bravely and to good effect.

The selection of *Times* obituaries for inclusion in this book has
been restricted by two unavoidable limitations. Many SOE agents
whose conduct in the field would certainly have merited their
inclusion died on active service and – for security reasons – no
obituary could be published.

Others of equal merit are fortunately still alive. A number of
obituaries of agents who have died since the war were surprisingly
brief or lacking in detail on the operations in which they took part.
This is due to restrictions on what information was in the public
domain at the time of publication of the obituaries, rather than to
any lack of appreciation of individual bravery and accomplishments.
Consequently, an effort has been made to alleviate such omissions in
the text introducing or commenting on these obituaries.

Despite these limitations, it has been possible to present a
relatively balanced account – through the obituaries – of SOE
operations in France, Italy, the Mediterranean, Scandinavia, the
Balkans and the Far East. Sadly, this cannot be said for Belgium and
Holland, as SOE operations in Belgium had only limited success
and the circuits in Holland were comprehensively penetrated by the
German Army intelligence, so that new agents parachuted into the
arms of the enemy, were handed over to the Gestapo and given the
option of co-operation or death. Some died in appalling circumstances but wartime security restrictions denied them an obituary,
other than in their personal file at SOE headquarters.

Chapter 11 on 'Speculative Ventures' explains the intriguing
attempts to find and establish co-operative contact with opposition
or resistance groups in countries that had joined Germany in the
Axis alliance, for example Hungary and Romania, or to establish
them there. The courage of the agents undertaking these forlorn
hopes was indeed remarkable. Some members of SOE served in
more than one theatre of operations, but in order to present their
obituaries as a whole their full wartime story has been told on just
one occasion.

Readers will note the number of women whose obituaries are included or whose service with SOE is mentioned where no obituary is available. This is not an attempt to present a gender-balanced account but to reflect the significant role undertaken by women in SOE operations. Although originally recruited as couriers – women being thought less conspicuous than men – or as radio operators, a role in which they were conspicuously successful, many showed magnificent courage and resource when thrown on their own devices in dire emergency, some becoming circuit leaders.

This book could not have been attempted without the trenchant support of *The Times*, in particular that of Ian Brunskill, editor of The Register section of the newspaper, Rose Wild in charge of the *Times Archive* and the enthusiastic help in seeking out obituaries and photographs – when dates of death or other aids to search were obscure – from Melissa van der Klugt and Fiona Wilson of *The Times* Obituaries Department.

For use of photographs from their archives, my grateful thanks are due to the Director-General of the Imperial War Museum, Ivor Kraglund of the National History Museum, Oslo, the President of the Special Forces Club and Clive Bassett of the Jedburgh Association. My thanks are also recorded here for the patience and care taken in the preparation and production of this book by Robin Baird Smith and the Staff of Continuum International Publishing Group Limited and David Defew, Kim Storry and my copy editor, Erika Cox, all of Fakenham Prepress Solutions.

Michael Tillotson

1

Structure and Communications

In an age where the establishment of a new Government Ministry is seemingly achieved almost overnight, it may be thought that the impetus of wartime ensured SOE was established quickly. In fact, the cabinet instruction was implemented only with considerable difficulty and amid controversy. It was the stated opinion of Dr Hugh (later Lord) Dalton, the first Cabinet minister to be given oversight of the project in his wider capacity of Minister of Economic Warfare, that, 'the war from within was more likely to be better conducted by civilians than by soldiers.'

Whether this was a matter of carefully considered opinion or an example of the unfortunately still prevalent view of many politicians and intellectuals that soldiers lack intelligence – otherwise why do they chose such a financially unrewarding and inherently dangerous profession – it is now impossible to say.

Civilians certainly had a significant hand in getting the project under way and many of the more successful agents in the field were drawn from the world of business. That said, it was not until a professional soldier was appointed Executive Director in 1943 that the organization began to run as smoothly as could be expected in a structure where the demands for secrecy were constantly at odds with those for detailed planning and consequent efficiency.

These conflicting requirements also inhibited the choice of location for SOE's London headquarters. A need to be as close as possible to the decision-makers of Westminster and Whitehall led to search for premises in St James's Street but this came to nothing and the more remote site of 64 Baker Street was selected with the cover name of the 'Inter-Services Research Bureau.' The title was not just bounced off the wall at the time, as the genesis of SOE is to be found in a pre-war branch of Military Intelligence in the War

1

Office entitled MI R, the 'R' being for Research. Its first chief was Lieutenant-Colonel J. F. C. Holland, an acknowledged expert in counter-irregular warfare in Ireland and India. While Baker Street was to remain the centre of SOE control and planning throughout the war, many other buildings in London and establishments elsewhere were used to interview potential recruits, for training them, for preparing agents for dispatch and for equipment design and testing.

Winston Churchill's choice of Hugh Dalton as the first Cabinet Minister responsible for the supervision of SOE was curious, as he is reputed to have both disliked and distrusted him, but Dalton's role as Minister for Economic Warfare gave him prior claim. Churchill was determined that SOE should not be encumbered by the bureaucracy of the War Office or the prejudice of the military hierarchy against the unorthodox. He also wished to keep his finger on the pulse of SOE and so arranged for the early Executive Directors to be men who could be trusted to be both innovative and energetic. The first was Sir Frank Nelson, a former businessman and Conservative Member of Parliament, under whom the command and control structure of SOE was developed, although not without a good deal of interdepartmental and personal infighting.

Nelson was succeeded by Sir Charles Hambro, a former Head of SOE's Scandinavian Section, until in September 1943 a professional soldier already working within SOE and an experienced expert on guerilla warfare was chosen.

Major-General Sir Colin Gubbins, KCMG, DSO, MC
(Obituary *The Times* February 12, 1976)

Major-General Sir Colin Gubbins, wartime leader of the Special Operations Executive, died yesterday at the age of 79. SOE was the mainspring of armed resistance in northern, western and southern Europe and in south-east Asia; and Gubbins has been well described as the mainspring of SOE.

Colin McVean Gubbins, a pure Scot by descent, was born in Tokyo, where his father was serving in the British legation, in 1896. He went from Cheltenham to Woolwich, and was commissioned in the Royal Artillery in 1914. He fought through the First World war on the Western Front, being awarded the MC, was wounded and promoted Major by 1917, and was a Brigade Major in Ireland during the Troubles. Here he got his first experience of irregular warfare;

its power impressed him. He spent part of the 1920s and 1930s on intelligence duties in the War Office, and in the spring of 1939 joined an old friend, Major J. F. C. Holland, in an obscure department there called MI R which examined the methods of guerilla warfare.

He made a reconnaissance of the states on Germany's eastern border in the spring; and wrote that summer three short pamphlets on partisan war and sabotage, of which hundreds of thousands of copies – in appropriate translations – were soon to be distributed all over German-occupied Europe by the RAF. Just before the war began, he left for Poland as chief of staff to Carton de Wiart's abortive mission.

He escaped from the Polish disaster, and headed an MI R mission to the Poles and Czechs in Paris; whence Holland withdrew him in April 1940 to command the independent companies in Norway.

These companies, small forces of shock troops later expanded into the first commandos, exercised a slight braking influence on the German advance. Gubbins was one of the few people to enhance his reputation in the Norwegian campaign; he was appointed DSO on return. His next task was more secret and still more difficult; he had to organize the small, secure parties of saboteurs who would stay behind the German lines in England, should the anticipated invasion take place, to disrupt the German communications and headquarters. By November the invasion danger had receded, and Hugh Dalton was able to secure his services for SOE.

Here he joined the governing council with the rank of Brigadier, as director of operations and training, with the symbol 'M'. Gubbins infused large parts of the organization with his own courage, tenacity, and will to beat the Germans. He kept up his relations with the Poles – SOE's Polish sections were under his command, and Sikorski was his personal friend – and it was he who set up the RF (République Française) liaison section to work with de Gaulle's Free French, who SOE had so far tried on Foreign Office advice to cold-shoulder. He made so strong an impression on his colleagues, superiors and subordinates that he was promoted Major-General in the summer of 1943, and that autumn was advanced by Lord Selborne to be executive head of the whole organization as 'D'.

Gubbins's task was as much diplomatic and political as military; he was in constant touch with the exiled allied governments in London, Algiers, and Cairo. Though his personal identity was kept a secret at agent level within SOE, he was able to set and maintain the stamp of his leadership on the organization; and he carries the credit, as well as the responsibility, for several outstanding operations by SOE. These included the arming and inspiring of the main bodies of Norwegian, French and Italian resistance; the original arming of Tito's partisans; several interesting coups against the Japanese; and above all, the creation all over occupied Europe of a willingness to resist the nazi invader that unsettled the German's rear areas, sapped their troops' morale, and caused significant drains on their manpower. In France alone, SOE's effort – with less than 2,000 agents deployed – was reckoned by Eisenhower as worth half a dozen divisions; and SOE's work undoubtedly shortened the war.

Gubbins, who was made CMG in 1944, was advanced to KCMG in 1946; he retired when SOE was disbanded in that year. He also held 14 foreign decorations, from all the principal Allied powers except the USSR.

He worked in London for many years as a textile merchant, and was assiduous in attending celebrations of past SOE successes; but he preferred to live in his Hebridean home. He was twice married, and leaves a son, whose elder brother was killed in action in 1944.

(He died on February 11, 1976, aged 79).

The operations planned and executed by SOE raised demands for a wide range of new equipment for sabotage and inserting agents into enemy-occupied territory. A special research department, known as Station IX, was established to undertake the work of design and testing of such items. George Ingham Brown was an example of a civilian drawn into its work.

George Ingham Brown
(Obituary *The Times* July 14, 2010)

A chemist with a degree from Magdalen College, Oxford, when called up in 1942 George Brown was initially destined to work in the army's gas warfare section. Wishing to avoid further unexciting work trying to improve the efficiency of the army gas mask on which he had been engaged while at Oxford, he volunteered to work for the Special Operations Executive and was snapped up by their Research Section, known as Station IX, situated at the Thatched Barn, an old road house on the Barnet bypass.

The work of Station IX concerned the design and manufacture of aids to SOE agents in German-occupied Europe in their role of sabotage and subversion – and also objects that might contribute to the undermining of German morale. Before embarking on any of that, Brown was required to complete the agents course of fieldcraft and survival, parachuting and the use of explosives for the industrial and communications sabotage, just in case he was called on to exercise his inventive aptitude in continental Europe or in the Far East against the Japanese.

He began work at Station IX with experiments on new methods of train derailment but was then directed to testing the electrically operated submersible canoe, known as the 'Sleeping Beauty'. This was a piece of equipment designed to meet a requirement set by the Combined Operations staff early in 1942. Brown was instructed to subject the craft to exhaustive tests in Staines reservoir. A photograph of him taken at the time revealed a figure emerging from the water in a diving suit looking rather like the man in the well-known Michelin advertisement. Although proved successful in practice voyages as a means of carrying an explosive device silently to the hull of a stationary enemy vessel, both occasions when it was used operationally were unsuccessful. A raid against Maaløy Island off the south-west coast of Norway and a second against shipping in Trondheim fjord, both in September 1944, ran into difficulties unforeseen by the planners and had to be abandoned. Extreme cold water conditions later that year precluded further attempts.

The technique was transferred to Australia, from where SOE attacks were being launched against the Japanese forces and their supporting shipping in South-East Asia, with Brown being sent to provide the benefit of his experience. Originally based in Melbourne, he was moved to the Australian Army advanced base on Morotai Island close to the equator. Later, he experimented with explosive charges by sinking a Chinese junk in Darwin harbour, which has a high rise and fall of tide. Attaching charges at high tide and recovering the vessel at low tide after it had been sunk, he was able to repeat his experiments until satisfied with each technique.

George Ingham Brown was born in Standish, Lincolnshire, and educated at Kingswood School, Bath, and at Magdalen College, Oxford. On demobilization, he was invited to teach Chemistry at Eton but considered the text books he had used at school difficult and out of date, so he wrote his own. His *Introduction to Chemistry*, Longmans 1952, had world-wide sales of around a million, with translations into Malay, Japanese, Czech, Hindi and Punjabi. Basing his method on the principles of Valency Theory – considered very forward-looking at the time – he enjoyed significant influence on the teaching of his subject.

He became a housemaster at Eton in 1956 and was Chairman of Committees for five years under Michael McCrum's headmastership, including the not-sought-after chair of the central feeding committee over a period of some 15 years. His calm was tested but proved when someone threw a bomb through his window and again when some adventurous Etonians fired a charge of debris at Manor House from the Crimean gun in Cannon Yard, having possibly acquired the means to get the ancient gun to fire from some aspect of his teaching of chemistry.

A letter of condolence sent to his widow after his death described him as 'A wonderful beak who radiated common sense, knowledge and wisdom in such a natural and easy-going manner and who created so much joy.' He had a lifelong preoccupation with crosswords and he and his wife would seldom pass a day without completing the one set in *The Times*.

He retired from teaching in 1985 and after living in Datchet for a while settled in Eton in 1993, occupying a converted flat in the Boat House. He continued with his writing but moved away from text books onto general scientific subjects publishing, first, *The Guinness History of Inventions*, then *The Big Bang: A History of Explosives*, *A Biography of Count Rumford and Invisible Rays: A History of Radioactivity*. (Rumfold was the American inventor of the Rumfold fireplace and created a count under the aegis of the Holy Roman Empire taking his title from his hometown in New Hampshire). A BBC documentary is to be based on his *Big Bang* but none of his later books achieved the acclaim or distribution of his *Introduction to Chemistry*. He married Barbara Earnshaw in 1944, who survives him with two daughters.

(He died on May 24, 2010 aged 90).

The training of SOE agents demanded special arrangements, facilities and instructors and an early step in this key area of provision was the establishment of a school of sabotage in Hertfordshire. One of the successful students was Victor Hazan, who was launched on an operational mission that evolved into one of training saboteurs in the area of potential operations.

Major Victor Hazan, MBE
(Obituary *The Times* December 8, 2006)

Recruited into the Special Operations Executive for his linguistic ability and familiarity with the region around Bordeaux, Victor Hazan was parachuted into Vichy–controlled France in 1942 to undertake a task for which he was temperamentally quite unsuited.

SOE agents sent earlier had built up circuits of local agents as opportunities allowed, inevitably with a number of territorial overlaps. Hazan's assignment was to sort out demarcation disputes and impress upon the circuit organizers the importance of strict compliance with directives from SOE headquarters in London. A scholarly and mild-mannered man, Hazan found himself shouted down or circumvented, so he turned his hand to something he was good at: training saboteurs.

After his parachute descent in early May 1942, he had, without much success, tried to impose some better co-ordination between the organizers of SOE circuits as widely dispersed as Clermont-Ferrand, Lyons and Montpellier. Fortunately, he had been a student of George Rheam, instructor in sabotage techniques at the SOE school in Hertfordshire, and knew where best to place explosives to inflict maximum damage to machinery, communications or railway systems. Volunteers were readily available for training but few had any knowledge of military equipment beyond the rifles they had used as conscripts in the French Army. Hazan was among the first to provide them with sound training in the use of plastic explosives.

The *Carte* circuit straggled uncertainly from the Lot to Les Bouches de Rhône. Avoiding its organizer, whom he had already found difficult, he established contact with the circuit's sub-agents and trained about 90 instructors in demolition techniques and Sten sub-machinegun handling during the winter of 1942-43. By this stage the RAF was supplying Sten guns to the Resistance by airdrop, virtually wholesale. (This simple, automatic weapon was cheap to manufacture but imperfect finish or careless handling could cause accidents).

Although the *Carte* circuit was to disintegrate through no fault of his, the instructors Hazan had taught were snapped up by adjacent circuits to make worthwhile contributions to sabotage and mayhem after Germany occupied the whole of France, following Operation *Torch*, the Allied landings in North Africa in November 1942.

Transferring his expertise to the *Spindle* circuit operating around Annecy, Hazan continued training French instructors until *Spindle* had to be wound up and it agents dispersed after a security fiasco at St-Jorioz, on the western shore of Lake Annecy. He and Adolphe Rabinovitch, a young Russo-Egyptian radio operator, closed down the circuit and literally headed for the hills, in this case the Pyrenees.

After taking a train to the foothills, the pair crossed the mountains on foot above the snow line and descended into Spain the hands of the Spanish police. They were interned in a fortress prison at Barbastro, in Huesca, then in a concentration camp for Allied escapers at Miranda de Ebro, south of Bilbao, until the British Embassy negotiated their release and return to England via Gibraltar.

Having signally failed in the mission he had been sent to France by SOE to perform, Hazan turned his talents to more practical issues that, in the final analysis, undoubtedly proved more useful. He was appointed MBE for his services, having not actually engaged the enemy at first hand, but France honoured him with the Croix de Guerre.

Victor Hyam Hazan was born in 1915 in Southport, Lancashire, the son of Lazaar Hazan, a cotton and shipping merchant. He accompanied his parents to Casablanca in the 1920s, eventually attending Rabat University. His father's links with Bordeaux took him there as a young man to read for his licencié ès letters (bachelor of arts).

On his father's death, he returned to his mother's birth-place of Manchester to teach French at the Berlitz School and the Manchester High School of Commerce. He was commissioned into the South Lancashire Regiment and served briefly with the 2nd Battalion before joining SOE.

After return from France in 1944, he went to Egypt to work in the psychological warfare department of GHQ in Cairo. Subsequently, he was the British Vice-Consul in Djibouti for two years before joining the Nato language service for translating work.

His wife Evelyn, whom he married in 1944, survives him with two sons and two daughters. His son, Raymond, blinded by a parcel bomb while serving with the Army in Northern Ireland, is president of St Dunstan's and of the International Congress of War Blinded Associations.

(He died on November 6, 2006, aged 91).

In the early days of SOE operations agents were delivered onto enemy territory mainly by sea, as the landing point could be precisely – or almost precisely – determined, but there were significant drawbacks. Submarines were ideal provided the landing beach shelved sufficiently steeply to allow an approach close inshore and the surf not so strong as to overturn the inflatable dinghy required for the final leg of the transfer. The Royal Navy was reluctant, however, to risk a valuable vessel of war unless the operation could be shown to be more than speculative, which was seldom the case in the early days. Nevertheless, submarines were used when appropriate.

This situation led SOE to seek cheaper and possibly expendable craft of its own. The former RAF seaplane tender No. 360 operating out of the Helford river, west of Falmouth, was an early acquisition, shortly to be joined by a French tunnyman, six other smaller fishing vessels – including one long-liner – and a motor-trawler. Commander Gerard Holdsworth, RNVR assembled and controlled the operations of this fleet mainly to the Brittany coast until he was transferred to the Mediterranean theatre and relieved by another RNVR officer, Bevil Warrington-Smith. Regrettably no

obituary for Warrington-Smith was published by *The Times* and
Holdsworth's in Chapter 5 deals only briefly with support for SOE
agents into northern and central France.

Another deterrent to the seaborne delivery of SOE agents into
France was the German-imposed *zone-interdite* established along
the full extent of the Channel and Atlantic coasts and diligently
patrolled day and night. Although this zone was penetrated
many times by agents entering and leaving France, it was an
additional hazard to be avoided whenever possible. That said,
a brisk exchange of incoming agents for refugees and escaped
prisoners was conducted between Gibraltar and the rocky inlets of
the south coast of France using *feluccas* captained by Lieutenants
Jan Buchowski and Marian Krajewski of the Polish Navy. Between
them they landed 52 passengers for SOE and brought out three
groups of evaders and escaped prisoners in eleven round voyages
from Gibraltar. Both won DSOs but did not receive obituaries in
The Times, although Buchowski featured in a report of 1 June
1943, when Polish Lieutenant Ludomin Cienski was acquitted of
his murder in a dispute over Cienski's wife.

The sea was the predominant means of SOE's communications
with Scandinavia throughout the war, although parachute drop
was used with striking success in the attack on the heavy water
plant in Norway that Germany had appropriated for their atomic
weapons development programme, as we shall see in Chapter 3.
The difficulties of operating in sparsely populated Norway predi-
cated that virtually all SOE agents there were Norwegian, but
they had to be supplied and regularly relieved. For this a small
fleet of Norwegian-manned vessels was assembled and many
daring deliveries and recoveries made. As with cross-Channel
operations, with the exception of Quartermaster Leif Larsen (see
Chapter 3), the survivors among the skippers did not feature on
the obituary pages of *The Times*. This may be due to the fact
that they were Norwegian rather than British heroes.

Mediterranean access to southern Europe was fully exploited
by SOE, with Cairo and later Algiers attempting to keep control
over the wide range of craft plying to and fro to the south of
France, Greece, Albania and Yugoslavia delivering and collecting
agents. Until the formation of the American and British 'Balkan
Air Force' based in Italy from 1944, when the parachuting of arms
and explosives to partisans became the norm, deliveries had to be
made by sea with varying degrees of success due to the vigilance

of the Luftwaffe and the hazards of carrying heavy loads inland to bases concealed in the mountains.

Delivery and extraction of agents to and from regions within range of aircraft based in the south of England, and in Algiers after the Allied invasion of French North Africa in November 1942, became a highly developed and increasingly used method. RAF Special Duties squadrons were formed for inserting agents by parachute or air-landing, delivery of arms and explosives to resistance fighters and the pick-up of agents or individuals any SOE section was anxious to evacuate from danger.

The skill required to navigate to improvised landing strips laid out and manned by the partisans, putting down safely and returning to England or North Africa cannot be better demon-strated than by the obituary of Group Captain Hugh Verity, who flew many of those missions.

Group Captain Hugh Verity, DSO and Bar, DFC
(Obituary *The Times* November 19, 2001)

The heroism of wartime Special Operations Executive agents has been rather better publicized than that of the Royal Air Force pilots who delivered then into occupied France and recovered some of the survivors. Operations flying agents into France using the single-engined Westland Lysander monoplane were run by Verity during the whole of 1943. Others had pioneered the techniques but he refined and perfected them, regulating his flights by the cycle of the moon.

A directive from the British Chiefs of Staff of May 1942 instructed SOE to build up and equip paramilitary organi-zations in the area of projected operations in western Europe. In France, the priority was to establish contact with the *Maquis* resistance movement – itself subject to some unhelpful internal rivalries – and prepare the more promising of its groups to sabotage the road and rail communications the German Army would need to reinforce their divisions facing the Allied bridgehead when the invasion was launched in Normandy in June 1944.

The Lysander had advantage over delivery of agents by parachute in that it ensured pin-point accuracy. Designed in the 1930s as an Army co-operation and reconnaissance aircraft, its short take-off and landing capability at around 80 mph and robust fixed undercarriage allowed it to put down on rough ground and, when fitted with an external fuel tank, its range was extended to 900 miles. The pilot also navigated and the rear compartment was modified to take two or, uncomfortably, three passengers.

In the period before he took over the Lysander flight of 161 Squadron RAF, pilot casualties had been sustained through what Verity assessed as an inadequately professional approach to a particularly exacting flying technique. He was determined to put this right yet he came to the task after, in his own words. 'a very unsuccessful year trying to be a night fighter pilot'. But he had accumulated invaluable night flying and navigation experience in that time and his quiet demeanour gave confidence to those around him. He also spoke fluent French.

Verity's flight flew from Tangmere airfield, near Chichester, where a cottage just outside the main gate of the airfield provided the pilot's with accommodation together with the privacy and security essential for such sensitive operations, The SOE and Secret Intelligence Service agents were delivered to the cottage to allow time to meet their pilots and familiarize themselves with the aircraft. The agents were not always on a first time mission, as it was usual to bring out any urgently needed for debriefing by the SOE's Baker Street headquarters.

Verity flew twenty-nine missions during 1943, using moonlight to navigate between several check points from the first landfall on the French coast through others perhaps an hour's flying time apart to the Loire and beyond. The final leg of only four or five minutes would be from a local landmark – a church or railway junction – down to the improvised landing ground, having first replied to a single Morse identifying letter flashed by a torch on the ground. Fires or flares were lit to illuminate the strip when the aircraft was heard approaching. After landing, the Lysander would be turned round at the end of the strip, taxied back to the point of touch down, turned into the direction of take off and, with engine running, the passengers would quickly climb out and the returnees scramble in. With no hitch, time on the ground would not exceed three minutes.

He had two narrow escapes from disaster during approach

flights. Once, while peering at his map to fix his position, he almost flew into a radio mast near Lyon. On another occasion, the field containing the landing strip had been ploughed since last seen by the *Maquis* leaving only a narrow strip of turf for landing. Returning one night to Tangmere with M. Jean Moulin, General de Gaulle's personal representative with the French resistance, he found the airfield shrouded in dense fog. Reckoning his wheels were just three feet above the runway, he cut the throttle only to feel the Lysander fall thirty feet and crash on the tarmac.

Luckily, neither pilot nor passenger was hurt. He apologized to Moulin in his always courteous French to be thanked equally courteously for having completed an 'agreeable flight'. For his calm courage flying what became known as 'l'avion de Londres', Verity received the DFC, the DSO and bar. His service to France was recognized by his appointment to le Légion d'Honneur and award of the *Croix de Guerre*.

Hugh Beresford Verity was born in Jamaica where his father was an Anglican clergyman. He was educated at Cheltenham, where he won a Laming Scolarship to Queen's College Oxford to read French and Spanish. His language ability attracted him to the foreign service but when war broke out during the summer vacation of 1939 he volunteered for RAF flying training.

While flying a Bristol Blenheim light bomber with Coastal Command in the autumn of 1940, engine trouble forced him to land in the Irish Republic where he was interned at The Curragh. Taking advantage of his guards celebrating their success at a race meeting, he made his escape and took a train to Belfast. This ensured his swift return to active service but his wife's Irish relatives long refused to meet him in the mistaken belief that he had broken his parole.

After command of the Lysander squadron he returned to the staff in 1944 to work in the air operations branch of SOE on deception measures for the Normandy invasion. These included flying twice as many sorties into France north of the Havre, rather than to the west, to give the impression that the invasion would be on that coast. He was granted a regular commission in the RAF after the war and commanded Number 541 Photographic Reconnaissance

Squadron, Number 96 Meteor Fighter Squadron and, in the early 1960s, the major RAF base at Akrotiri in Cyprus. After a staff appointment in the MoD, he retired from the RAF in 1965 and joined the Industrial Training Board. He eventually settled in Kew, where he and his wife often entertained friends from the French resistance, with whom he maintained contact throughout his life. He frequently represented the Special Forces Club at the unveiling of memorials to heroes of the resistance in France and, in 1978, published his memoirs of the Lysander flights in *We Landed by Moonlight*. He retained his wit and courteous manner to the end. His wife Audrey, who he met at Oxford in 1940, survives him with two sons and three daughters.

(He died on November 14, 2001, aged 83).

Occasionally, SOE was able to seize an opportunity to take the enemy at a disadvantage outside the organization's established field of operations.

Such an opportunity arose in early 1942, with a most successful outcome.

Peter Lake MC
(Obituary *The Times* July 14, 2009)

At a perilously low point in the war for Britain – January 1942 – Peter Lake was the Vice-Consul on the Spanish Island of Fernado Pó (now Bioko) in the Gulf of Guinea, when an opportunity for a positive publicity coup came his way. He was already working with the Special Operations Executive (SOE) and saw his chance when the 7,000-ton Italian liner *Duchessa d'Aosta* unexpectedly put into the island's harbour accompanied by a German tug and lighter. Being Axis owned, the vessels were legitimate targets but Spain's neutrality was a sensitive issue, not least as the British Ministry of Economic Warfare was seeking ways to restrict supplies of Spanish wolfram to German factories.

Recognizing a violent takeover of the ships was out of the question, even had he the wherewithal to hand, Lake began the discreet distribution of funds ashore to attract the crews into town on a chosen night while arranging, through SOE channels, for two small craft to make the 400-mile voyage from Lagos to bring boarding parties to overcome the skeleton crews. A little further largess ensured that the harbour lights would go out at the critical moment. The craft carrying a total of thirty-four men – half of them trained SOE operators and the rest civil service volunteers from Lagos – entered Fernado Pó harbour on time, overcame and locked up the skeleton crews without violence and sailed the liner and her attendant vessels quietly away into the African night. Once on the high seas, they were ostentatiously arrested by the corvette HMS *Violet* and carried off as valuable prize captures. The publicity brought some cheer in England during a grim winter that had seen Rommel advance to Gazala and Singapore surrender. Lake remained aside from events and there were no diplomatic repercussions from General Franco's administration in Madrid.

Peter Ivan Lake had been chosen for the Fernado Pó assignment as he was a fluent Spanish speaker, having been brought up on Mallorca where his father Ivan Lake was the British Consul at Palma. Educated at Clifton and St John's, Oxford, where he read modern languages, he was working with the Standard Bank of West Africa in Accra on the outbreak of war in Europe. Determined to enlist, he made his way overland to the Mediterranean, then home by sea to arrive as the troops evacuated from Dunkirk were flooding through the south coast ports. Told to await call-up, he worked for some months on a farm until directed into the Intelligence Corps, where his languages could be put to use.

From there, it was a relatively short step into SOE. The organization's Baker Street headquarters having decided that opportunity for a second coup in Fernando Pó was unlikely, recalled him to prepare for more hazardous duties in German-occupied France. He was dropped by parachute into the Corrèze in April 1944 to join the SOE *Author* circuit in the countryside north of the Dordogne.

In the previous summer, SOE had established contact with a group of the French Resistance around Tulle led by the French novelist and politician André Malraux. This appeared such a promising prospect, as Malraux's group was anxious to receive arms by parachute, that the *Author* circuit was formed by SOE's Major 'Harry' Peulevé in September. Unfortunately the Gestapo caught Peulevé, in company with Malraux's brother Roland, while he was operating the circuit's radio in a house near Brive in March 1944. The circuit was taken over by his assistant Jaques Poirier and renamed *Digger*, while Lake and a second SOE agent Ralph Beauclerk were dropped on April 9 to help him. They faced formidable difficulties. Although they would not have been informed of even the approximate date of the forecast Allied landings in northern France, Lake and Beauclerk knew they were imminent. Therefore time was against getting the local Resistance groups armed and organized in readiness to begin acts of sabotage in co-ordination with the invasion.

The local Resistance groups included a good many Spanish veterans of the Civil War likely to harbour leftist sympathies. Arguably, this aligned them with the communist FTP (*Francs-tireurs et partisans*), suspected of being less interested in sabotage against the occupation forces and their lines of communication than in acquiring weapons with which to seize political power after the Germans had withdrawn or been driven out.

Finally, the countryside of the upper Dordogne was already in a ferment of anticipation of the Allied invasion, which allowed the German *Abwehr* to insert informers into the disparate Resistance groups with the aim of eliminating SOE agents and preventing the supply of weapons by parachute. This required the three men to keep changing location to limit the risks of betrayal.

Despite these difficulties, all the groups were armed and ready for operations by early June. Lake's group in particular proved adept at guerilla warfare. As soon as they received the coded signal from London, the lateral railway line running through Perigueux and Coutras to Bordeaux was kept under constant attack and denied to the enemy's use until after the withdrawal. Lake was awarded the Military Cross and the *Croix de Guerre* for his preparatory work and direction of the local Resistance in support of the Allied invasion. He was later appointed to the Legion of Honour in recognition of his wartime service to France.

On demobilization, he applied to join the Consular Service and was accepted for a cadetship in Mozambique. His acceptance for a full career in the service was not long in coming and he served subsequently in Madagascar, Paris, Iceland, Aleppo and finally as British Consul in Venice. After his retirement in 1975 he worked with the Cambridge Wild Life Trust and developed his hobby of book binding. He married Kathleen (Kay) Sheffield in 1944. She survives him with two sons and a daughter.

(He died on June 26, 2009, aged 94).

Brave and resourceful as they were, the SOE agents operating in enemy occupied territory depended on the guidance and support of their country section working in 64 Baker Street. Each of these was known by an identifying letter: 'F Section' for France, 'N Section' for The Netherlands and so on. With widely differing prospects for successful subversion and sabotage and acutely sensitive about their individual plans, the Section Heads clamped their cards to their chests and sometimes found themselves in competition with each other for allocation of aircraft and resources. The most well known Section Head was Colonel Maurice Buckmaster, Head of F Section.

Colonel Maurice Buckmaster, OBE
(Obituary *The Times* April 20 1992)

Colonel Maurice Buckmaster, OBE, head of the 'independent French' or F section of the Special Operations Executive from 1941 to 1945, died on April 17 aged 90. He was born on January 11, 1902. As spymaster of the French Section of the Special Operations Executive it was Maurice Buckmaster's task to organize the activities of the British agents sent to spy, carry out sabotage and recruit resistance groups in occupied France. This had to be done without the advantage of being able to make use of such Frenchmen as succeeded in escaping from France, for although the SOE worked alongside the Free French movement they were entirely separate. It was regarded as remarkable that the SOE was able to find more than 150 British officers whose French was good enough for them to be passed off as Frenchmen and who had, at the same time, the courage and capacity for such hazardous tasks. Among the more famous of SOE's recruits were Odette Hallowes, tortured by the Germans and received the George Cross, and Violette Szabo, awarded a posthumous GC after being tortured and shot by the Germans in Ravensbrück in 1945.

Every care was taken to ensure that the individual agents knew only what was necessary to enable them to carry out their particular task. Buckmaster alone had to contrive to know, from London, what was going on in every district of France. There was no easy system of passwords to establish camaraderie between one agent and another. Although the special agents themselves undertook many specific jobs of sabotage, they sought, on the whole, to get the French to work for themselves, thereby enabling them to fight for their self-respect as well as their freedom, while at the same time the agents showed, by their presence, that they were willing to share the peril and to aid them to do the utmost with arms and other materials. Nearly everywhere the response was magnificent the great problem became how to control them.

The cost of the SOE's cloak and dagger activities was high. Out of some 400 agents operating under Buckmaster's command in more than 80 networks, 117 were killed, many of them being tortured beforehand. Years after the war Buckmaster and the SOE came under attack at home. Accusations were made in 1958 that the SOE had been run in an amateurish manner, that it was infiltrated by German intelligence, that it suffered betrayals which led to the arrest of many men and women, and that these shortcomings had been deliberately concealed. Buckmaster responded by saying that the SOE was no more amateurish than many other wartime units. He confirmed that the Germans had penetrated one important *reseau,* but only one (Holland). He described as monstrous and categorically denied the allegation that 47 British agents had deliberately been dropped to the Germans to distract their attention from other undercover operations.

Maurice James Buckmaster was educated at Eton and made an early intellectual mark by teaching French to those few boys younger than himself who were trying to pass Common Entrance. This natural talent for languages was to set the pattern for the rest of his life. As a young man he worked on *France-Soir* and then, from 1923-29, for the merchant bankers J. Henry Schroder & Co before becoming publicity manager, then manager of the Ford motor company's French operation and, from 1936-39, head of its European department. When the second world war began he was commissioned into the Intelligence Corps and was one of the last officers to be evacuated from the French coast near Dunkirk. His linguistic skills, he had by then perfected German, made him a natural candidate for the highly specialised work of the SOE into which he was co-opted, first as a staff officer in F Section and then as head of the Belgian section and, from December 1941, as head of F Section.

His knowledge of France and the French, his gift of leadership, immense energy and enthusiasm, instinctive love of people and, ultimately, his extraordinary capacity for achieving what he believed to be right, made him an extremely effective leader of what was a critical area of operations and proved to be one of the greatest thorns in the side of the Nazis. It was said that Hitler so reviled Buckmaster that he had put him as the third person on a target list if the German invasion of Britain had gone ahead.

Buckmaster's critics complained that he found it hard to delegate, had no first-hand experience of the clandestine life of his agents and favoured some agents above others. He certainly had favourites and was equally highly regarded by them. Buckmaster was that sort of man. His fierce and sometimes uncompromising loyalty to his own people could at times upset and irritate the military establishment. He was four rungs down the SOE ladder of command and the SOE system was such that officers, like Buckmaster, who commanded country sections' had to be left to make most of their own decisions about men and measures, within broad outlines laid down from above, and often in dangerous ignorance of each other's doings.

One of the sections with which he had to liaise, representing the Gaullists, regarded F Section as a tiresome rival. Indeed, de Gaulle was openly critical of F Section. But the SOE maintained F's separate identity, in spite of de Gaulle's protests. Such political ripples undoubtedly contributed to the fact that the OBE was the sole British honour accorded to Buckmaster, inadequate recognition of his contribution to the war effort. The French were later to make him an officer of the *Legion d'Honneur* and streets were named after him in France. Running any of the SOE sections was an intensive and 24 hour a day task. By the summer of 1944, in spite of a determined effort by the Gestapo to suppress them all in the previous winter and spring, about half of the *reseaux* were still operational. Their strength and breadth of operation caused severe disruption to vital German military movements to the north at the time of the D-Day landings and they gave invaluable assistance to the advancing allied armies.

After D-day all SOE's forces in France were amalgamated under General Koenig, who had Buckmaster as one of his three chiefs of staff. Following his demobilisation, Buckmaster returned to work for the Ford motor company this time in Britain and became head of the company's public relations department, serving a number of chief executives before moving to London where he became a public relations consultant. His love affair with France continued and in 1961 he was invited by the governing body of the Champagne industry to represent them in London. He held this post until the early 1980s.

Buckmaster appeared as himself in Herbert Wilcox's film *Odette* in which Anna Neagle played the leading role. Their friendship lasted the rest of her lifetime. He published two books on the Resistance, presenting F Section's work in semi-fictionalised form; indeed, while he was happy and at ease to talk about certain aspects of his work during that critical period of history, he maintained a reluctance to reveal any 'secrets'. Failing health prevented him travelling to Annecy for the unveiling, in May 1991, of a memorial to the Resistance attended by the Queen Mother, who wrote a note reflecting her personal sadness at his absence. It was a personal touch that reflected the affection felt for Buckmaster by the royal family during the second world war.

From his first marriage he had a son and two daughters and he married again in 1944, a marriage that was to last more than 40 years until he was widowed in 1988. There were no children of this marriage. Although a man of his time, Buckmaster had that rare quality of inspiring affection and respect, none less than among the young French people he met at the annual Resistance reunion in Paris.

(He died on April 17, 1992, aged 90).

This chapter would be incomplete without some mention of the tensions and eventually distrust that developed between SOE's headquarters in Baker Street and its strategic outposts in Cairo and Meerut, then later in Algiers, Bari and Kandy and its representational stations in Moscow and Washington and also between them and the in-country missions. In any context, the views of those on the ground seldom match those 'back at base' and the intricacies of covert operations involving partisan groups with rival political aspirations inevitably exacerbated misunderstandings.

Individual characteristics also played an often unhelpful part, with career officers trying to impose peacetime military discipline on adventurous and hard-pressed former civilians with no time for financial accounting. The unreliability of radio contact with remote bases in mountainous country and the unavoidable cancellation of airdrops without prior notice could have infuriating consequences, not least the loss of confidence of the partisans who had been persuaded to co-operate by the promise of arms, explosives and supplies.

As the war ground on and communist influence gained ground in Italy and the Balkans, suspicions that those at base favoured the communist partisans or, alternatively, their opponents – as in Greece – fuelled the doubts of agents in the field that they were being fully supported, either morally or materially. Remoteness, loneliness and the uncertain loyalty of the often rag-tag insurgents they were urging to fight had their place. In all these circumstances it is scarcely surprising that there would be disappointments, failures, turncoats and the inevitable traitor.

Some operations did not realize their potential because circumstances turned out to be different from what was expected; these could be ranked as disappointments or failures according to scale. The turncoats were principally agents dropped literally into enemy hands and given the option of collaboration or death. Penetration of the entire SOE network in Holland by German military intelligence and their Security Service led to most of these. As to traitors, the long suspected Henri Déricourt admitted having 'conversations with the enemy' – but on the orders of SOE; he was tried and acquitted after the war. There were tragic incidents of ill-luck and miraculous escapes from capture, some due to German negligence and others to sheer chance.

2

France – Early Days

Of all the Axis-occupied countries in which SOE sought to foster subversion and sabotage, France appeared to offer the best opportunities. Almost all the region south of the Loire and inland from the Atlantic coast lay under Vichy government control until – in response to the Allied invasion of French North Africa – the German Army arrived in November 1942 to forestall any landing on the Mediterranean coast. This is not to say that SOE had an open target in this region; the Vichy police and security service jealously guarded its integrity – such as it was – but at least there were few Germans around.

The region's countryside of rolling hills and woodlands offered good dropping zones for parachutists and the air-drop of weapons and explosives. Night landings for the delivery and extraction of agents by Lysander and Hudson aircraft were not too difficult for expert pilots to achieve, so long as the Resistance reception parties had marked out the landing strips and shown the requisite identification signals.

Once on the ground, SOE agents could merge into the populations of the industrial cities and ports, usually adopting cover identities that gave them local credibility and excuses for apparently not having to earn a living. There were difficulties, of course. The Resistance expanded rapidly once conscription for forced labour in Germany was introduced in late 1942, prompting young men to take to the hills, but it was divided into the pro-Gaullist *Forces françaises de l'intérieur* (FFI) and the communist *Francs-tireurs et partisans* (FTP). Suspicions that the latter would use any arms delivered to them to seize political power after the liberation impeded development of London's dependence on their reliability.

There were also sensitive issues in London. General de Gaulle strove to insist that no clandestine operations be undertaken in German-occupied or Vichy-controlled France without his approval, a guarantee impossible to give. De Gaulle nevertheless held to this view throughout the war, operating his own secret intelligence service in France, co-operating with MI 6 and SOE only as far as he judged expedient to his advantage. Given these pros and cons, France eventually emerged as the most fruitful ground for SOE operations.

The first SOE agents delivered into occupied France arrived in the late spring of 1941 with missions to establish 'circuits' (or networks) of local helpers and resisters willing to carry out acts of sabotage – once they were supplied with the requisite explosives. The *Autogiro* circuit was formed west of the Seine with a detachment far away on the Doubs, near the Swiss frontier. *Ventriloquist* lay in the loop of the Loire south of Orleans, and in August and September that year, six circuits were launched in the then unoccupied southern region administered by the Vichy government.

One of the early arrivals, who was also to become one of the greatest heroes, was an Englishman working with André de Waverin, the head of De Gaulle's intelligence and operations staff. SOE was demonstrating support for the Free French leader's efforts to establish his authority in occupied France.

Wing Commander F F E 'Tommy' Yeo-Thomas, GC, MC and Bar
(Obituary *The Times* February 27, 1964)

Wing Commander Forest Frederick Edward Yeo-Thomas, GC, MC, who died yesterday in Paris at the age of 61, three times parachuted into France during the war of 1939-45 to organize and work with the French resistance movement; betrayed eventually to the Gestapo, who shamefully used him, he spent some time in Buchenwald and in a Jewish extermination camp. Finally, after some further heartbreaking adventures he reached the American lines

The citation which accompanied the award of his George Cross in 1946 stated, "… he endured brutal treatment and torture without flinching and showed the most amazing fortitude and devotion to duty throughout his service abroad during which he was under constant threat of death." In addition to the GC he was awarded the MC and Bar and the Croix de Guerre. In July last year he was promoted Commander of the Legion of Honour.

Yeo-Thomas was born on June 17, 1902, of an English family which had lived in France since 1865. He was educated in France and in England.

Although under age, he served with the Allied armies in the latter part of the 1914-18 War and fought with the Poles against the Russians during 1919 and 1920. He was captured by the Bolsheviks and sentenced to death but escaped the night before he was due to be shot – an experience that was to be repeated two decades later. Between the wars he worked in Paris, from 1932 as a director of the fashion house of Molyneux.

SEIZED BY THE GESTAPO

He enlisted in the RAF in 1939, became a sergeant-interpreter with the Advanced Air Striking Force and was later commissioned. Early in 1943, he dropped by parachute into France to get in touch with the underground movement and on his return in April he brought with him a United States Army Air Corps officer who, having no French, was in danger of capture.

Later the same year he went back to France to find out what the *Maquis* needed in the way of weapons and supplies. Six times he was all but captured but continued to keep his liberty and returned to England.

In February 1944 he made his last visit to France, and a month later he was betrayed and seized by the Gestapo. He was interrogated for four days, was beaten and tortured. The Germans attempting to break his spirit by immersing him head-downwards in ice-cold water while his legs and arms were chained. They were unsuccessful. The questioning went on for two months and he was offered his freedom on condition that he gave the Gestapo the information they wanted.

He all but lost an arm through blood poisoning caused by the chains cutting one of his writs. After twice attempting to escape Yeo-Thomas was confined in solitude in Fresnes prison for four months, for some weeks he was given little food. Throughout all he remained steadfast, inspiring his fellow prisoners by his infectious spirits.

After further attempts to escape from Compiègne, where he had been transferred with a party of prisoners, he was sent to Buchenwald where, in his own words, "I conveniently died of typhus on October 13, 1944, after getting into the 'guinea pig' block and changed my identity to that of a Frenchman named Choquet." Next day his execution order arrived.

He was now moved to a work commando at Gleina and Rehmsdorf, where as a hospital orderly he almost miraculously survived. With 20 others, whom he led, he escaped in April, 1945, from the train in which they were being moved once more. On his recapture he impersonated a dead French officer and succeeded for the last time in escaping and thus regained the allied lines. This period of his life is recorded in Mr Bruce Marshall's book *The White Rabbit*, one of his many soubriquets, *Shelley* being the one by which he was most often known.

After the war he first returned to Molyneux and in 1950 he joined the Federation of British Industries as their representative in France, which he remained until his death. To his new task he brought his characteristic qualities of loyalty and service and his understanding of the French scene, and the special regard in which he was held enabled him to render great assistance to the Federation of British Industries and to its members

(He died on February 26, 1964, aged 61).

Our next two heroes were not directly associated either with subversion or sabotage but initially with the uniquely established circuit *Carte* with its headquarters at Antibes. *Carte* was a completely home-grown circuit formed by the French patriot and painter André Girard. With sabotage or anything else anti-German in mind, Girard had enlisted acquaintances all over Vichy France but they had no arms, explosives nor any sense of security. Captain Peter Churchill was landed by submarine in January 1942 to investigate the organization's potential.

Captain Peter Churchill, DSO
(Obituary *The Times* May 2, 1972)

The son of W. A. Churchill, Peter Churchill was educated at Malvern and Caius College, Cambridge, where he read modern languages for which he had a marked gift. His courier during his secret work in France was Odette Sansom, better known as *Odette*, who was later captured by the Germans on the same day as he.

In 1947 she and Captain Churchill were married. They were divorced in 1956 and both remarried, he to Jane Hoyle and she to Geoffrey Hallowes. During his last illness she visited Captain Churchill in hospital in Cannes.

Peter Churchill was among the first of the gallant men and women who, during the 1939-45 War, volunteered for service with the French Section of the Special Operations Executive (SOE). In 1941, he had not long been down from university and, like so many of his contemporaries, was not content to play a passive role nor accept the comparative uneventfulness of life in the Services. He was an idealist, but a very practical and matter-of-fact idealist, never entering an assignment until he could see the practical steps which he would have to take to carry it out successfully.

From the point of view of an organizer of underground activities in enemy-occupied territory, he was a 'natural'. His French was perfect, he was quick to grasp the complexities of a problem and, above all, he had an intuitive sense of responsibility and initiative.

To say that he was a particularly brave man gives only a superficial description of his character. He was a man who saw, with devastating clarity, the dangers of the work involved and who had the ability to accept these risks without letting them interfere with his judgment. He never took needless chances; his actions were deliberate and balanced. He knew his own ability and used it to the full.

In the early days of subversive activities in France we needed to know, from practical experience, which were the best methods of introducing agents clandestinely into the country – by fast naval craft to the coast of Brittany – by submarine and rowing boat to the Mediterranean shores – by *felucca* from Gibraltar – on foot across the Pyrenees (which involved also a clandestine journey through Spain) – by Lysander aircraft landing in a small field in France   or by parachute, 'blind' or to a reception committee.

Peter volunteered to try them all and his assessments of advantages and disadvantages were of incalculable value to the section. Between missions he would report to a 'secret' flat shared with a London friend, where, ensconced very often for privacy in the bathroom with The Times crossword, he would unwind and dictate his reports, which frequently had a Damon Runyonesque flavor.

But Peter was no playboy. He loved life and was prepared to undertake any kind of mission which he felt would speed the liberation of his second mother-country, France. An excellent athlete – with an ice hockey blue – he made light of the physical hardships of living in occupied France, where the *Côte d'Azur* of those days was no luxury region but one of the physically toughest areas of France.

Here and in the snowy foothills of the Alps he originated the first groupings of young men who sought to avoid being taken away for forced labour to German factories. We knew them later as the *Maquis*. The first arms drop to the *maquisards* was organized by Peter, with help of *Odette*, his courier, whom he subsequently married.

Throughout the period of his confinement to a concentration camp after his capture he displayed great fortitude. For his bravery and devotion to duty he was awarded the DSO. From the French he received the insignia of the *Légion d'Honneur* and the *Croix de Guerre*.

After he had recovered from his war sufferings he returned to the *Côte d'Azur* where he married and made his home. Always an active man, he combined authorship of several books with estate agency work, in which he excelled.

On hearing of his death, a friend wrote, "I knew Peter better, probably, than any of the other 500 British men and women who undertook SOE duties in France. I have for him the loving respect born of trust in his willingness to venture. He will be immensely missed, both by his many French friends and colleagues and by his former companions in Great Britain."
(He died on May 1st 1972)

Characteristically of many of the early SOE obituaries published by *The Times*, the above lacks detail of what he actually achieved in France. This was due to the restrictions of information at the time of publication of the obituary.

Due to concerns over the circuit's security, only a limited quantity of arms and explosives were delivered to Girard and his fellow patriots but their extensive coverage – Girard boasted a 3,000-strong membership – gave those at SOE's Baker Street headquarters, and through them, the British Chiefs of Staff, confidence in what might be achieved in France.

Peter Churchill's courier in his mission to *Carte* was Odette Sansom who, together with an SOE agent named Roger Bardet, got into difficulty while Churchill returned to London to report on *Carte*. Working with an offshoot of *Carte* near Annecy, they were tricked by German intelligence into a security breach that led to Churchill's arrest and her own.

Odette Hallowes, GC, MBE
(Obituary *The Times* March 17, 1995)

Born in Amiens on April 28, 1912, of all the women who took part in wartime special operations in France, Odette as she was universally known in spite of having borne three married surnames in her lifetime perhaps best symbolised the indomitable spirit of resistance to the horrors of Nazism. Captured by the Gestapo in France in 1943 and consigned, after being cruelly tortured in Paris's notorious Fresnes prison, to Ravensbrück concentration camp, she emerged emaciated, weak and gravely ill at the end of the war.

But in the years that followed, her undiminished mental and moral energy, combined with a complete absence of bitterness towards her tormentors and the nation that had spawned them, became a beacon to others who had suffered disfigurement, pain or bereavement. Indeed, the theme of her post-war working life, with its service to various charities and help for the underprivileged, was the healing of those wounds, both physical and mental, which had been inflicted upon individuals by the war.

Her George Cross, she always maintained, was not to be regarded as an award to her personally, but as an acknowledgement of all those, known and unknown, alive or dead, who had served the cause of the liberation of France. Her wartime experiences had taught her two great truths: that suffering is an ineluctable part of the human lot, and that the battle against evil is never over.

Fame came to her notably through the film 'Odette' which celebrated her life but she never sought it. In her entry in Who's Who she styled herself simply: housewife.

She was born Odette Marie Celine Brailly in Picardy, the daughter of Gaston Brailly, who was killed towards the end of the First World War. She was educated privately and at the Convent of Ste Therese in Amiens.

She always said that she had been determined at the outset to marry an Englishman, after a series of young British officers were billeted on the family house during the First World War. At any rate, when the son of one such man, whom her mother had nursed back to health, visited the family after the war to improve his English, romance soon blossomed. She married Roy Sansom, who worked in the hotel industry, in 1931 and settled in London, where she had three daughters.

British domiciled she might be, but her heart remained French. After the catastrophe to French arms in the early summer of 1940, she longed to do something more active than looking after her young ones. By a stroke of luck she got in touch with the independent French section of the Special Operations Executive.

Yet when she was first interviewed there were some doubts about her suitability as a clandestine SOE courier. Would she be able, as a mother of three young daughters who might be constantly on her mind, to undertake missions requiring steely nerves and an ability to concentrate on the task in question to the exclusion of all else? On the other hand, from certain points of view she seemed an ideal candidate. She was young, attractive, vivacious. She knew France; she had a winning manner. Furthermore, she had a burning desire to redeem by direct action the disgrace her country had suffered in its capitulation of June 1940.

Accepted, she joined the First Aid Nursing Yeomanry (since membership of a service organisation was a prerequisite of working for SOE and the FANY provided basic training in such matters as driving, wireless operation, etc) and did well in all her courses. She returned to France secretly, by small boat from Gibraltar to Antibes, on the last night of October 1942, with orders to join a new circuit in Burgundy. There she got on so well with Peter Churchill, SOE's organiser on the spot, that he secured London's leave to keep her on the Riviera.

Within a fortnight, the Germans and Italians overran all southern France. Churchill and Mme Sansom continued to try to provide contact between London and a large as it turned out, a purely imaginary secret army that was supposed to be organised by a friend of Churchill's codenamed *Carte*, the father of Danielle Darrieux the film star. Unfortunately quarrels among *Carte's* friends became so acute that next February Churchill took Mme Sansom and his wireless operator, Adolphe Rabinovitch, away to St Jorioz near Annecy in the French Alps. Churchill then returned to London for instructions.

While he was away, Odette was approached by a 'Colonel Henri', who represented himself to be a German officer who wanted to defect to the Allies. She was highly suspicious of 'Colonel Henri' with some justification since he was in fact Sergeant Bleicher of the *Abwehr*. But one of the more impetuous of the *Carte* members was taken in by him and imparted some names and numbers of the members of the circuit in and around Annecy. Churchill returned to France by parachute on April 14-15, 1943, and was met by Odette, with whom he returned to St Jorioz.

He had already been warned against 'Colonel Henri' in London. But their operation had been fatally undermined by the indiscreet disclosures of their *Carte* comrade. After dark next evening Bleicher and a detachment of Italian troops arrived at the hotel in St Jorioz where Odette and Churchill were staying. He arrested her in the hall and going upstairs, where he found Churchill sound asleep in bed, arrested him too.

Churchill and Odette passed themselves off as married, and as relations of Winston Churchill (he claimed to be Churchill's nephew). They were, therefore, for a time treated with a mixture of savagery and deference. Odette was sent to Paris where, at the notorious Fresnes prison, she endured excruciating torments including having her toenails pulled out (for a year after her homecoming she could not wear shoes and had to walk on her heels until several operations restored her normal mobility).

Both she and Churchill were eventually sent to the vast concentration camp at Ravensbrück, north of Berlin, where, in June 1943, Odette was condemned to death. That sentence was not carried out but for the remainder of her stay there her lot was one of alternate molly-coddling and beating which is the traditional procedure of the interrogator. Neither of them, however, made any admissions of importance. Meanwhile Rabinovitch, who had evaded arrest, escaped to England only to be dropped back by an unhappy staff error straight into the arms of the Gestapo next year.

At the end of the war, when the Red Army's advance approached Ravensbrück, Fritz Suhren, the camp commandant, drove in a sports car with Odette beside him into the American lines, in the hope that he could use her charm to save himself. She at once denounced him and he was hanged after trial.

Odette became a national heroine, subject of innumerable newspaper articles, a book by Jerrard Tickell and the film 'Odette' (1950) which starred Anna Neagle in the title role. She was appointed MBE in 1945 and in the following year awarded the George Cross. In 1950 she was made an officer of the *Legion d'Honneur.*

She believed that the George Cross had been given to her, not because she had been especially gallant, but because she had had the good fortune to survive; unlike 11 other women in her section who had died in German hands, some of them shot within earshot of her cell.

Her first husband died and she married Peter Churchill in 1947. In 1956 that marriage was dissolved and she married Geoffrey Hallowes, a wine importer, who had also served in another section with the SOE in France. He was a constant support to her throughout the years when her life was lived in the glare of often unexpected bursts of publicity, not all of them welcome; there were, for example, criticisms of the effectiveness of SOE's operations in southern France.

But there was also publicity of a more light-hearted kind. On one occasion her mother's house in Kensington was burgled, the thief making off with some silver spoons and Odette's George Cross and *Legion d'Honneur.* Distraught at the loss of her daughter's treasures, Mme Brailly appealed through the press for their return. The thief, evidently a humane soul, obliged His letter accompanying the decorations read: "You Madame, appear to be a dear old lady. God bless you and your children. I thank you for having faith in me. I am not all that bad it's just circumstances. Your little dog really loves me. I gave him a nice pat and left him a piece of meat out of fridge. Sincerely yours, A Bad Egg."

Odette was active in many organisations: she was on
the committee of the VC and GC Association; she was a
vice-president of the FANY; an honorary member of the St
Dunstan's Ex-Prisoners of War Association; and President of
282 (East Ham) Air Cadet Squadron.

Last year, though already frail, she revisited Ravensbrück.
For her it was the first time since 1945. The occasion, the
unveiling of a plaque remembering the courage of the SOE
women who had died there, was for her a profoundly moving
experience.

Her husband and the three daughters of her first marriage
survive her.

(She died on March 13, 1995)

The crucial importance of radio operators in the work of SOE
agents in the field needs no emphasis. They were also highly
vulnerable to arrest, even if they kept their transmissions to the
absolute minimum length to avoid detection by the German
direction finders, as their aerials could not always be concealed and
local 'gossips' on the lookout for strangers in their district were
notoriously careless when speaking of them.

All that said, the experiences in France of the young radio operator
Derek Baynham and his companion were quite extraordinary.

Brigadier Derrick Baynham, GM
(Obituary *The Times* July 13, 2006).

Friends of Derrick Baynham warned him that he was
unlikely to become a general as he had too many interests
outside the Army. While this proved true, he enjoyed a
varied career. But his personal determination and strength
of character were shown to best advantage as a schoolboy
and as a young man.

In June 1940, aged 16, he joined the crew of a river cruiser,
captained by his Walton-on-Thames bank manager, on three
cross-Channel trips to Dunkirk to help to evacuate troops of
the British Expeditionary Force. From an assembly point off the
Medway, they were guided by a Royal Navy picket boat to the
beaches.

On their third trip they were overloaded to such an extent
that there was imminent risk of sinking, and their cargo and
crew, other than the bank manager and Baynham, were taken

off by a destroyer. They reached Dover and he returned to school at St George's College, Weybridge.

While on holiday at Anglesey in August the following year, he and a friend, John Wood, put to sea in a dinghy in an attempt to rescue the crew of an RAF bomber that had crashed off the coast. After 45 minutes hard rowing they reached the almost submerged aircraft to find a single survivor – a Polish airman – clinging to the fuselage, the rest having been swept away. In the course of the prolonged struggle to get the exhausted airman into the dinghy it capsized. The airman was drowned but the two boys eventually reached the shore. Both were awarded the George Medal and the Royal Lifeboat Institution's silver medal for their bravery and tenacity in daunting sea conditions.

As soon as he was 18 Baynham enlisted in the East Surrey Regiment but soon transferred to the Royal Corps of Signals. He volunteered for special duties, and an introduction to sabotage and the techniques of silent killing was followed by instruction at the Special Operations Executive (SOE) signals school.

In the autumn of 1942 he and a female SOE radio operator/courier were flown by RAF Lysander to a landing strip in the unoccupied zone of France, south of the Loire. In the memoir he wrote 50 years later, he referred to her by the codename 'Angel', although this was not the name allocated by SOE. They expected to be met by an agent on landing, but he had already been arrested.

Baynham was still short of his 19th birthday and 'Angel' was younger. Their instructions were to report to the SOE circuit operating around Limoges. At the time this was codenamed *Ventriloquist*, extending eastwards as far as the Rhône and under command of the Baron Philippe de Vomécourt. Despite help from French civilians, Baynham and Angel did not succeed in establishing contact with the circuit and only narrowly escaped capture by the Vichy Government's security police, the *Milice*.

After testing the reliability of a local farmer, Baynham sent 'Angel' to him with a message while he reported to London. As he was rigging up his aerial from a disused pigsty, he turned to see a *Milice* officer covering him with a revolver. Suddenly there was a shot and the man fell dead in front of him. 'Angel' had returned, sized up the situation instantly and shot the officer. A second *Milice* man was shot as he came to investigate and the bodies disposed of in the *Milice* van, which was tipped off the road into a wood 50ft below.

After hiding their two radios in a ruined farm, the pair set out for Perigueux. Their inability to establish contact with the local SOE in either place led London to order them to move northwards and await pick-up by a Lysander. On the way, 'Angel' developed a serious chest complaint and Baynham felt obliged to leave her in the care of a convent, where she stayed until the end of the war. He caught the flight home.

When set against the record of most SOE operations in France, Baynham's account of his has to be rated a failure, but not through lack of courage or initiative. After return to England, he was commissioned in the Royal Signals and served with the Guards Armoured Division in the North-West European campaign, in which he was wounded by a grenade. He was briefly taken prisoner but escaped and was mentioned in dispatches.

Subsequently he served in Palestine and for a period was an ADC to Field Marshal Earl Wavell when Viceroy of India. His post-war career concluded with command of the 11th Signal Group of the Territorial Army in the rank of brigadier and appointment as an honorary ADC to the Queen. In retirement he was bursar at London University's College of Speech Sciences, and ran computer courses from his Hampshire home.

He was separated from his wife, Ann, who survives him with two sons and a daughter; also his long-term partner, Sue. Another son predeceased him.

(He died on May 16, 2006, aged 82)

Whether agent or radio operator, the risks of betrayal and capture were part of the everyday existence of every SOE man or woman in the field. Yet one of the most remarkable aspects of their character and conduct was the manner in which they accepted these hazards and reacted after the worst happened. Sydney Hudson was a fine example of such courage and determination to persist.

Sydney Hudson, DSO
(Obituary *The Times* June 8, 2005)

Sydney Hudson's first mission into wartime France for the Special Operations Executive (SOE) might have been his last, for he was betrayed and then arrested by the Vichy police – the despised *Milice* – and imprisoned. He escaped and later returned by parachute to France. As the war in Europe was drawing to a close he volunteered for operations of uncertain outcome in Japanese-held Thailand. A man of laconic humour, insatiable curiosity and intense interest in human relations, he turned his talents after the war to business and to politics, becoming involved in establishing the Social Democratic Party in Scotland.

Charles Sydney Hudson was the son of Theodore and Ella Hudson. Brought up near Montreux, Switzerland, where his father was a businessman, Hudson was a member of the British ski team at the 1936 Winter Olympics and took first place at the Swiss Amateur Open Golf Championships in 1939. At the outbreak of war, he came to England to enlist and was commissioned into the Royal Fusiliers.

By then France had fallen and when he found military life more regimental than he had expected in wartime, he answered a discreet invitation to fluent French speakers to undergo training for operations of a hazardous nature. He was parachuted into the Puy-de-Dome, west of Clermont Ferrand, in charge of a three-man team of agents code-named *Headmaster*. His task was to make contact with the local Resistance movement and guide its sabotage work, but he was arrested by the French police only two weeks after arrival.

Counting himself fortunate not to be handed over to the Gestapo, he was sent to a prison camp at Essye, near Toulouse, for dissidents actively opposed to the Vichy regime, where he remained until he and Baron Jean de Vomécourt – of the Resistance – organised a mass escape on January 3, 1944. Largely through the co-operation of one of the warders whom de Vomécourt had been able to compromise, about 50 prisoners got out. After making contact with the SOE circuit operating northeast of the Pyrenees, the party was led, in atrocious weather, into Spain. Once there it was relatively easy to go on to Gibraltar and England.

Hudson returned to France in May 1944 with a mission to

re-establish the *Headmaster* circuit around Le Mans. Given the day-to-day expectation of the Allied landings in northern France, he and his 20-year-old colleague Sonya d'Artois were welcomed by the local Resistance and blew up the Le Mans telephone exchange, forcing the German Army to transmit by radio with its inevitable security risks. When the American 3rd Army under General George Patton reached Le Mans in August, the *Headmaster* circuit was on hand with local intelligence.

Recalled to England, Hudson volunteered for service with Force 136, the SOE arm in South-East Asia. In May 1945 he made his third parachute drop into enemy-held territory, this time into northern Thailand.

By then a lieutenant-colonel, he was in charge of a group – including Thais – with instructions to arm and train resistance fighters for operations against the Japanese but hold them in check until the time was right. His team trained selected local volunteers and, with the aid of 1,400 villagers, built a runway to receive Allied troops. But Japan's surrender after the atom bombs on Hiroshima and Nagasaki rendered this unnecessary.

He was later involved in an operation with Force 136 concerned with repatriation of Allied PoWs from Thailand. He thought that South-East Asia Command was too hesitant about using Thai irregulars against the Japanese. A Foreign Office perception that the Siamese must work their passage – having been forced by the Japanese to side with them ostensibly – was cited by Hudson as inhibiting Force 136 activity in Thailand.

He received the *Croix de Guerre* for his work in France and was awarded the DSO in 1945. He stayed on in South-East Asia, practically governing a province of Laos, until he was offered a post with the Allied Control Commission in Germany in 1947, where he helped to establish de-Nazification programmes in the mining areas of the Ruhr. This developed his fascination with industrial relations and in 1953 he joined the human resources division of Shell International, subsequently working in Israel, Gabon, Trinidad and the United States.

When faced with a Shell appointment to Vietnam in 1969, he opted instead for a post with the Bank of Scotland's training and development department. This provided him with all the stimulus he needed up to retirement in 1980 in the East Lothian town of North Berwick. That is until the formation of the Social Democratic Party by the 'Gang of Four' the following spring. He immediately threw himself into establishing the SDP in Scotland. As a former represent-ative on the Scottish Council of the CBI and later chairman of CBI Scotland, his clout was considerable.

He was twice married and is survived by his German-born second wife, Ruth, and by a daughter of his first marriage.
(He died on April 7, 2005, aged 94).

The French railway system proved vulnerable to sabotage instigated by SOE agents, as the railway workers could usually be persuaded to wreck their own lines or rolling stock, just so long as their liveli-hoods were not threatened. This became a valuable weapon against the German forces after they had occupied the whole of Vichy-controlled France following the Allied invasion of French North Africa in November 1942.

Anthony Brooks, another youthful recruit to the ranks of SOE became something of a specialist in railway disruption.

Anthony Brooks, DSO, MC
(Obituary *The Times* May 22, 2007)

Tony Brooks was recruited by the Special Operations Executive (SOE) largely because of an act of personal initiative in France. Subsequently, despite his youth and inexperience he became one of SOE's most successful agents, methodi-cally combining caution with imagination – seldom natural bedfellows.

He specialised in sabotage of railway systems, but it was his meticulous reception arrangements for airdrops of arms and explosives that won him the confidence of SOE's London headquarters, the Royal Air Force and the resistance fighters so supplied.

Brought up in Switzerland and fluent in French, he was working in his father's timber business in the French Jura at the time of the Franco-German armistice in June 1940. He met by chance a British private soldier who, having avoided capture at Dunkirk, was gamely making for the Pyrenees on foot, reading the maps inside French telephone boxes and following road signs. Brooks had heard of an escape line to

England being set up in Marseilles, so put the soldier in touch with a local contact and then followed him out, reaching England in late 1941.

Although he was only nineteen, SOE snapped him up as ideal material, trained him in silent killing and sabotage techniques, briefed him on the French trades union structure and dropped him blind – that is without an arranged reception party – into the Garonne on the night of July 1-2 1942, shortly after his twentieth birthday.

His first task was to establish a circuit of local agents, then to assess the likelihood of persuading French railway workers to sabotage traffic northwards from Marseilles to Lyons and Toulouse, to be exploited as opportunity offered.

His only contact, made in a Toulouse café by exchange of a codeword, turned out to be a former acquaintance and the two set up one of SOE's most successful circuits, codenamed *Pimento*. Having no radio link with SOE in London, Brooks formed a courier line using trusted railway staff to deliver messages to a communication point in Geneva. For local cover he co-opted another family friend, a Montauban garage-owner, for whom he worked as a mechanic. This conveniently allowed him to travel widely in the south, ostensibly to collect parts from vehicles abandoned in the 1940 exodus south.

Knowledge of trade union practices, his excellent French and persuasive manner gave Brooks ready access to workers on the Marseilles-Toulouse-Lyons rail network. This became their framework for sabotage after German occupation of southern France in November 1942, following the Allied landings in French North Africa, when the railways became critical to German re-supply and – after the Allied invasion of Normandy in 1944 – their movement northwards.

Brooks had a narrow escape when the train from Toulouse on which he was travelling entered Lyons. The platform was thick with Gestapo but the *Pimento* agent waiting for him pretended to be a plain-clothes French policeman, bundled him into a police car and spirited him away.

During 1943 Brooks arranged for more than 30 airdrops of weapons and explosives. In fact he received more weapons than he could usefully deploy to the *Maquis* youths who had taken to the hills to avoid conscription for German labour camps, most of whom became partisans.

Abrasive axle grease and explosives were used to dislocate the railways in the Garonne until Brooks returned to London by a Hudson aircraft in August 1943 for re-briefing and to get married. He was awarded the Military Cross for the sabotage he had organized or undertaken during his first period in occupied France.

He returned in January 1944 to direct sabotage operations against the railway yards at Lyons. During his absence the *Pimento* circuit had suffered some losses of French sub-agents to the Gestapo, but without serious damage to the circuit as a whole. He had two further narrow escapes in the months before and shortly after the Normandy invasion. In May, an airdrop container of grenades exploded on impact, leading to a vigorous search of the area by a German SS unit, obliging him to hide up a tree for twenty-four hours.

More alarming was his chance arrest during a street spot check in Lyons in late July, by which time the Allied invasion had heightened the alertness of the occupying forces. He was unarmed and carrying no incriminating documents but the 72,000 French francs in his pocket aroused suspicions. His German interrogators kept him without food for 48 hours before questioning him but were unable to break his original cover story of being a mechanic from Montauban. He explained the francs as the price of a suit on the black market he was hoping to buy. He was released and the cash returned.

Sabotage by the *Pimento* circuit resulted in the derailment of every train carrying German troops or equipment at least once in its journey from Marseilles to Lyons after D-Day (June 6, 1944) Consequently, the journey of key elements of the Das Reich 2nd SS Panzer Division from Toulouse to the Normandy battlefield took more than two weeks.

By mid-August 1944, the position of German troops in southern France had become so perilous that Brooks decided to break cover. Planting a Union Jack on the bonnet of a car he had requisitioned, he led attacks on enemy German transport vehicles using phosphorous grenades while his *Pimento* partisans engaged withdrawing troops in street ambushes. He was awarded the DSO for his service in France in 1944.

After the war Brooks helped to wind up SOE and transferred to the Secret Intelligence Service (MI 6). He served in Sofia between 1947 and 1950. In 1952, after ten years of constant stress and domestic pressure of a failing marriage, he resigned and returned to the French company which had employed him before the war.

During this period he remarried. But by 1956 the scars of wartime had faded and Brooks was bored by commerce. By good fortune SIS was at time looking for someone with Brooks's experience and skills in the context of the Suez invasion and civil unrest in Cyprus. He was re-employed in Cyprus, and successive governors sought to prolong his service there.

It was a triumphant return, but the rest of his service was something of anti-climax. He was a distinct success, not unsurprisingly, in Paris between 1959 and 1963. But spells in London and Geneva were less happy. It was if the preoccupation with secrecy which had kept him alive in wartime France had come to dominate his view of peacetime operations. His last few years in the service were spent on secondment to the Security Service (MI 5). He finally retired in 1977and returned to a business career.

Anthony Morris Brooks was born in Essex in 1922. He was educated at Chillon College, near Montreux, and at Felsted School in Essex.

His first marriage, in 1943, was dissolved and he is survived by his second wife, Hélène (Lena), whom he met in Lebanon. There were no children of either marriage.

(He died on April 19, 2007, aged 85).

There were a number of instances of SOE wireless operators or women couriers showing outstanding initiative and courage when abruptly left in charge of the circuit with which they had been working in France. This reflected well on the organization's selection and training processes common to all its members to be deployed in the field. Roger Landes rose to the challenges of command with distinction but lived to regret not killing a traitor when he had the opportunity.

Roger Landes, MC and Bar,
(Obituary *The Times* July 17, 2008)

There was little of the archetypal hero in Roger Landes's appearance. Of medium height with the air of a shrewd but possibly accommodating bank manager, he spoke English with a decidedly French accent. It was his fluency in French that first drew him to the attention of the Special Operations Executive (SOE). He was to fulfil the expectations of the SOE authorities not just as a radio operator, for which he was recruited, but as the leader of an SOE circuit in German-occupied France.

At the time of the 1938 Munich crisis, he was living with his brother Marcel in Paris, their parents having moved to England after the failure of their father's jewellery business in the Depression. Born in Paris, the son of a British subject, Roger had dual nationality, so joined his parents in England and secured a post with the architect's department of the London County Council as a quantity surveyor. When war came, this employment delayed his call-up but he joined the Royal Corps of Signals in March 1941.

His French and familiarity with France having been noted, he was interviewed for training as a radio operator in the German zone of occupation and given five minutes to decide whether or not to volunteer. He agreed and began specialist radio training and instruction in the use of plastic explosive. After parachute training and commissioning, he and another agent were dropped south-west of Orleans on October 31, 1942. His instructions were to join the SOE *Scientist* circuit in Bordeaux.

His codename was *Aristide*, confusingly shared with other agents, and initially his responsibility was to maintain radio contact with SOE headquarters in London, working from varied locations and on irregular schedules to avoid detection. The low-lying Bordeaux region was unsuited to radio transmission, but he found an unoccupied bungalow on high ground ideal for his purpose. Shortly after establishing himself in Bordeaux, Landes was introduced by the leader of the *Scientist* circuit, Claude de Baissac, to the local head of Organisation Civile et Militaire, André Grandclément, an association that subsequently was to have dire consequences.

Anxious to avoid compromise of his bungalow transmission site through over use, Landes set up three more and used all four to no discernible pattern. Then, in August 1943, Claude de Baissac was flown to England by a Lysander aircraft for consultation. Landes was promoted to captain and appointed leader of the *Scientist* circuit.

The circuit extended its range of agents under his direction, and the chance arrest of one revealed the involvement of Grandclément. First arresting his wife, the Gestapo put it to Grandclément that France's real enemy was communism, so why did he not join the war against the threat from the east? Whether the Frenchman was taken in by this (he was of strong right-wing opinions) or by his wife's being in Gestapo hands is arguable. He agreed to reveal Resistance arms caches in return for his life and that of his wife and, on being let go, promptly informed a senior *Scientist* agent of this intention.

Landes was witness to this event and his instinct to shoot Grandclément on the spot was restrained only by the presence of the agent's wife and daughter. Through some prompt communication, Landes and the *Scientist* agent were able to get a substantial proportion of the arms away from the caches before the Gestapo reached them, but the whole circuit was by then at serious risk.

With Grandclément under Gestapo control, Landes knew his own arrest would be only a matter of time so he dropped out of sight and changed his alias to Roger Lalande, a real but absent person with authentic papers and registration. The Gestapo arrested other *Scientist* agents, however, leaving Landes no alternative but to cut all connection with the circuit and Grandclément, while informing London what had occurred. He was instructed to make his way out through Spain.

The journey was physically demanding and fraught with bureaucratic hazards. After a period in a Spanish prison, he reached Gibraltar on December 31, 1943. On return to England, suspicion in the SOE hierarchy that he might also have been 'turned' by the Gestapo led to his interrogation until able to prove his loyalty. With the Allied invasion of France only five months away, SOE was acutely security sensitive and preoccupied with preparations to bring much of the French railway system to a halt, to curtail the movement of German reinforcements to the intended Normandy beachhead.

After re-briefing, Landes and a radio operator were dropped on the night of March 1-2, 1944, to a Resistance reception party near Auch in south-west France. A strong wind caused him to land awkwardly and sprain his ankle. Two weeks rest and medical attention in a safe house restored his mobility and enabled him to return to Bordeaux. By the end of March he had made contact with the survivors of the *Scientist* circuit and had begun to call for arms drops, but Grandclément was still active.

The Frenchman was persisting in his efforts to turn the Gaullist FFI Resistance against the overtly communist FTP throughout the region. Despite this, Landes restored his circuit and gave instructions for attacks on rail and other communications immediately after the invasion on June 6, 1944. The security of this action could not be risked, so when informed that Grandclément, his wife and bodyguard had fallen into the hands of the Resistance near Arcachon he at once went there to take charge. Grandclément admitted his treachery and with Bordeaux still in German hands, Landes had no option other than to order the execution of both the Grandcléments.

After the German evacuation of Bordeaux and the establishment of a provisional government under General de Gaulle, the French leader visited the city – in which he enjoyed no great personal popularity – on September 17, 1944. Landes was presented only to be greeted by the words: "You are British. Your place is not here."

Landes was awarded the Military Cross for his first period of SOE service in France and a Bar for his second. He was also appointed to the Legion of Honour and awarded the Croix de Guerre with palm. He was advanced to Officer of the Legion of Honour in 1992 in recognition of his wartime services to France.

Born on December 16, 1916, Roger Landes was the second of three sons of Barnet Landes, whose grandfather had emigrated from Russian Poland in 1848 to avoid conscription into the Tsarist army. His father spoke English only hesitatingly and preferred to live with his Russian wife in Paris. Roger was educated in Paris and graduated from *L'Ecole des Beaux Arts* in the year after his parents' departure for England.

He married Ginette Corbin, daughter of the French *Scientist* agent Charles Corbin to whom André Grandclément had revealed his intention to betray the arms caches to the Gestapo. She died in 1983 (obituary March 12); Landes married Margaret Laing in 1990. He is survived by her and a son of his first marriage.

(He died on July 16, 2008, aged 91)

Claude de Baissac, the leader of the *Scientist* circuit when Roger Landes joined, had a remarkable sister, Lise, who was sent to France to establish a new circuit which she was to control from the outset. She was to become one of the most successful of SOE women agents.

Lise de Baissac
(Obituary *The Times* April 14, 2004)

Lise de Baissac – as she was before she married – had a special place among the women secret agents sent to France to work for Special Operations Executive (SOE). She went not as a courier or a wireless operator working under a circuit leader, but to set up her own small circuit. The commandant at SOE's Beaulieu 'finishing school', which prepared agents for the clandestine life, wrote that she was "quite imperturbable and would remain cool and collected in any situation... she was very much ahead of her fellow students".

De Baissac was one of the first two women agents to be parachuted into France on the night of April 24-25, 1942 – Yvonne Rudellat had arrived by boat two months earlier. She was dropped with the 22-year-old Andrée Borrell south of the Loire.

Her mission was to establish a safe house in Poitiers where new agents could be settled into the secret life. Her cover story was that she was a widow, Madame Irene Brisse, seeking refuge from the tension of life in the capital. With characteristic nonchalance, she moved into an apartment on a busy street near the Gestapo HQ, and even became acquainted with the Gestapo chief – Grabowski – "hated by everyone", she said. In Poitiers she made many friends, entertaining them at her flat, so agents visiting her would not seem unusual. She had presciently chosen a ground-floor apartment in a block without a concierge and even her cleaning lady, there every morning, never suspected her clandestine work. As well as receiving new agents, she organised reception committees for arms drops.

Being without a wireless she had to travel to Paris to send and receive messages and collect funds, or to Bordeaux where her brother Claude was building up the large *Scientist* circuit, organising sabotage and providing copious reports on submarines and shipping.

On August 16, 1943, she returned with her brother by Lysander to London just as her circuit in Poitiers had been penetrated by the Germans. A second one she had established in Ruffec remained intact.

She was dropped back into France on the night of April 9-10, 1944, to work with the active and successful *Pimento* circuit run by the SOE agent Anthony Brooks. However, in one of those seismic quarrels that occasionally broke out among agents, she found herself completely at odds with her new colleagues. Brooks thought she was far too smartly dressed to fit in with the railway and industrial workers in his circuit. She thought they were militant socialists with political aims and was not willing to work simply, she said, as their postman.

Instead, "black with rage", she joined her brother Claude, who had gone to Normandy to reconnoitre large landing grounds that could be held for 48 hours while airborne troops established themselves. Now with the codename *Marguerite*, de Baissac found herself living in a village beside the Germans. One day she found a German soldier sitting on her sleeping bag – made from a parachute. Fortunately he had no idea what it was.

For her brother she cycled twice to Paris, going through numerous checkpoints and heavy German formations, escaping detection even when frisked, thanks to her sang-froid.

Captain Blackman, the leader of an SAS party that parachuted behind the lines in July 1944, wrote that "she risked her life daily" carrying wireless material and secret documents. He added: "The part she played in aiding the *Maquis* and the British underground movement in France cannot be too highly stressed and did much to facilitate the *Maquis* preparations and resistance prior to the American breakthrough in Mayenne."

She organised several groups in Normandy and continued liaison until liberation, contributing with zeal to the provision of military information for the Allied forces. "She was the inspiration of groups on the Orne and by her initiative caused heavy losses to the Germans with tyre bursters on the roads near St Aubin-le-Desert, St Mars, and as far as Laval,

Le Mans and Rennes. She also took part in several armed attacks on enemy columns," runs a resumé on her SOE personal file.

Colonel Buckmaster, the head of SOE's French Section, proposed her in April 1945 for a George Medal. "A very courageous woman, very diplomatic ...She did everything, sabotage, arms drops, receptions, looking after airmen and wireless operators, even guerrilla work." Instead a recommendation put forward for an OBE was downgraded in September 1945 to an MBE by the War Office. The valiant work of SOE's women agents was first chronicled in M. R. D. Foot's *SOE in France (1966)*.

De Baissac belonged to the impressive group of agents – many like her from old French families – who came from the island of Mauritius, which had been British since 1810.

Before the war she had fallen in love with a dashing young artist, Henri Villameur, but her parents had refused to give their blessing to the match. After the war he married another girl, but they separated and Lise was soon reunited with him. Villameur by this time had become a fashionable decorator and they lived in an apartment he created under the eaves of a block on the Quai de Rive Neuve overlooking the port of Marseilles.

She quickly settled into normal civilian life after the war, making light of her war work (and never telling the full story of it), continuing to lead an active social life into grand old age.

Nonetheless she was extremely proud to be guest of honour at a parachute drop organised by the FANYs (First Aid Nursing Yeomanry) in 2002 to commemorate her original drop 60 years before. She was granted her French parachute wings and entertained at the Chateau Nanteuil.

She was vice-president of the Association France-Grande Bretagne in Marseilles for many years. She was a *Chevalier de la Legion d'honneur* and awarded the *Croix de Guerre avec palme*.

Her husband predeceased her. There were no children.
(She died on March 28, 2004, aged 98).

By the autumn of 1942, shortly before the *Wehrmacht* came storming into the previously unoccupied zone of France, SOE had sixteen circuits operating there and two in the north, one immediately south of Paris and another based on Orleans, plus a third that was on the point of collapse.

In the south, the circuits were operating well in and around Bordeaux, in the Garonne and Toulouse, Lyons and St Etienne as well as in the deep south-east around Nice and Toulon. The *Ventriloquist* circuit that Derrick Baynham and his young companion had been assigned to join, stretched from Limoges through the Haute Loire and eastwards across the Rhône and even then did not satisfy the territorial aspirations of its organizer, the indefatigable Philippe de Vomécourt. Close to the inter-zonal border, the *Monkeypuzzle* circuit was well established around Tours and *Detective* north of Poitiers. But the situation was about to change.

As we shall see in Chapters 8 and 9, the occupation of the whole of France awakened the population to the prospect of liberation through an Allied victory, while Germany, desperate for more workers for her defence industry, began conscripting young Frenchmen for forced labour in the Reich. This measure gave an immense boost to the Resistance movements, as those likely to be put on trains to Germany literally took to the hills. There they became the *Maquisards,* a name taken from the scrub covering their areas of refuge, and the more determined and robust of them joined the local Resistance groups and began to clamour for arms.

In turn, SOE operations took on a sharper focus, changing from acts of sabotage where support of the Resistance movements could be found, to preparation of plans specifically designed to hinder the redeployment of the German occupation forces from south and central France to the north, where everyone knew the Allied invasion must eventually come – many Frenchmen and women hoping for liberation as early as 1943.

3

Scandinavia

Britain and France turned their attention to Norway and Sweden during the opening months of the war, although for different reasons. Winston Churchill, First Lord of the Admiralty, argued that halting the export of Swedish iron ore from the Gällivare mines through the Norwegian port of Narvik would bring the Ruhr's war industry to a halt. This proved not to be the case, but a minefield was duly laid off Narvik with disastrous results for Norway and Denmark. The French Commander-in-Chief, General Gamelin, urged Premier Daladier to open a Scandinavian flank to divert Germany's attention away from the European Western Front.

After Denmark and Norway had been overrun by Germany in April 1940, following Britain's intervention in Norway's territorial waters and Hitler's anticipation of the Western Allies occupying the Norwegian ports, SOE began to look seriously into opportunities in Scandinavia.

The Secret Intelligence Service (MI 6) had probed Germany's reliance on Swedish iron-ore before the war, and the results of this and some of the staff were transferred to SOE on its formation. As Britain became more isolated with the fall of France in June 1940, SOE priorities focused on:

a. adopting a low but friendly profile in Sweden so as to facilitate the export of high quality technical products required by the British war industry – and striving not to provoke the Swedish authorities into action against SOE agents in Sweden or escaping from Norway.

b. supporting the Norwegian resistance, the 'Military Organization' or '*Milorg*', with the primary objective of inhibiting German use of the Norwegian ports for submarine and battle-cruiser operations against British shipping in the Atlantic. In 1942 SOE mounted a series of operations against German atomic weapon development facilities at the Norsk Hydro plant at Vemork in the province of Telemark.

c. supporting the Resistance movement in Denmark, although this proved remarkably difficult due to the population distribution and the limited number of places suitable for parachute drops or landings from submarines or small boats.

SOE's first triumph – and it was a remarkable one – based on Sweden was Operation *Rubble* to secure the sailing of five Norwegian ships loaded with urgently needed technical goods from Göteborg harbour to British ports without interception by the German Baltic Fleet in 1941. The key individual concerned was Mr (later Sir) George Binney of the British Iron and Steel Control working in Sweden before and during the war.

Strictly speaking, Binney was not a member of SOE when *Rubble* was planned and accomplished in co-operation with the Executive's man in Stockholm but he later became even more closely involved and received the DSO in addition to his knighthood after suffering a heart attack in 1944. His obituary in *The Times* scarcely does justice to his achievements in wartime, perhaps a reflection on the editorial approach at the time.

Sir George Binney, DSO
(Obituary *The Times* September 30, 1972)

Sir George Binney, DSO, FRGS the explorer died on Wednesday. He was 72. During the twenties he took part in three Oxford expeditions to the Arctic – two of which he led.

In 1924 on the third expedition the party explored the little-known North–East Land of Spitsbergen by making aerial surveys, surveys from the coast, and sleigh journeys. He later described the exploration which occurred in conditions of round-the-clock daylight in *With Seaplane and Sledge in the Arctic* (1925). The sledging parties accomplished their arranged journeys, but the seaplane was less successful.

Binney received the Back Award of the Royal Geographical Society and the Gold medal de la Rocquette of the Geographical Society of Paris for his journey across North East Land.

He served with the Hudson Bay Company from 1926 to

1931 and as a result of his journeys through Eskimo country published *The Eskimo Book of Knowledge* in 1931.

During the Second World War he served in the Royal Navy Volunteer Reserve while he was assistant commercial attaché in Stockholm from 1940 to 1942. He was knighted for 'special services in the supply of valuable war material' and is said to have been the brains behind the blockade-running attempt by ten Norwegian ships from Göteborg in 1942.

He was awarded the DSO for outstanding leadership and skill.

(He died on September 27, 1972, aged 72).

The blockade-running incident mentioned in the obituary was much less successful than that of 1941. SOE was responsible for mounting the second operation, code-named *Performance*, in which ten Norwegian ships were loaded in Sweden with urgently required goods not available from the United States under the Lend-Lease Agreement.

Germany applied great pressure on the Swedish authorities after the success of Operation *Rubble* and, in consequence, the Swedish Navy escorted the convoy with fully-lighted warships and made it impossible for them to take refuge in Swedish territorial waters when the German Navy made an appearance. As a result only two reached British ports.

Other operations were conducted from Sweden, where Colonel Andrew Croft, whom we will encounter again in the final chapter, looked after SOE interests after he became the Assistant Military Attaché in 1941. In July that year, a train taking supplies to the Germans in Norway blew up while still on Swedish territory, an incident not appreciated in Stockholm. From that point onwards, the SOE Scandinavian Section in Baker Street gave its attention very largely to supporting the *Milorg* in Norway, which was reported to have reached a membership of some 20,000 men and women.

One of the most intriguing characters working for SOE in Norway was Gunnar Sønsteby, who at the time of publication is still alive and well. His book *Report from No. 24*, his number when he began working for SOE, explains his exploits in German-occupied Norway, involving sabotage and preparations for the liberation of his country. He was given the task of specifically monitoring the building of a U-boat base at Trondheim. He also organized the sabotage of the Messerschmidt aircraft parts storage depot at Korsvoll and an oil depot inside the Oslo dockyard.

Arguably the most important SOE operations carried out in Norway during the whole of the Second World War were those to destroy the industrial plant at Vemork, which had been turned over to the production of heavy water for the atomic weapon programme in Germany. This had many heroes, including:

Einar Skinnarland, DSO, MM
(Obituary *The Times* February 4, 2003)

As an engineer at the Vemork hydro-electric plant some 50 miles west of Oslo, Einar Skinnarland provided a vital link in the struggle to frustrate Germany's production of plutonium to develop an atomic bomb during the Second World War. The electrolytic process for the division of water to obtain hydrogen for the manufacture of ammonia at Vemork produced, simply as a by-product, small quantities of heavy water. This differed from ordinary water only in that the hydrogen atom is heavier than normal, but the heavy water was essential for Germany's production of plutonium.

In May 1940, shortly after the German occupation of Norway, British Intelligence learnt that the Vemork plant had been ordered to increase production of heavy water to 3,000lb per year, a figure advanced to 10,000lb in January 1942. Six weeks later, a group of young Norwegians planning to join one of their units in Britain hijacked the coastal steamer *Galtesund* and sailed her to Aberdeen. Among them was Einar Skinnarland on one month's annual holiday from the Vemork plant. The layout of the plant was already known in Britain, thanks to information from Professor Lief Tronstadt, a Norwegian scientist who had left Norway before the occupation. But Skinnarland was able to provide details of the German guarding system and, even more important, was prepared to return to Vemork to act as guide for a future sabotage operation.

After a comprehensive debriefing on the current situation at Vemork and very basic parachute training, he was dropped over the Hardanger Vidda mountains by an RAF aircraft on March 28, 1942. This was 11 days after he had reached Aberdeen and just in time for his return to work at the end of his 'holiday'. Because of the mountainous terrain and swiftly changing weather conditions, Skinnarland's return was only the second operation the RAF had been able to accomplish on behalf of special forces in Norway at that stage of the war.

Moreover, the summer nights were too short to give adequate cover, so no attempt could be made to capitalise on the intelligence Skinnarland had provided until the autumn of 1942. He, meanwhile, befriended the chief engineer of the plant, gleaned from him additional information necessary for a *coup de main* operation and relayed this by radio to the Special Operations Executive (SOE) in London.

The first operation, in November 1942, ended in disaster. A four-man team of the Norwegian SOE, led by Lieutenant Jens Anton Poulsson, had been dropped successfully in October and established contact with Skinnarland. Their task was to select and prepare landing sites for two gliders carrying British commando-engineers and – based on latest information from Skinnarland – guide them to the Vemork plant. Both gliders crashed in bad weather and the survivors were captured and executed.

A second operation, carried out by a six-man team of the Norwegian SOE parachuted on to the Hardanger Vidda in February 1943, was completely successful. The second team met Poulsson and his companions, who had existed on the mountain throughout the winter, and carried out a copybook sabotage action that put the heavy water producing plant out of action without the loss of a Norwegian life. When General Nikolaus von Falkenhorst, commander of the German forces in Norway, inspected the site he declared it a military operation -the best piece of sabotage he had seen – and ordered the release of the Norwegian hostages rounded up by the local Quisling leader.

When the SOE teams returned to Britain, one of them through Sweden, two members remained behind to train and arm volunteers for the Norwegian Home Army, as the resistance movement was known. One of those to remain, Knut Haukelid, teamed up with Skinnarland in a mountain hut until the spring thaw of 1943, when they moved to a farm on the lower slopes, where they were better placed to gather information to relay back to SOE headquarters in London.

In July they received an inquiry about reports that production of heavy water at the Vemork plant had restarted. It was decided to attempt to destroy the plant by a United States Army Air Force bombing raid. This wrecked the factory but failed to destroy the heavy water plant, which was protected by seven concrete floors above it.

Norwegian technicians were able to convince the German authorities that the plant as a whole was no longer viable but, on January 29, 1944, London advised Skinnarland that it was to be dismantled and shipped to Germany, together with the Vemork stocks of heavy water.

Haukelid and he took great risks in entering local towns, where both were well known, to gather information about the planned shipment. Eventually, they discovered that it was to be conveyed in a Norwegian ferryboat which would have to traverse Lake Tinnsjo on its way to the open sea. Assisted by others recruited locally, Haukelid placed charges on the keel of the ferry, which blew up and sank in 1,000ft of water in Lake Tinnsjo in February 1944, sadly with the loss of several Norwegian lives.

The exploits of Skinnarland and Haukelid and their resistance colleagues were immortalised in the film *The Heroes of Telemark* (1965), with Kirk Douglas and Richard Harris.

Skinnarland continued to maintain radio contact between the local elements of the Norwegian resistance and SOE headquarters in London until the end of the war in Europe, when the Norwegian Home Army took over the emergency administration of their country.

After the war, Skinnarland emigrated to Canada. He is survived by his wife and five children.

(He died in Toronto on December 5, 2002, aged 84)

All who took part in the second raid received decorations from Britain and Norway. The leaders were Joachim Rønneberg who led the *coup de main* party from Britain, who is still alive at the time of this publication, and the staunch commander of the reception team who had wintered on the Hardanger Vidda waiting for Rønneberg's group to arrive.

Colonel Jens Anton Poulsson, DSO
(Obituary *The Times* February 17, 2010)

As a young officer of the Special Operations Executive, Jens Anton Poulsson led the in-country support team for two attempts to destroy Hitler's heavy water plant in German-occupied Norway. The first operation proved a tragic failure, the second a resounding success.

Poulsson's outstanding contribution was to keep his team alive and highly motivated during the intervening three months – living on what they could scavenge or snare above the tree line on Norway's uninhabited Hardanger Vidda mountain range.

Towards the end of 1941, secret intelligence sources in occupied Norway reported a marked increase in the production of heavy water – essential for the manufacture of plutonium – at the Norsk Hydro plant at Vemork, fifty miles west of Oslo. Operation *Freshman*, using glider-borne engineer commandos, was the first attempt to halt Hitler's atom bomb development programme. At 6 pm one evening in early November 1942, duplicate teams of engineer commandos boarded two gliders which were to be towed by Halifax bombers to landing zones within skiing and marching distance of Vemork.

Three weeks earlier, Poulsson and his team of three Norwegian NCOs – all from SOE – had been parachuted at night onto a nearby plateau. Their task was to prepare the operational base and landing zone, to which they were to guide the towing aircraft using a Eureka homing device. But as the aircraft and gliders crossed the Norwegian coast on the night the operation was launched, icing on their wings forced them to lose height. The first glider crashed near Stavanger and the second tug aircraft, after briefly picking up the Eureka signal, hit a mountainside. All nine survivors of the second glider were executed on Hitler's order. Poulsson and his team were left to their own devices on the mountain.

Knowing they would be hunted by German troops following the glider catastrophe, he took his team up above the tree line where they found an empty trapper's hut. Here they survived, living on snared small game and a reindeer he shot just before Christmas. News received from London by radio in early January gave warning of a new plan – a great boost to their morale and resolve to survive.

Meanwhile at the Commando training base at Aviemore in Scotland, a new sabotage group was forming up under Lieutenant Joachim Rønneberg. He trained his team of five Norwegians on a scale model of the Vemork plant prepared by Professor Leif Tronstadt, who had worked there and knew it intimately. Rønneberg's group was parachuted over the Hardanger Vidda on the night of February 16, 1943. Except for one weapons container falling wide but recovered, the drop was perfect. After sheltering in an empty hut during a three-day gale, by good chance they met two members of Poulsson's group on the mountainside.

Working together, the two teams carried out the destruction of the heavy water plant with ruthless efficiency. Carrying the explosives Rønneberg's group had brought, they set up a forward base close to the plant and climbed up to it from the bed of the Maan river. While Poulsson's group gave cover and stood ready to intervene should anyone try to interfere, Rønneberg's group entered the plant via the electricity supply tunnel and placed the charges alongside the heavy water plant.

Both parties were on their way down to the valley when the explosions were heard and the plant's alarm siren did not sound until after they had re-crossed the river. By dawn they had collected their skis from the forward base and set out for the mountain. Before dark, after struggling through a snow storm, they reached their main base on the Vidda, where the radio operators were waiting to send the success signal to London.

The German reaction to the SOE triumph was predictably furious. The local Quisling leader, co-operating with the occupation forces, ordered Norwegian hostages to be taken for reprisals. But when General Nikolaus von Falkenhorst, commander of German forces in Norway, had inspected the damage and pronounced it a purely military operation and one of the best acts of sabotage he had seen he ordered the hostages to be released.

Leaving three men behind to train the local Resistance and distribute equipment they could not take back, the two teams split up for return to Britain. Rønneberg's group returned via Sweden and Poulsson's by sea to Scotland. Both Poulsson and

Rønneberg were awarded the DSO and their respective team members either the Military Cross or the Military Medal.

An attempt was made in February 1944 to move from Norway to Germany the stocks of heavy water produced before the plant was sabotaged. When this intention became known to Knut Haukelid, one of the SOE team who had remained behind after the 1943 operation, he informed London and, with the help of the local resistance, placed charges on the keel of the ferry carrying the two railway trucks with the heavy water across Lake Tinnsjø. The ferry sank at a point where the lake is 1,000 feet deep.

This episode and the earlier sabotage of the of the heavy water plant were dramatized in the film *The Heroes of Telemark* (1965), starring Kirk Douglas, Richard Harris and Michael Redgrave. Poulsson appeared as himself in a French-made drama documentary about the sabotage mission, *Kampen om tungtvannet* (1948, The struggle for heavy water). In 1982 he published Aksjon Vemork, *Vinterkrig på Hardangervidda* (Winter war on the hardangervidda), an account of his wartime experiences.

Jens Anton Poulsson was born in Gransherad in the Telemark region of Norway in 1918. He continued to serve in the Norwegian Army after the war and eventually retired with the rank of colonel.

He is survived by his wife Bergljot and two daughters.
(He died on February 2, 2010, aged 91).

One member of Poulsson's team who displayed such rugged stoicism while waiting on the Vidda for Rønneberg and the *coup de main* party to arrive by parachute was Knut Haugland, who was take part in the famous Kon-Tiki Expedition. The greater part of his obituary in *The Times* was taken up with a description of his part in this epic sea voyage but the following extract deals with his service with the SOE.

Lieutenant-Colonel Knut Haugland, DSO, MM
(Obituary *The Times* December 29, 2009)

Knut Haugland was a wartime hero of the Norwegian resistance and the last living member of Thor Heyerdahl's Kon-Tiki expedition across the Pacific Ocean on a balsawood raft. Born in Rjukan, Telemark, in 1917 he had survived a life full of danger and excitement well before the invitation to sail the Pacific on a balsawood raft.

In 1938, after taking his *examen artium*, he enrolled on a military course to study radio communications. His posting to Setermoen in the far north early in 1940 coincided with the German invasion of Norway. He fought in the battles near Narvik as a part of the Norwegian campaign, but once the German occupation was established he retreated to work at the Havding Radiofabrikk factory in Oslo. He bitterly opposed the invasion and occupation of his country and was obstinately determined to do all in his power to thwart it. He joined the Norwegian resistance movement and in August 1941 was arrested by the Statspolitiet, escaping from custody, crossing into Sweden and from there reaching Britain. There he enrolled in the Norwegian Independent Company, the Kompani Linge.

With nine other Norwegian resistance fighters he embarked on the now famous raid to demolish the first plant in the world to mass-produce heavy water at Vemork, higher up the same valley where he was born in the rugged Telemark countryside. Although early in the war the use of heavy water in the development of nuclear energy may not have been fully understood by the Resistance, a German intention to develop a nuclear capability later became clear.

Haugland was parachuted into Hardangervidda in October 1942 with three other resistance members who were codenamed Operation *Grouse*. Their orders were to await a British operation codenamed *Freshman* which would use gliders. When this proved a disastrous failure, another team, Operation *Gunnerside*, was sent and in February 1943 the Vemork plant was successfully sabotaged. Haugland remained in Hardangervidda for two months before moving to Oslo where he helped to train marine telegraphers.

He made a return visit to Britain to collect more radio equipment and then flew back to Norway, parachuting near Skrimfjella to help with communications work with the Resistance. In Kongsberg he was arrested for a second time by the Gestapo but escaped and continued his efforts to train radio operators. On April Fool's Day in 1944 he again narrowly escaped from the Gestapo when one of his transmitters hidden in the Oslo Maternity Hospital was located by a German radio direction finder.

After this series of close shaves Haugland fled to England and did not return to Norway until after the war. His record of service twice won him Norway's highest decoration for military gallantry, the War Cross with two swords. Britain acknowledged his war record with the Distinguished Service Order and the Military Medal, while the French awarded him the *Croix de Guerre* and *Legion d'honneur*. He also received the Royal Norwegian Order of St Olav.

After the war Haugland returned to normal military life with a break for the Kon-Tiki expedition before transferring to the Royal Norwegian Air Force where he headed the electronic intelligence service in northern Norway, holding the rank of major and then lieutenant-colonel

He left the air force in 1963 to become acting, and subsequently the permanent, director of Norway's Resistance Museum. He was also director of the Kon-Tiki Museum beside Oslo Fjord where the famous raft now rests. He later became board chairman until his retirement in 1991.

Significantly, perhaps, all but one of the Kon-Tiki expedition members were keen supporters of the Scout movement. Haugland himself was an attaché to the 12th World Scout Conference in Elvesaeter and his taste for adventure and obstinate refusal to bow to authoritarian government or accept received wisdom at face value were marks of an exceptional man in the Scouting tradition. He is survived by his wife and his three children.

(He died on December 25, 2009, aged 92).

SOE communications with the Resistance in Norway were never easy, but the establishment of the 'Shetland Bus' sea link with the northern coast of Norway proved the most reliable method of sending in agents and quantities of stores and getting agents out. The link was run almost entirely by former Norwegian fishermen in often extremely hazardous sea conditions and under constant threat of interception by marauding aircraft of the Luftwaffe or interception by the German Navy.

Co-operation between SOE and the *Milorg* Resistance increased as the war began to turn in the Allies' favour and the 'bus' became the most reliable means of shipping volunteers from Britain to support sabotage in Norway to keep the German 300,000-strong army of occupation busy and not drawn away to strengthen Hitler's

'Atlantic Wall' defences against the inevitable Allies invasion. Many brave men were lost in the service of the Shetland Bus but the greatest hero was Leif Larsen.

Quartermaster Leif Larsen, DSO, DSC, CGM, DSM and Bar
(Obituary *The Times* October 17, 1990)

No one, British or foreign, ever received quite the range of British military decorations Leif Larsen did. He was awarded many Norwegian honours as well, and it was only because he was not British that he could not have the VC his bravery so richly deserved.

From 1940, after the German invasion of Norway, to the end of the war, Larsen was part of a small, secret organisation based at Lunna and Scalloway in Shetland, working under the aegis of the British Special Operations Executive. Norwegian fishing boats and their crews crossed and re-crossed the North Sea always in winter, benefiting from darkness but enduring appalling weather to smuggle SOE agents, arms and radio transmitters into occupied Norway, and to take refugees, Norwegian volunteers wanting to come to Britain for training and information out.

Larsen made 52 such voyages across the North Sea, surviving two shipwrecks off the Norwegian coast in foul weather. Among the operations in which he was involved was an attempted attack on the German battleship *Tirpitz*, anchored in Trondheim fjord, in 1942. This failed at the last minute, when heavy weather snapped the cables towing two-man 'chariot' submarines. Larsen was forced to scuttle the towing boat, but was able to get his crew back to Britain via neutral Sweden.

For Norwegians, 'taking the Shetland bus' became a synonym for escape in the last resort, and a small but significant aid to national morale. The crews and skippers themselves had no thought of escape: operating the 'Shetland bus' was their way of fighting back. Normal naval rules and discipline did not and could not apply to these indepen-dently-minded men. Crews were invited by British officers to elect their own skippers, and they seldom made a mistake. Larsen was the first to be elected by the men who had sailed with him, and he turned out to be the finest leader of them all.

He did not look the part. Then in his early thirties, he was a stocky man, with china-blue eyes, a broken nose, a wide humorous mouth, and so modest a manner that his talents might never have surfaced. But he had first gone to sea in fishing boats at the age of 16 in some of the most inhospitable seas on earth and when he joined the Norwegian navy's special service unit to operate with the SOE he soon showed astonishing qualities of rough and ready leadership and unshakeable courage. These, with a combination of confidence, bravado and luck brought him through one adventure after another in conditions which would have broken most men's nerve. By the end of the war he had become the subject of legendary stories in Norway and the object of devotion among the crews, affection and admiration among his British colleagues, and a certain natural jealousy and mistrust among officers of the Norwegian navy. All of this left him unchanged and unspoilt.

The most notable quality of his character was its stability. He was always the same, with people of every rank, whether talking to the commander-in-chief Home Fleet, the Norwegian crown prince, an ordinary Shetlander or a British private, he remained himself, never raising his gentle voice to his juniors, never obsequious or over-awed by his seniors. His men recall that he was the same in battle unruffled and quiet as he stood at his wheel while the wheelhouse was shot to matchwood around him, or as he sat in a cabin discussing with a German officer the cargo of peat which hid weaponry, explosives and British sailors. He was equally unruffled, hove-to in a hurricane, in a dinghy with wounded and dying comrades, or having to abandon his sinking ship a hundred miles from shore and four hundred from home.

Yet his was not the calm which can be shown in danger by people of little imagination, and which sometimes passes for bravery. He once said in confidence that he had been scared stiff in his most recent adventure, and indeed he had the sense often to be afraid; but he always overcame his fear by that mixture of sense of duty and self-respect and of strength of will which is true courage.

Larsen continued with his daring exploits right to the end of the war and was one of the most decorated men in the entire allied forces, holding the uncommon Conspicuous Gallantry Medal among his honours. After the war he ran a small factory in Norway.

He is survived by his wife, Anna, and three daughters.
(He died at Bergen on October 12, 1990, aged 84)

The German battleship *Tirpitz* posed a threat to Allied shipping in the North Atlantic for much of the war, keeping warships of the Royal Navy's Home Fleet on watch as she lay in a Norwegian fjord waiting for an opportunity to emerge. On the one occasion she did – to attack a Russia-bound convoy – she was forced back into her refuge. The first attack on the *Tirpitz t*o impose significant damage as she lay at anchor in the fjord was an exceptionally hazardous and demanding operation. Royal Navy X class midget submarines placed explosive charges beneath her hull in September 1943.

Lieutenant Basil Place commanding HM Submarine X7 and Lieutenant Donald Cameron commanding HM Submarine X6 both received the Victoria Cross for their part in the action. The German warship was finally put out of the war when attacked by Lancaster bombers of the Royal Air Force on November 12, 1944, leading her to capsize.

As the date for the Allied invasion of North-West Europe approached, SOE became concerned with increasing the scope and range of sabotage in Norway, so as to keep the 300,000-strong German garrison tied up there, rather than withdrawing – all or in part – to reinforce Hitler's 'Atlantic Wall' of defence along the coast of Holland, Belgium and France. One of the key figures in working towards this aspiration was Max Manus, who had been with SOE since 1940.

Max Manus, DSO, MC and Bar
(Obituary *The Times* October 2, 1995)

A well-nigh legendary hero of wartime Norwegian resistance, many of whose exploits would seem at home in an Alistair Maclean novel, Max Manus made his adventures the theme of two books he wrote after the war. He risked his life in a series of acts of sabotage during the German occupation of Norway from 1940 to 1945.

That he survived the war was, in his view, due less to skill than a great measure of luck. If so, it was a luck aided by intelligence, quick reactions and a nonchalant disregard for personal danger. "Others live on proteins and vitamins," he wrote in one of his books, "but my life has been based on adrenalin."

Manus's relentlessly pursued campaign against German occupying forces brought him to the top of Norway's Resistance movement. He was involved in a variety of activities including sabotage, the underground press, counter-intelligence and propaganda directed against German soldiers. As a result he was high on the list of men the Germans wanted captured. But he always managed, sometimes by a mere hair's breadth, to escape.

Manus had just returned from the Winter War of 1939-40 in Finland, where he had fought as a volunteer against the invading Russians, when Germany attacked Norway. He took part in the armed resistance until Norway capitulated and then almost immediately became involved with the underground, particularly with the publication of clandestine newspapers.

When the Quisling state police arrived at his flat in Oslo in January 1941 to arrest him he threw himself out of the window, but was captured and taken to hospital. But with only a matter of hours to spare before he was due to be passed to the custody of the Gestapo, Manus escaped with the aid of hospital staff and friends on the outside, and got away across the border to Sweden. An eventful journey halfway round the world took him to Canada, then to Britain. Here he was trained in commando tactics and sabotage. In March 1943, as a member of the famous *Company Linge*, he arrived back in Norway with the specific purpose of conducting naval sabotage.

With the use of limpet mines Manus and a friend, Gregers Gram, succeeded in sinking the German ships *Ortelsburg* and *Tugela* (Operation *Mardonius*). Further acts of naval sabotage followed (Operation *Bundle*, October 1943 to April 1944) and a failed attempt in June 1944 at sinking the troop carrier *Monte Rosa*. In January 1945 Manus's most spectacular and dramatic act of sabotage took place – the sinking of the troop carrier *Donau* in the Oslo Fjord. This was a ship which had been used for years to transport large numbers of Norwegian prisoners of war to concentration camps in Germany.

From the spring of 1944 Manus was one of the driving

forces behind the Oslo Gang – a group working on behalf of Norway's military resistance – which performed a number of daring acts in the last year of the war. In May 1944, together with a team of Allies, Manus succeeded in destroying by fire the offices and archives of the Employment Service, nominally an organisation set up to prepare young people for work, in reality a facade for the mobilisation of Norwegian men to serve as soldiers on the Eastern Front.

As the fire was just catching hold the police arrived on the scene. Manus told his accomplices to exit via the back while he, continuously firing his machine-pistol in the direction of the police, ran out of the main gate. Along the road he held up a passing cyclist demanding "your bicycle or your life", and got away.

A number of years in his youth had been spent in the West Indies and South America, where among other things he worked as a plantation manager and carpenter. Here he was also involved in the smuggling of weapons – a useful training for his later subversive activities. His two books, published in Norway immediately after the war, were later translated in English as *Underwater Saboteur* and *Nine Lives before Thirty*. They sold in vast numbers in Norway, and the income from them was used by Manus to found a successful computer and office equipment business where he employed many of his wartime colleagues.

When, at the end of the war, the King and his family returned to Norway from exile, Manus was appointed to guard Crown Prince Olav against snipers. If a grenade was thrown into the car carrying the prince, Manus's instruction was to throw himself on top of it.

For his war services Manus received Norway's highest gallantry award, the Norwegian War Cross. His funeral was attended by Olav's son, King Harald.

He is survived by his wife Tikken, whom he had met during the war in Sweden, where she was working for the Norwegian consulate, helping to ease the plight of Norwegian fugitives in that country.

(He died on September 20, 1996 aged 81)

Unlike Norway, after German occupation in 1940 Denmark offered little scope for sabotage and subversion. The Danish authorities in Britain were hesitant about any enterprise that might damage their eventual post-war recovery or divide the nation politically. Yet, despite this daunting prospect, persistent efforts were made by SOE to establish contacts with the Danish Resistance and give what help it could.

Ronald Turnbull, OBE
(Obituary *The Times* March 11, 2004)

Recruited into the Special Operations Executive when it was created in 1940, after careers in journalism and the Foreign Office, Ronald Turnbull was appointed the SOE's Danish organiser in Stockholm, where he arrived in 1941. In the Swedish capital his task was the sometimes delicate one of co-ordinating relations between the SOE and the Danish Resistance for the remainder of the war.

In a climate which was sometimes one of misunderstanding between the SOE leadership in London and its Resistance contacts in Copenhagen about each others' expectations and intentions, he played his part in helping Danish Resistance to develop more teeth, as the war progressed. From an early disastrous attempt to insert two agents into Denmark in 1941, he saw operations take on a more vigorous and more professional hue, and in the end become much more effective.

Ronald Bruce Turnbull was born in Edinburgh in 1914. He was educated at Cargilfield School, Cramond, and Fettes College, where he excelled at sports, mountaineering and history. In 1935 he went to Gonville and Caius College, Cambridge, to read history. While still at Fettes he had struck up a friendship with a visiting Danish schoolboy and, when a rugby injury forced him to take time out from his university studies, he spent the summer at Copenhagen University as a lektor, reading out texts to Danes studying English literature.

At Cambridge he acted in Elizabethan plays with the ADC and Marlowe Society, and he also edited the student newspaper Varsity. On leaving Cambridge, he stood (unsuccessfully) as a Liberal MP in the East End of London at Bethnal Green. He next began work as a journalist on the London Evening Standard. His fluency in Danish also enabled him to broadcast for the BBC until he was posted in October 1939 as a press attaché to the British Legation in Copenhagen. From there, in the aftermath of the German invasion of Poland, he reported to the Foreign Office in London on attitudes to German aggression among leading members of the Danish Government.

In the spring of 1940 Turnbull had just become engaged to Maria Thereza do Rio Branco, daughter of the Brazilian Ambassador. On April 9, 1940, he was awoken in Copenhagen at 7am by the sound of aircraft. He rushed to the window of his apartment to see German bombers flying over the city. Soon neutral Denmark was at the mercy of the Nazi invaders.

Turnbull eventually got away in a sealed train through Germany to Belgium and so to London. There he was joined by his fiancée and they were married in London on May 22, 1940.

When, in July, SOE was brought into being with the Churchillian injunction to "set Europe ablaze", Turnbull was recruited. On September 30 he was appointed to Stockholm, there to assess, and if possible to build up, the Resistance organisation in Denmark. From his knowledge of the country he had already presented to the head of SOE's Danish section, Lieutenant-Commander R. C. Hollingworth, a comprehensive analysis of the Danish people's likely reaction to what was, certainly at first, a relatively benign occupation. In it he had emphasised the necessity of making contact with and encouraging organisations which might combine to create an attitude of greater hostility towards the occupying power.

At that stage of the war, with the Germans in the ascendant everywhere, the journey from London to Stockholm was more difficult than the distance as the crow flies might suggest. Turnbull left England on December 15, 1940, accompanied by his new (and pregnant) wife and his assistant Pamela Towers. Their route was by sea to Cape Town where his party was taken by flying-boat up Africa to Cairo. They then reached Istanbul by car and train through Palestine. On February 15, 1941, his son was born in Istanbul.

On March 6 he took the last Soviet ship to Odessa via Bulgaria and then travelled by train to Moscow where he was put up at the British Embassy by Sir Stafford Cripps. From there, on March 12, he was flown to Stockholm.

This roundabout journey was treated to the derision of Lord Haw-Haw in one of his propaganda radio broadcasts, as having been made necessary by German control of the Continent and the skies over Europe.

Once in Sweden, Turnbull proceeded to set up the SOE outpost at the British Legation. Denmark was not at that time high on SOE's list of priorities. The assessments about resistance possibilities issuing from Hollingworth's London office were, as he admitted, somewhat optimistic, given the fact that the Germans held the country with a light hand, leaving it to govern itself.

One of the difficulties was in recruiting agents to be trained and then dropped in by parachute. And when, in December 1941, SOE was ready to mount its first insertion by agents, it was a disaster. Of the two agents parachuted in from an RAF bomber as part of an air raid, one was killed when his parachute failed to open. His radio operator was left isolated, unable to function since the two man unit's radio had been carried by his comrade, and had been smashed in his fatal fall.

In 1942 Turnbull made the first contact with members of the Danish General Staff Intelligence Organisation. This meeting laid the basis for further work in Stockholm. In April 1942 (Operation *Table Top*) the first complete three-man team of Danish Resistance personnel, trained in England, was dropped into Denmark.

Turnbull's main goal was to co-ordinate the efforts of Danish Intelligence (LIGA) with those organised in London. He was authorised to act as the only authentic channel of communication between Denmark and London and also had to ensure that no breach occurred between Danish amateurs and professionals in the field.

With the arrival in 1943 of a new Danish agent, Flemming Muus, satisfactory co-ordination and a new impetus was at last achieved in the field. Danish Resistance and sabotage were stepped up, culminating in the August uprising of that year, as a result of which the Germans took over direct control of the government of the country. There were by then many more agents in Denmark, and large supplies of explosives and weapons were dropped to help the underground.

About this time, the Danish Freedom Council was formed to co-ordinate resistance activities and prepare for liberation. In August 1943 LIGA supplied Turnbull with drawings of the V1 flying bomb which had been fired from Peenemunde and had crash-landed without exploding on the Danish island of

Bornholm. These were sent immediately to London, some ten months before the V1 attacks on London began.

Meanwhile, Turnbull had for some time been trying to persuade the Nobel prize-winning nuclear physicist, Niels Bohr, to escape from Denmark to Stockholm and join the British and American scientists already working on the atom bomb. This Bohr did on September 30, 1943, and was put on an RAF Mosquito aircraft for London by Turnbull.

As the defeat of Germany drew closer, Turnbull urged the Foreign Office, via the Ambassador in Sweden, of the desirability of establishing a British presence in the country as soon as possible after a German collapse. There had been rumours of a plan to delay going into the country with a military force until 35 days after a German surrender, on the grounds that the Danes would be able to restore order themselves. Turnbull pointed out that the Danes would regard the absence of a liberating force as a sign of indifference by the Allies, and would undoubtedly resent such a presence if it occurred only after they had picked up the pieces themselves. Turnbull's arguments carried the day: British diplomats returned to Copenhagen on the heels of the German surrender, while Montgomery's victory parade in the capital on May 12, 1945, set the seal on the country's liberation. Turnbull was appointed OBE, awarded the American Medal of Freedom and created a Knight of the Dannebrog.

Turnbull returned to Denmark, now as a representative of the Foreign Office following the closing down of SOE at the war's end. But on September 29, 1945, his wife was killed in a motor accident. He left government service and with his son and newly born daughter went to his wife's homeland where he set up a thriving advertising business with Danish and American colleagues.

In December 1946 he married Maria Helena Arantes Negrao, and they had two sons and three daughters. In the 1970s he moved into commercial translation, at which he became a recognised expert. His wife died in 1982. In February 2003 Turnbull returned to Scotland for recuperation from a long illness. He died in a nursing home in Pencaitland, East Lothian. He is survived by nine children, including two sons from a third relationship.

(He died on March 2, 2004, aged 89)

The Dane mentioned in Turnbull's obituary – Flemming Muus – was a founding member of the Danish liberation council established in the country in 1943 and a stalwart worker for the Danish Resistance until liberation in 1945.

Flemming Muus
(Obituary *The Times* September 25, 1982)

Mr Flemming Muus, one of the leading figures in the Danish Resistance movement during the Second World War, died in Copenhagenon September 23 at the age of 74.

Born on November 21, 1907, Muus found himself in Liberia on April 9, 1940, when Denmark was occupied overnight by the Germans. A businessman, he had been working in Liberia since 1931, holding among other posts the local shipping representation for the Elder Dempster Lines.

After initial frustration, Muus managed finally to make his way to England in the spring of 1942, and enlisted immediately in The Buffs (of which regiment the King of Denmark was the Colonel-in-Chief). He reached the rank of major after undergoing training as a parachutist agent.

In March 1943, he returned to Denmark, being parachuted by the British over north Jutland as a member of the Special Forces Unit with the express object of organizing Danish resistance to the Germans in preparation for the allies' later liberation of the country. His *nom de guerre* was 'Jorgen' during the long assignment, which was to take Muus, whose facial traits had been disguised by plastic surgery, a central figure in the Danish underground movement.

He brushed often with death, forming Danish sabotage groups, moulding them into an effective co-ordinated force, and working closely with the British; among his tasks were organizing the receipt of containers of arms and explosives and maintaining radio contact with the Allies.

A measure of Muus's role is given by the fact that recorded sabotage operations against the Germans by the Danish Resistance force increased from 14 in January, 1943, to a monthly figure of 198 by August of the same year.

Muus was also in close contact with the Danish government under German occupation, and was largely responsible for provoking the collapse of its policy of collaboration with the occupying power in August 1943, and the beginning of open

Danish resistance to the Axis from then onwards. On August 29, the Danish government resigned and was succeeded by an overt German military regime, so that all semblance of Danish connivance with th Nazis came to an end.

Muus was a founding member of the 13-member *Frihedraad*, the Danish liberation council established in 1943 by the Resistance, and thus was one of those largely responsible for the reorganization of Denmark after its liberation by the British under Montgomery in 1945.

After the war Muus spent some years in South Africa, returning to Denmark in 1949. He lived there until his death, writing over 20 books, mainly autobiographies, travel books, and children's literature. Muus became a member, and later vice-president, of the board of the Danish Resistance Museum in Copenhagen. He edited one of the museum's publications, called *Resistance Veterans*. He was a member of the Special Forces Club in London.

Muus is survived by his half-English wife, Varinka, whom he married in 1944.

(He died on September 23, 1982, aged 74)

Another Dane who made a courageous contribution to the work of the Resistance in Denmark was Svend Truelson.

Svend Truelson
(Obituary *The Times* January 31, 1997)

One of the principal figures in the resistance to Germany's wartime occupation of Denmark, Svend Truelsen spied for the Allies there before, in 1944, he was forced to flee the country, hotly pursued by the Gestapo. Escaping via Sweden to Britain, he co-operated closely with the Special Operations Executive (SOE) in organising Danish Resistance activities. In particular he did valuable work helping to plan RAF bombing raids on German targets in occupied Denmark.

Notable among these were the spectacular low level attacks on various Gestapo headquarters in Denmark which, by destroying all secret police records and killing Nazi and collaborationist personnel, prevented the Gestapo from moving against members of the Danish Resistance. Perhaps the most completely successful of these was the raid – conducted with almost surgical precision – on the Gestapo

HQ situated in the Aarhus University building, which totally wrecked it and took severe toll of Gestapo life, without inflicting collateral damage. It was, thereafter, impossible for the Gestapo to know who Resistance members were, since their organisation in Jutland had been completely destroyed.

Germany had occupied Denmark in 1940 with little resistance, and the government initially adopted a policy of Vichy-style peaceful collaboration with the Nazis, much to the anguish of Truelsen and the burgeoning Resistance movement. But as secretary-general of the Danish Agricultural Council, the umbrella organisation for Denmark's powerful farming lobby, Truelsen had at his disposal a ready-made network of contacts throughout Denmark when he took over the leadership of the unofficial Danish secret service in August 1943.

"Our (farmer) contacts sent in reports of German troop movements and other activities written on the back of meat production forms sent in to the Agricultural Council," Truelsen wrote later. "The information was processed by 50 resistance officers whom I employed and sent on to SOE in Baker Street in London."

During the early years of the German occupation, the resistance movement gradually grew in Denmark, opposed to the government's policies of appeasement and determined to place Denmark on the Allied side. In August 1943, with Germany experiencing military reverses in all the theatres of war and Danish Resistance propaganda and sabotage beginning to take effect, the collaborationist government finally collapsed. An underground freedom council was formed by Danish resistance leaders to direct the struggle against the Nazis. By the liberation in 1945, the Danish Resistance movement numbered some 50,000 fighters.

After his escape, from May 1944 Truelsen was one of a group of exiled Danes working with the SOE in Britain, which included the politician Christmas Moeller, later to become foreign minister in Denmark's first post-liberation government. Truelsen underwent parachute training, being commissioned as a major in The Buffs (Royal East Kent Regiment) and was leader of Danish operations at Special Forces Headquarters in 1944-45.

Besides liaising with Danish resistance, he helped the RAF in planning three crucial air raids on Gestapo headquarters in occupied Denmark: at Aarhus on the Jutland peninsula; in the Shell Building in Copenhagen; and at Odense on the island of Funen. The Aarhus attack which took place at noon on October 31, 1944, was prompted by fears that South Jutland resistance groups were about to be uncovered. Twenty-four RAF Mosquito aircraft, attacking from rooftop level, totally destroyed their target and its archives. In the process they killed more than 100 Germans, including the Gestapo chief Schwitzgebel and his next in command.

After a tip-off that the Gestapo had infiltrated the entire Copenhagen resistance, the RAF sent 18 Mosquito and 28 Mustang fighters to Copenhagen on March 21, 1945. The mission was complicated by the presence of imprisoned Danish resistance fighters in the building; nevertheless, more than a hundred Gestapo officers and their Danish accomplices were killed in the raid. Seven of the Danish resistance fighters, held in the loft of Shell House, survived miraculously, two of them after jumping from the fourth floor of the building.

The raid was again a success but, tragically, one of the low-flying RAF planes crashed on the French School in the city, setting fire to the building, which some of the other incoming British aircraft then mistook for the target. Many bombs were dropped on the school, killing 112 people, 88 of them schoolchildren. The RAF lost seven aircraft with a death toll of 12.

The Odense raid was staged without loss of life or materiel on April 17, 1945, just weeks before the liberation of Denmark by British forces.

In 1945-46, Truelsen was a member of the Danish Freedom Council, which supervised the return to civilian government. After the war he served as a reserve officer in the Royal Danish Life Guard with the rank of major until 1975. He studied law, later practising as barrister and lecturing in the subject at Copenhagen University. He joined the boards of the once illegal Information Resistance Newspaper and of the Danish subsidiaries of many international corporations, Schweppes, Coca Cola and others.

Though he had, until a quite advanced age, been an active sportsman, he was crippled by a stroke in his seventies and spent the last eight years of his life in a wheelchair.

He is survived by his second wife Eva, whom he married

in 1987, and the son and daughter of his first marriage with Maud, who died in 1977.

(He died on January 21, 1997, aged 81)

Finally, before leaving Denmark, here is the obituary of Ole Lippmann who also left a significant imprint on the history of the wartime Resistance in that country.

Ole Lippmann
(Obituary *The Times* October 25, 2002)

It was as chief of Special Forces in occupied Denmark and local representative of the Special Operations Executive (SOE) that Ole Lippmann welcomed Major General R. H. Dewing, the incoming Commander of British Forces in liberated Denmark, on his arrival at Copenhagen airport on May 5, 1945.

In the years of occupation Lippmann's most significant exploit had been to persuade the RAF to bomb the Gestapo headquarters in Copenhagen in March 1945. The operation was successful but there were high civilian casualties, with 88 schoolchildren among the dead after one of the low-flying RAF aircraft crashed on to a school.

Lippmann had travelled widely in the 1930s as a student, visiting Britain, the United States, Japan and the Soviet Union. He experienced at first hand Japan's invasion of China in 1937 before continuing his travels to the Soviet Union, where evidence of the purges and terror of the Stalin era thoroughly disabused him of any sympathy with communism.

After the breakdown of Denmark's policy of appeasement of its Nazi occupiers, the underground Resistance movement formed the Freedom Council in 1943. It aimed to rid Denmark of the German presence, supervise the return to civilian government after the war and ensure that thereafter the country was firmly on the side of the Western allies.

Lippmann's task was initially to reorganise military espionage activities in Denmark, purchase arms from neutral Sweden and distribute supplies flown in by the RAF for sabotage operations. In 1944 he was summoned to London for training as a parachute trooper, attaining the rank of major in The Buffs (Royal East Kent Regiment). In January 1945 he returned via Sweden to Copenhagen to become successor to Flemming Muus as Allied observer on the Freedom Council and SOE's chief agent in Denmark.

Lippmann also carried a message to King Christian X from King George VI, secreting it in a tube in his rectum to hide it from German searches.

In peacetime Lippmann returned to his business career as owner of the medical and hospital equipment firm Simonsen & Weel. In 1956 he organised and participated in Danish Red Cross ambulance services in Budapest during the Soviet intervention.

(He died on September 3, 2002, aged 86)

Aside from all that Denmark had done to assist the Allied cause since the change of policy in Copenhagen in 1943, the country had regained its self-respect and returned to peace without any internal political conflict. The price of her co-operation with the Allies – and SOE in particular – had been high, however. There were serious numbers of Danish casualties from the RAF bombing raids on the Gestapo headquarters and other targets and an unknown number of hostages had been shot by the occupying German forces in retaliation for acts of sabotage.

Fifty-seven SOE-trained Danish agents had been infiltrated into the country during the course of the war, of whom thirteen were captured and six killed. The encouragement and then support of the Resistance movement had required delicate handling by SOE headquarters in London, due to the early policy of reluctant Government collaboration with the German occupying forces but relations rapidly became easier and more positive after the end of this attitude came with the resignation of the Danish Government in 1943.

The fact that it was the British Army that entered Denmark to take the German surrender was celebrated for many years on the May anniversary as the 'coming of the light', with candles burning in the front windows of every house in every town. Free at last, many Danes joined British regiments with the intention of fighting the Japanese, as although the war in Europe ended in May 1945 that in the Far East continued until August.

Links with comrades in SOE were maintained by Danish SOE veterans by membership of the Special Forces Club in London and attendance at occasions of remembrance for the fallen. These were welcome signs of the continued friendship between the two countries; welcome because it was due to British and French intentions towards Norway in 1940 that led to Denmark being invaded by Germany in the first place and subsequently occupied for five long years.

4

The Low Countries and Escape Lines

As we shall see, the history of SOE in the Low Countries and in Holland in particular does not make happy reading. Before the sequence of disasters and disappointments began, however, an act of strategic sabotage not conducted by SOE – as the organization had yet to be established – was executed with such dash and success that it may have been the inspiration for Winston Churchill's order to 'set Europe ablaze'.

Major Robert 'Peter' Keeble, DSO, MC, TD.
(Obituary *The Times* October 29, 2004)

Robert Keeble was named after a godfather but called 'Peter' in childhood and known by no other name. He was born in Kenilworth, Warwickshire, educated at King Henry VIII's School, Coventry, then indentured to Alfred Herbert Machine Tool manufacturers.

At the outbreak of war he was a captain commanding a field company of the Kent Fortress Royal Engineers who, together with other Territorial Army artillery and engineers units, were required to man sections of the country's coastal defences. His first experience of active service was of a quite different nature, however.

The surprise German invasion of the Low Countries and northern France, in May 1940, alerted the War Office Military Operations branch to the risk of vast oil stocks stored in continental ports falling into enemy hands, so the Kent Fortress Engineers were ordered to send demolition parties to France and the Netherlands to destroy them. Keeble's party of 18 NCOs and men was embarked in the destroyer HMS *Whitshead* with their explosives, arms, ammunition and equipment piled on the deck. His mission was to destroy the oil stocks at Amsterdam.

Withdrawal arrangements were clearly not the immediate priority, and *Whitshead*'s captain had orders not to hazard his ship unnecessarily. There was no guaranteed return ticket.

Despite zigzagging at speed, *Whitshead* was hit on the port quarter by a German bomb as she neared the Dutch coast, and half a dozen of the crew were blown into the sea. The ship turned round to pick them up but, when she was attacked again, some floats were put over the side and the ship raced on for IJmuiden where her efforts to come alongside were further delayed by enemy air attack. Once ashore, Keeble and his men were sent with a naval covering party of an officer and 16 ratings on a single-carriage train to Amsterdam, where Keeble was taken to meet the Dutch naval commander-in-charge.

As soon as his mission had been cleared by The Hague, Keeble toured all the installations, met the managers to get information on the layout and types of oil stored, without giving away his real intention, allowing it to be inferred that he was there to help to protect the oil from German parachutists. At dusk on May 12 he moved his small force to their objectives, allocated tasks, gave the signal for action and outlined the tentative withdrawal routes. Early next day, the British naval officer responsible for the whole demolition programme telephoned Keeble and ordered him to carry out his demolition tasks but to try to inform The Hague as a matter of courtesy. Keeble got straight through to The Hague and heard an anxious voice say: "Do it now."

His sappers used gun cotton to blow off the filler cocks to the oil tanks, flooding the concrete surrounds, then fired Very-light cartridges into the air above them. The fuel ignited and burnt furiously about 50ft above each tank, and every now and then, with an enormous blast, a whole tank would take off into the air, roll over and fall down. After the destruction of the outlying tanks, the demolition party made its way to the rendezvous. There Keeble was waiting to fire the last group of storage tanks.

Three launches had been put at their disposal for withdrawal down the canal system to the coast, but Keeble had heard that the Luftwaffe had mined the canals. He therefore commandeered the first good-size lorry he saw and drove fast for IJmuiden. On arrival he appreciated that the prospects of evacuation were not good, but eventually found a 32ft motor boat and put two sappers aboard. After firing the remaining oil tanks, he and his complete party headed out to sea with no navigational instruments or charts, only a compass. They motored due west throughout that night and the following day until the destroyer *Havoc*, fortuitously on passage from action off Norway, sighted them and took them to Harwich.

Keeble and two other sapper officers who had led demolition parties were all recommended for the Military Cross. But when Winston Churchill, who had been much concerned about the oil stocks while First Lord of the Admiralty, heard of the successful demolition operations he sent for a report and put a pen through the citations, deleting the MC and writing 'DSO' across each.

In consequence of his success in the Netherlands, in August 1940 Keeble was sent round the Cape to Cairo to advise HQ Middle East on possible demolition of the British-owned Iraqi oil fields around Kirkuk. Although the German invasion of the Soviet Union did not occur until the following June, Churchill believed that Hitler might strike eastwards in his quest for oil. This was a clandestine operation, so Keeble travelled around Iraq in civilian clothes armed with a handbook on oil drilling bought at Foyles before leaving London, as he had no knowledge of how to destroy oil wells as distinct from oil tanks.

He and the local manager devised a contingency plan for putting the 53 wells not currently in use out of action by dropping the end of the boring drill down the shaft, hardened end uppermost, then cementing in the hole. He was mentioned in dispatches after his return to England, where he rejoined his former unit. He went back to the Continent with the Second Army, on the invasion of Normandy in June 1944, and commanded No 582 (Kent) Field Company Royal Engineers in the North-West Europe campaign, in which he was twice wounded, awarded the Military Cross and again mentioned in dispatches.

As with other members of the Kent Fortress Engineers, he joined the cement industry on demobilisation. He was a director of Associated Portland Cement Manufacturers, 1970-74, a governor of Hull University, an honorary Brother of Hull Trinity House and also a Freeman of the City of London and a Liveryman of the Company of Fan Makers. Keeble was an indefatigably humorous and restless man. He water-skied until he was 90, and then mastered windsurfing. He was unmarried.

(He died on August 23, 2004, aged 93).

The disastrous performance of SOE in Holland arose through refusal of the staff of Baker Street's N Section, responsible for Holland, to believe radio traffic evidence that their network of agents had been compromised. The German *Abwehr* had taken it over and were sending false messages back to London from 1942 to 1944. New agents dropped by parachute were arrested on arrival by the Gestapo and, in turn, put to work against their true masters. Those who refused to co-operate were shot as spies.

This dreadful situation was eventually recognized in London, following the arrival in early 1944 of two SOE agents who had escaped from enemy custody the previous August. SOE was subjected to rigorous inquiry but survived. The Secret Intelligence Service (MI 6) would have been glad to see this organization of 'enthusiastic amateurs' disbanded or at least put under SIS control but, ironically, at the latter's insistence all SOE signals traffic had initially been routed through MI 6 in London. For this reason, some blame for the security failure became attached to both services.

A myth grew up in Holland that the whole fiasco was either a deliberate and cynical ploy to deceive German intelligence over the site of the impending Allied landing in north-west Europe, to which the lives of many Dutch agents had been ruthlessly sacrificed, or the result of inter-service rivalry between MI 6 and SOE. The following article published as late as 1974 explains what happened while incorporating the misguided views as to the reasons of a supposedly reputable Dutch historian.

Rivalry in London led to deaths of agents
(*The Times*, May 2, 1974, Sue Masterman, The Hague)
Rivalry between the different branches of' the British Secret Service operating in London in the first half of the Second World War has been blamed for the arrest of almost all the Dutch agents they sent out to the Netherlands and to the deaths of many

members of Dutch Resistance groups. The allegation is made by the Dutch historian Dr Lou de Jong, head of the Institute of Wartime Documentation in Amsterdam. He is the author of *The Kingdom of the Netherlands in the Second World War*, an official history in 12 volumes.

In the second half of volume five, published today, a chapter deals with the 'capital blunders' of both MI 6 and the Special Operations Executive, Dutch section, between March, 1941, and July, 1942. Of the 11 agents sent out by MI 6 and its associates in this period, eight were arrested, one killed and two succeeded in returning to England. Of the 19 agents sent out by the SOE 16 were arrested, seven immediately after they were parachuted into the Netherlands, two were killed and one managed to return. The absolute lack of security training for the agents meant that they unwittingly led the German occupying forces directly to the Dutch Resistance movements with whom they were in contact.

The incompetence of the SOE operation gave the Germans the chance to set up, what is known as the *'Englandspiel'*. Various radio operators were arrested complete with all their codes. They were persuaded, often in exchange for promises that the lives of friends, relations or fellow agents would be spared, to transmit messages back to SOE and to act as though they were continuing their activities. The MI 6 radio operators (actually SOE) arrested managed to indicate either by omitting certain agreed 'mistakes' from their messages or failing to include security checks, that they had been arrested. M1 6 disregarded their information. But M1 6 failed to warn the SOE of the arrest of agents and SOE ignored the security checks omitted or the mistakes made by their own agents.

They continued to send secret messages involving Dutch resistance groups straight into German hands – and announced the parachuting of successive groups of agents who, after March, 1942, were intercepted immediately by the Germans on landing. Thirty-six agents and radio operators were arrested. This 'game' was a source of information about Dutch resistance activities to the Germans until late in 1943; The Germans built up a total of 18 'lines' with London.

Dr de Jong adds in SOE's defence that, after 1944, the Dutch section contributed considerably to the organization of sabotage and of a competent Resistance movement in the Netherlands. SOE also made a series of potentially fatal mistakes in equipping its agents. All radio operators were given a transmitter in a standard case, which was of such unusual size and shape that it attracted attention immediately. The Germans soon stopped people and searched them if they saw a case of roughly the same type. The identity card which the agents were given was obviously forged. The watermark showed the Dutch lions both facing the same way instead of facing one another.

Hubertus Lauwers, the first SOE radio operator to be arrested and to try in vain to warn the London headquarters of his arrest, later described to a post-war committee of inquiry how he and the agent Thijs Taconis, when they remarked on the badly forged identity cards, were told by one of the officers in London: "No one will blame you if you don't go." They were dressed almost identically in what is described as a supply of standard second hand clothing which was obviously not Dutch. SOE was also unaware that new zinc coinage had been issued in the Netherlands and that the Dutch were hoarding their silver coins. This made any agent who arrived loaded with silver coinage suspicious. In general, the agents had no ration books, not enough money, and were poorly equipped with contact addresses. They had no training in elementary security precautions, and the selection of agents also left much to be desired.

Only with the return of agent (George) Dessing to London in 1943 did SOE realize that their apparently efficiently working radio network in the Netherlands was a German-controlled farce and they had been feeding their agents and their information direct into enemy hands. Dr de Jonge does not believe that there was more behind the SOE failure than bitter inter-service rivalry. He discounts the theory that there could have been some purpose in the sacrifice of Dutch agents in exchange for the release of British agents in German captivity. Nor does he associate it with the activities of George Behar, better known as George Blake, who is Dutch born and possibly associated with the Dutch section of SOE at this time.

The fact of the matter was that Hubertus Lauwers decided co-operation with the *Abwehr* was preferable to death, as omission of a security check in his first supervised message to London would give warning that he was operating under duress. Unfortunately his omission was ignored.

--

Meanwhile, patriotic Dutchmen and–women were registering their opposition to German occupation by the best means available to them. One such person was:

Jos Mulder-Gemmeke
(Obituary *The Times* January 14, 2011)

Jos Gemmeke was still in her teens when catastrophe overwhelmed the Netherlands in May 1940, but she knew what she ought to do. Her father, well off, was a paper merchant and introduced her to a friend and customer of his, who early started up *Je Maintiendrai* – a motto of the Dutch royal house – which became the largest and most successful of the underground newspapers with which the Netherlands teemed.

She undertook to distribute the paper. This was a task of constant peril, for to be caught with even a single copy of it carried a death sentence under Nazi regulations. From the summer of 1940 to the autumn of 1944 she risked her life every day. She recruited on the old boy – or old girl – net, for there was nothing else safe to do; her friends all trusted her, as well as each other, and took care only to recruit those whom they themselves knew and trusted. So stubborn were Dutch *resistants* that, by the summer of 1944, *Je Maintiendrai* was able to circulate up to 15,000 copies of each issue.

After the failure of Montgomery's Operation *Market Garden*, that did not manage to seize both ends of the bridge at Arnhem, Gemmeke decided to make her way southwards by bicycle. She carried, hidden in her shoulder pads, some microfilm messages for the main Dutch external Resistance organisation, the *Bureau voor Bijzondere Opdrachten* (office for special orders), intended for their chief Prince Bernhard, the exiled Queen's son-in-law. When she got to the River Waal, a German sergeant told her the bridge was closed to civilian traffic. As she tried to charm him into letting her cross all the same, Allied aircraft attacked the bridge. The guards all dived for cover; she cycled quietly across it, picked her way through the fighting lines, and delivered the microfilms to the Prince's headquarters near newly liberated Brussels.

She was sent across to England, where as a matter of routine she was sent first to the Royal Victorian Patriotic School at Wandsworth. Her first interrogators there found her 'a very level and cool-headed young woman, completely unemotional, very reserved and determined'. SOE (the Special Operations Executive) snapped her up at once, and its training schools all thought highly of her. At the most secret of them at Beaulieu, Hampshire – now the National Motor Museum – she was judged out-standing. She was given the inappropriate codename of *Cackle* and went back to the still-occupied northern half of her home country by parachute on the night of March 10-11, 1945. Her mission was to press forward into Germany to see what she would do about alleviating the lot of Dutch forced labourers there.

She was received by friends; but made an unlucky parachute landing, and took some weeks to recover her health. By the time she was again fully mobile, the war was in full local confusion in its closing stages, and she never did get into Germany, although she collected some fearsome atrocity stories about what was happening to her compatriots there. (Sauckel, the Nazi Labour Minister, was tried and hanged at Nuremberg for the way he ran their camps). Gemmeke's part of the Netherlands was overrun by the Canadian Army, and she could go home.

She and Queen Wilhelmina were the only female members of the *Willensorde,* the principal Dutch military order; the Queen appointed her to it in recognition of her crossing of the Waal. She readjusted rather gingerly to peacetime life. In 1947 she was married to Jaap Mulder, another member of the *Willensorde* who had been flying fighter-bombers in the Free Dutch Air Force – they were the only married couple who belonged to the order. They had a son and a daughter. Gemmeke spent a lot of time making sure that none of her wartime companions in the resistance struggle were left in any sort of difficulty, social or financial.

She grew into a formidable grande dame, suffering no fool gladly, calling spades spades, and refusing to admit that the resistance struggle was marginal and not central to the conduct of the war. She belonged to the Special Forces Club in London, and made sure that it too did not forget the work of Dutch as well as other resistance forces. A large military guard of honour was present at her cremation on December 27.

(She died on December 20, 2010, aged 88).

An unusual character who joined SOE from Number 10 (Inter-Allied) Commando escaped the Gestapo trap because he parachuted into France, rather than into Holland.

Guido Zembsch-Schreve, MBE
(Obituary *The Times* April 3, 2003)

Guido Zembsch-Schreve had a variegated wartime career that ranged through the commandos and Special Operations Executive (SOE) to sabotage work as a slave labourer in the Harz mountains before he went into the oil industry.

Born in Switzerland in 1916, Zembsch-Schreve was the youngest son of a Dutch neurologist who settled in Belgium after the First World War. As a boy he travelled widely and picked up several languages; his education included a degree from the Harvard Business School. The German invasion of Belgium in May 1940 caught him working as a shipping clerk in Antwerp. He escaped by car, to friends in Provence; thence to Spain and so to North America.

He joined the Dutch Forces in exile in Canada as a private, was posted to the Prinses Irene Brigade at Wolverhampton, found it dull, and volunteered for the commandos. He joined the small-scale raiding force that operated across the English Channel and was able to capture a prisoner, in a raid on Sark, and subjected him to his first interrogation during the journey back to England.

The SOE then put him through specialist training, under the meticulous Leslie Humphreys, in how to run a secret escape line, and parachute training as well. He jumped into France in July 1943, with a wireless operator and a dual task. He was to run a parcels line from Geneva to Barcelona and in the longer term set up a line to run agents from Holland through to Spain. Like Humphreys, he was a perfectionist; he was not quite satisfied that his wireless operator's papers were in perfect order and, until they were, they both marked time.

He made what might have been a fatal error, however, and was arrested in a Paris café, when a secret transmitter was discovered hidden in his trouser leg. He was dispatched to Buchenwald concentration camp, and then sent the Mittebau-Dora camp in the Harz mountains, where thousands of prisoners were made to manufacture V2 rockets.

Though every slave labourer had a German soldier at his elbow, more than half the V2s made in Dora misfired, so badly had they been built. Zembsch-Schreve's own team was once suddenly visited by Wernher von Braun, who spotted at once that they were saboteurs; they were all instantly shot by von Braun's Gestapo companions, except for Zembsch-Schreve, who had taken the precaution of standing back against the wall behind the gunmen, and was overlooked.

At the tail end of the war Zembsch-Schreve was able to escape from one of the forced marches under guard that most surviving concentration camp prisoners were put through, and rejoined the Allied lines, miserably ill for months. He made himself useful to Dutch and British Intelligence, trying to probe some of the disasters that had overtaken SOE's penetrated circuits, but was then released to civilian life.

He worked in the oil and gas industries until he was 65. In retirement he wrote, originally for his grandchildren, a telling account of his wartime career, *Pierre Lalande* (one of his cover names), which was published by Leo Cooper in 1996. The British appointed him MBE, the French to the Legion of Honour, but more than either he prized having had a star named after him by an astronomer friend.

When, on February 13, 1996, Queen Elizabeth the Queen Mother unveiled the memorial in Westminster Abbey cloisters to the dead of SOE, he was one of the dozen stalwarts who escorted her through from the service in the nave.

He was happily married to Jacqueline Reynaud, a Provençal friend who bore him three sons.

(He died on February 1, 2003, aged 86).

Another Dutch patriot recruited by SOE was sent to Holland with the aim of re-establishing something of the organization's network there.

Jacob Beekman
(Obituary *The Times* December 2, 2010)

Jacob Beekman, who survived for over seven months as a secret radio operator in the Dutch underground, belonged to a large Dutch family – he had eight brothers and four sisters – at Zwolle, in the eastern Netherlands, and grew up to be six feet two inches tall. He went into the army in 1938, serving as a hussar, and transferred to the police in June 1940, just after the German army had trounced the Dutch in five days in May. From the police he was persuaded, by some French prisoners of war on forced labour in Holland, to desert in May 1942, and managed to reach Spain across occupied Belgium and France by July. He took ship to Curaçao, whence he managed to reach England that December; and volunteered at once for secret service in his home country.

SOE took him on, put him through the usual paramilitary, parachuting, and technical courses, and trained him also as a clandestine wireless operator. His school reports described him as shrewd and cunning but no intellectual. During his training, it became clear to his commanders – British and Dutch alike – that SOE's work into Holland so far had been hopelessly penetrated by the Germans; he was one of those sent, rather late, to try to pick up the pieces and rebuild effective resistance.

While under W/T training, he fell in love with a fellow student, the Swiss Yolande Unternährer, whom he married. She went to France by Lysander light aircraft in September 1943 to assist the unforgettable Canadian Major Biéler, was arrested with him next January, and murdered in Dachau next September. Beekman had heard of her arrest, but not fate, when he parachuted on the night of 28/29 August 1944, into the Veluwe, the heath-land that lay between the Zuyder Zee and Arnhem – the one part of Holland suitable for guerillas.

Codenamed *Maurits*, he was to operate his set for his two companions, Luykenaar and Hinderink, whose task it was to make touch with local units of the *Raad van Verzet*, the best of the Dutch resistance movements on the spot, and to supply them with arms. The RAF was to drop the arms under detailed arrangements to be made by Beekman, who kept himself apart from his colleagues, and took care never to spend more than a few minutes on the air at a time. He also sometimes provided supplies for a parallel SOE venture, the 'Jedburgh' team headed by Major Brinkgreve north of Arnhem, which had expected to be in the field for a few weeks but in fact lasted for most of the winter.

They managed to impose a few delays on German reinforcements hurrying to the Arnhem battlefield – a battle which surprised them as much as it surprised their enemies – and to provide some useful tactical intelligence and guides for the allied armies when they eventually broke out north of the Rhine in the closing weeks of the war. Beekman crossed into allied-held territory on 5 April 1945.

He did not hear for certain what had happened to Yolande until 1946. He went back to Zwolle, went into business, flourished quietly, and remarried. By his second wife, Kathleen Mary Pickering, who died before him, he had two sons and three daughters; he leaves thirteen grandchildren. He was a familiar, stalwart figure at meetings of former Resisters, retaining a stolid good humour to the end.

(He died on November 15, 2010.

The record of SOE in Belgium was better than for Holland but problems arose that set limits on what might be achieved in the way of sabotage and subversion. The frustrations faced by those who, in turn, headed T Section, responsible for Belgium, are well illustrated by the following obituary.

Claude Knight
(Obituary *The Times* November 29, 1993).

Claude Knight was head of the Special Operations Executive's Belgian section, 1941-43, and later a Sussex farmer, The year 1941 was a bad one for SOE in Belgium and 1942 was worse. The basic trouble was that in so small a country everyone, who was anyone, knew everybody else. The result was that secrets were all but impossible to keep, and the Gestapo's many double agents had an easy run.

Moreover, in London, the Belgian government-in-exile, at odds with its monarch who had stayed behind to share his occupied subjects' lot, was riven by incessant, internal squabbles. One of the worst of these was that fought out between the defence and the security authorities about which of the two should control secret work in Belgium.

It was into this maelstrom of conflicting interests that in the spring of 1941 Claude Knight was thrown by the Special Operations Executive. The then head of the Belgian section of SOE a former manager of the Antwerp gas works suddenly fell out with his superiors and Knight replaced him in November 1941. Zealous and loyal, he could exercise little influence on the various quarrels that were going on beyond the softening effect of good manners. Despite his stammer he did his best to smooth over differences which, alas, turned out to be insuperable.

Eventually his health broke down and he was moved in September 1943 into the calmer waters of the Belgian section of the Political Warfare Executive. For his work with SHAEF in Belgium from 1944 to 1945 reviving the indigenous information services he was mentioned in dispatches and made an officer of the Order of Leopold.

Claude Thorburn Knight was born in Didsbury, Manchester. He went from the army class at Marlborough to Trinity Hall, Cambridge, where he continued his military studies and took a pass degree. He then spent six years, 1930-36, as a Coldstream Guards officer, left the Army to travel and was recalled from the reserves at the outbreak of war. He served on the War Office's military intelligence liaison staff, working with the French, the Dutch, the Belgians and others until he was taken on by SOE.

He had married in 1935 Patricia Dodson, daughter of the second Lord Monk Bretton and grand-daughter of Sylvain van der Weyer, long the Belgian minister in London. This gave him standing in Belgian as well as in British society.

After the war he turned his back on metropolitan life, and settled on a farm near Lewes in Sussex, where his brother-in-law's estate lay. He managed a large dairy farm with enterprise and success for 35 years, and served on the East Sussex County Council. He and his wife retired from their farm in 1981 and in recent years both struggled against protracted illness. She survives him, together with a son and three daughters.

(He died on November 17, 1993, aged 83).

After a pause, Knight was replaced as Head of T Section by the then Major Hardy Amies, who had earlier been a member of the team planning SOE operations in Belgium. Inevitably his obituary, published many years later, focused on his success in the world of *haute couture*, but this extract does something to capture his contribution to the work of SOE.

Sir Hardy Amies, KCVO

(Extract from *The Times* obituary of March 6, 2003). Although his father worked in the valuers' department of the London County Council, Amies's grandfather had a manufacturing plant in Maidstone making the Dandy Roll, the machine which put the watermark on paper money. His mother worked in a court dressmaking establishment, rising to the rank of vendeuse (saleswoman) – a position of considerable power. Hardy's business acumen came from his father's side; his creative flair from his mother's.

He was educated at Brentwood, where he had a reasonably successful but by no means brilliant academic record and a somewhat less impressive impact on the school's sport. Always an individualist, he had no success at team games, but his determination to succeed made him a minor star on the tennis court. He took up tennis again when he was 40 and continued to play until well into his eighties – which is about when he stopped sailing. His great enjoyment of the company of young men also sustained him and lasted well into his old age.

His gifts were those of a journalist, although many felt that he should have continued with his theatrical triumphs at school and become an actor. Had he done so, he would have undoubtedly been in the Gielgud tradition of grandeur. He did dip a toe into the journalistic pond after leaving school by going to see R. D. Blumenfeld, then Editor of the Daily Express; but since he was hoping to go up to Cambridge to read English, he was told firmly: "We do not want academics as journalists. We want men of the world." Blumenfeld then turned to Amies's father and said: "Send him abroad, make him learn languages and make him work."

All three things were done. Hardy spent time in France and Germany, became proficient in French and fluent in German and then worked for Avery's, the weighing-machine manufacturers in Birmingham, as a travelling salesman for three of the unhappiest years of his life. He became a dress designer as a result of his skill as a writer. A description he wrote of the dress worn by the wife of the owner of the sportswear firm *Lachasse* came to her ears, and as a result he joined the firm, halving his income, in 1934, as managing designer. He knew nothing of fashion but learnt by talking to the customers and giving them what they wished to wear, a simple stratagem that was the basis of his long business success.

His time at *Lachasse* was interrupted by the war. His French recommended him to the Intelligence Corps, from which in April 1941 he went to the Special Operations Executive. His first post was as liaison officer between SOE's London HQ and the French and Belgian trainees at Beaulieu and elsewhere. In November 1941 he joined the Belgian section as training and recruiting officer, becoming acting section head in August 1943 and head in January 1944. As such he was one of a number of section heads who were involved in 'Ratweek', a project to assassinate Gestapo officers and collaborators in occupied territories. In the event, although a small number of such executions were carried out in Norway, Belgium and France, they could not be categorically ascribed to 'Ratweek' planning, and the operation was eventually put on ice.

In September 1944 Amies was put in charge of SPU47, the SOE unit which was set up in liberated Belgium to infiltrate Belgian agents into Germany. He returned to London in May 1945 and signed off in July.

(He died on March 5, 2003, aged 93).

Escape lines for refugees from Nazi tyranny, Allied airman shot down over enemy-occupied territory, escaped prisoners of war and anyone else seeking to reach freedom were organized by individual groups in the countries concerned and – for reasons of security – were usually quite separate from Resistance groups. The organization in Britain responsible for providing advice and funds to these groups – and to Allied servicemen in enemy hands – was a branch of Intelligence titled MI 9. Responsible for both escape and evasion in enemy territory, MI 9 worked closely with SOE in London and maintained a cell within its Baker Street HQ.

A number of escape lines began in the Low Countries as they lay on the route taken by Allied aircraft on their return from bombing missions over Germany and were consequently routinely in receipt of Allied airmen dropping by parachute from aircraft shot down or too badly damaged to reach their base airfield. Such escape lines had to cross international borders, with attendant difficulties, in order for the escapers to reach the frontiers of neutral Spain or Switzerland. Early in the war, the Channel was looked on as the most readily available route, but this became more difficult owing to restricted access to the coast imposed by the German authorities. Andrée Peel provides an example of individual initiative.

Andrée Peel
(Obituary *The Times* March 10, 2010)

The youthful Andrée Virot, as she was then, was running a beauty salon in the Breton port-city of Brest when Germany invaded and overran northern France in May-June 1940. Being adventurous and high spirited, she was an early recruit to the Resistance movement but her work was initially confined to the distribution of an underground newspaper. Later she worked for an escape line smuggling shot-down Allied airmen out of France to Britain and the reception and dispatch to safety of the occasional agent of the Special Operations Executive (SOE).

The main escape routes led south to the Pyrenees, then to Spain and Gibraltar, and also to Switzerland. Brittany offered a shorter route from northern France but the sea crossing presented formidable obstacles. Although there were many small isolated coves with steeply shelving beaches allowing easy access for small boats, the German Army had imposed a 25km forbidden zone along the coast into which French citizens from elsewhere ventured at risk of immediate arrest, trial and dispatch to a concentration camp.

Mlle Virot so impressed her superiors by her work for the underground newspaper that she was promoted head of a section of the Breton escape route known as the VAR line, which ran a highly efficient service over the beaches of northern Brittany in the winter and spring of 1943-44. Success depended on the use of 'safe houses' where escaping airmen or SOE agents could wait in relative safety until arrangements were complete for their next move. Each move was managed by a working member of the line protected by a cut-out system, so that those involved in one leg of the route knew no one in the preceding leg or the one that followed.

Codenamed Agent *Rose*, Virot was one of about 150 members of the VAR organisation in Brittany. Her role was at the dispatching and reception end of the line, where it was necessary to signal by torch to small naval craft approaching the beach. Submarines were rarely risked in such unpredictable operations and then only if a senior agent or political figure had to land or be taken off. No passengers were lost on any VAR line operation during the time Virot was working on it. 102 men passed through the section in her charge. She came under suspicion of the Gestapo in early 1944 and moved to Paris, changing her identity but – unwisely as events were to prove – retaining her codename Agent *Rose*.

In Paris she was betrayed by a fellow agent who had been arrested by the Gestapo and threatened with the torture of his family. Virot was herself arrested and sent to the Ravensbrück concentration camp for women. Later, she was moved to the Buchenwald camp and saved from death in one form or another only by the timely arrival of the US Army on April 11, 1945.

She returned to Paris on her release and after her health was restored worked in a restaurant on the Rive Gauche. It was there that she met her future husband, John Peel, a student studying in Paris at the time. They were not married until several years later but eventually he brought her to live in Long Ashton, southwest of Bristol, where she died.

Her bravery in Brittany and her stoicism in Ravensbrück and Buchenwald were recognised by her appointment to the Legion of Honour – later advanced to Officer, and presented by her brother, who was a French four star general – the *Croix de Guerre*, the American Medal of Freedom, the *Ordre de la Libération*, the Medal of the Resistance and, from Britain, the King's Commendation for Brave Conduct. She also received a letter of appreciation for her work with the Resistance from Winston Churchill. Her autobiography, *Miracles Do Happen*, was published in France as *Miracles Existent*. The English version was translated by Evelyn Scott and was made into a film by William Ennals.

Her husband predeceased her; there were no children.
(She died on March 5, 2010, aged 105).

Although he became a controversial figure in his reminiscences after the war, Gaston Vandermeerssche achieved extraordinary personal success in establishing an escape line from the Low Countries through France and into Spain as far as Barcelona. He maintained to the end, however, that SOE had deliberately sent Dutch agents to their deaths in Holland.

Gaston Vandermeerssche
(Obituary *The Times* December 2nd, 2010)

The death of Gaston Vandermeerssche in Milwaukee on November 1st briefly revived the fallacy that as part of some campaign of deception during the Second World War, the Special Operations Executive (SOE) deliberately sent agents into German-occupied Holland aware that they would be captured on arrival.

It is true that German Army intelligence (the *Abwehr*) had penetrated and later took over SOE's network in Holland. After arresting an SOE wireless operator, Hubertus Lauwers, and forcing him on threat of death to radio false intelligence to London using his own set and ciphers, the *Abwehr* duped London into sending more agents and supplies. Even when subsequently captured operators did not use their security checks – as instructed if captured – suspicions were dismissed. Thus it was London's refusal to accept the possible scale of the disaster that led to the continued despatch of agents – not a feature of some Machiavellian plot.

Born in Ghent in 1921, Vandermeerssche left the local university to answer Leopold III's call to arms when the German Army swept into Belgium in May 1940. As the Belgian and British forces were overwhelmed by the onslaught, he crossed into France and headed south for Toulouse. Although the Franco-Belgian frontier was policed after the French armistice with Germany in June, it was a less formidable obstacle than the heavily defended Channel coastline. In consequence, Belgian escape lines adopted this route, as it gave eventual access to the Vichy-controlled part of France, the Mediterranean and Pyrenees.

Vandermeerssche became a courier along such a route, working from Brussels to Toulouse. Security being of paramount importance, each line kept exclusively to itself with agents knowing only the absolute minimum contacts and safe houses along it. Vandermeerssche developed his own line, concentrating on delivering microfilmed intelligence from Belgium through Toulouse to the Belgian consul in Barcelona and ultimately to the Belgian Government in exile in London.

It has to be acknowledged that relations between the Belgian representatives in London and SOE headquarters in

Baker Street were fractious and untrusting. There were organizational and personal reasons for this and a similar situation persisted in SOE's dealings with the exiled administration of the Netherlands. It was therefore hardly surprising that when Queen Wilhemina – 'the only man in her Government' decided to set up her own Resistance movement in Holland she turned to Vandermeerssche who, by mid-1942, had established a reputation as a successful Resistance operator that even the Gestapo acknowledged.

He rose to the challenge, adopting the codename *Rinus*. Within months he had established a courier line from Holland through Belgium and France – wholly occupied by Germany after the Allied invasion of the North African coastline in November 1942 – over the Pyrenees to Barcelona. Dutch and Belgian agents were involved but the line was independent of the SOE circuits operating along much of its length, as were other courier and escape lines for reason of mutual security.

Vandermeerssche served Holland and his own country's interests well but was never able to come to terms with SOE's continued reservations about the security of his network, or the value of the information his agents were providing. The extent of the German takeover of SOE's network in Holland was revealed only when two SOE agents captured there escaped and made their way to Switzerland in November 1943. By then Vandermeerssche had fallen into the hands of the Gestapo, having been unluckily caught up in a routine police action against black-marketeers in Perpignan.

Subjected to interrogation and physical abuse for many months in prisons in France and Germany, he resolutely continued to conceal his identity and those of his agents and the safe houses along his courier chain. He was sentenced to death for espionage in July 1944 but, no doubt with an eye to the likely outcome of the war by that time, the governor of the German prison where he was being held kept him alive. He was finally released at the end of the war in Europe on May 8th 1945.

He returned to Belgium and the University of Ghent, where he earned a PhD in physics and became the director of electron microscopy. Some years later he moved to the United States to work for the multinational finance company 3M. On leaving there, he returned to Belgium to become an expert on surface abrasion with the brewers of Schlitz beers who were seeking a way to reduce damage to their product labels in transit. Schlitz later moved him to Milwaukee where, from 1980, he served as the honorary French consul.

His wartime exploits on behalf of Belgium and Holland were acknowledged by decorations bestowed by both countries, also by France and Luxembourg. In 1988 he published *Gaston's War,* written in collaboration with the author Allan Mayer, which described not only his part in the conflict but also set out his long-held suspicions of SOE's motives for continuing to send agents into occupied Holland long after doubts about the security of the network there had been aroused. A film of the same title was made in 1997.

After the war he married Violette Castiaux, the daughter of a Belgian Resistance worker. She survives him with a son and three daughters.

(He died in November 1ˢᵗ, 2010, aged 89).

A spirited but unlucky MI 9 agent who fell straight into enemy hands put up a consistently brave and resolute personal resistance to her captors.

Beatrice Terwindt
(Obituary *The Times* May 4, 1987)

Trix Terwindt, a Dutch wartime secret agent, who was captured on her first mission for MI 9, survived two years of imprisonment and torture. She was a KLM air hostess in her middle-20s when Germany overran the Netherlands in May 1940. She was keen to play a part in resistance, and managed to escape to London, where she was recruited by Airey Neave into MI 9, the secret escape service.

Neave was attracted by her air of calm and competence. He explained to her how she could help to organize escape lines running from Holland into Belgium, where M1 9 already active posts at work. As no other channel was open, she had to reach the Netherlands by a parachute drop organized by the Special Operations Executive. Nobody in London knew that SOE's work into Holland had at this stage been completely penetrated by the Germans. Early on February 14, 1943, she dropped from an RAF bomber into the arms of the Gestapo.

Her training as an air hostess saved her: long mentally prepared for sudden shock, she kept her head. The enemy tricked one address out of her before handcuffing her; thereafter she told them nothing of interest through several days' continuous cross-questioning. She never breathed a word about her mission, and they did not discover what it was.

They imprisoned her for a year at Haaren, near Eindhoven; she was then taken to worse concentration camps, at Ravensbrück and Mauthausen. From the last of these she was rescued, emaciated but still very much alive, by the Swiss Red Cross a few days before the war's end.

KLM gave her back her job, at which, calm and unobtrusive as ever, she continued to work for some years. She was briefly married, but had no children. Trix Terwindt never complained about what had happened to her; she had tried to do her duty to her country. As she wrote to Neave after the War: "I was an amateur, but in war risks have to be taken. I played a game of cat-and-mouse with the Gestapo with the only difference that I was caged and the cat was free."
(She died on April 8, 1987, aged 76)

Arguably one of the most resourceful organizers of an escape line was also a swift-thinking master of deception.

Major-General Albert Guerisse, GC, KBE, DSO
(Obituary *The Times* March 29, 1989)

Guerisse was a medical officer in the Belgian cavalry when Germany overwhelmed Belgium in May 1940. But he managed to escape to England through Dunkirk, and secured entry into the British Navy and was commissioned as Lieutenant-Commander Patrick Albert O'Leary.

He served in HMS *Fidelity*, a converted French trawler which performed various secret assignments in the Mediterranean. On one of these, in April 1941, Guerisse got left behind on the beach at Collioure after landing a couple of agents for the Special Operations Executive.

He passed himself off to the French as an evading Canadian airman. He escaped from custody and set up from a Marseilles base a system that became highly efficient for moving escaped Allied POWs and shot-down airmen who had evaded capture, out of France into Spain and to Britain.

He built the 'Pat line', as it came to be called, round a mixed group of men and women French, Scots, Jews, Australasians, Greeks and even Germans opposed to Hitler and his firm and unobtrusive leadership inspired them all. The line expanded to cover occupied as well as unoccupied France, and carried over 600 people to safety, including the late Airey Neave on his way back from Colditz.

To inspire the confidence of his colleagues Guerisse travelled frequently between the Dutch frontier and the south of France through numerous German controls, himself escorting the escapers. But eventually it all drew too much attention, both from the French and from the still more dangerous Gestapo. An English defector, Harold Cole, cost it 50 casualties in the winter of 1941-2, and a French defector caused 'Pat's' own arrest at Toulouse early in March 1943. This broke up the line.

Guerisse was tortured to make him reveal the names, duties and whereabouts of the other members of the line. He was put in a refrigerator for several hours and then beaten continuously but did not disclose any information of use to the Germans. He was then held under the Nazis' infamous Nacht und Nebel procedure in a series of concentration camps, beginning at Natzweiler and ending at Dachau.

He was again tortured at the Bavarian camp and sentenced to death, though the war ended before he was executed. Even the SS had failed to break his irrepressible spirit, and when the Allies in April 1945 reached Dachau they found the camp taken over by 'O'Leary '. As the prisoners' 'president,' Guerisse refused to leave until he had ensured that all possible steps had been taken to relieve his fellow inmates' condition.

Albert Marie Edmond Guerisse was born in Brussels on April 5, 1911, and read medicine at Brussels University before joining the Belgian Army. He decided to take the alias of Patrick O'Leary after a peace-time Canadian friend. After the war Guerisse returned to serve in the Belgian Army. He was wounded in the Korean War while rescuing a casualty. He was to become head of the Belgian Army's medical service, before retiring in 1970 with the rank of major-general.

Guerisse remained always a gentle, humorous, unassuming man, unless a tyrant or a villain roused him; then his anger could be terrible. He was awarded the George Cross in 1946

for his outstanding wartime gallantry, and had received the
DSO in 1942. He was once described as the most decorated
man for bravery alive and held 35 decorations in all from
various countries. In 1964 he figured in the television series
This Is Your Life. He was made an honorary KBE in 1980
and, not long before he died, King Baudouin of Belgium
ennobled him as a count.

In 1947 he married Sylvia Cooper Smith, who predeceased
him. Their son survives him.

(He died on March 26, 1989, aged 77).

On April 3, 1989, Mrs Helen Long wrote this letter to *The Times*:

'Sir, Further to the obituary on Major-General Albert
Guerisse, who ran his escape line from the flat of my uncle,
Dr Georges Rodocanachi in Marseilles, I well remember
interviewing him at his home in Belgium in connection with
research for my book *Safe Houses Are Dangerous*.

Having been provoked into landing a punishing blow to
the traitor Paul (alias Harold) Cole in the Rodocanachis' flat
in 1941, Guerisse was left with a fractured and mis-shapen
right hand. Why, I asked him when he displayed the deformed
knuckles at my request, had he not got Doctor Rodocanachi
to set it for him then and there? His reply was that his cover as
Lieutenant-Commander Patrick O'Leary was all-important.
"As a fellow doctor, I would surely have betrayed myself and
been unable to hide from him my medical knowledge and
both of us would have been compromised since my cover
would have been blown," he explained. As it was it served
him through years of unparalleled gallantry till victory.

When his English wife, Sylvia, was taken terminally ill I
accepted that his promised foreword for my book would no
longer be forthcoming. And yet I felt that he would never fail
me. Nor did he. A man who could spring his friends from
captivity despite all the odds was not going to let me down as
my book was going to press. Like many, I shall never forget
his legendary charm and audacity.'

Marseilles was the destination for a number of escape lines
through France. It was from the rugged coast to the east of the
port-city that two Polish Naval officers, Lieutenant-Commanders
Marian Krajewski and Jan Buchowski, operated two fishing craft

– local feluccas – transporting refugees and escaped servicemen to Gibraltar and landing SOE agents.

They began in the summer of 1941, when Krajewski captained *Seawolf* on 18 voyages to and from the French coast to evacuate some 300 Polish soldiers trapped in France by the French armistice of 1940. A second craft *Seadog*, captained by Buchowski, joined in and, among many similar exploits, put ashore four SOE agents at Cap d'Antibes in July 1942 and over four nights in September landed an agent and 2,000lbs of sabotage stores at Agay, south-west of Cannes, and collected five other agents. Then, on 4 September, he picked up agents from the beach at Narbonne and an RAF Lysander pilot who had crashed while flying in SOE agents.

Both these enterprising officers were awarded the DSO for their intrepid voyages between July 1941 and October 1942. Krajewski survived the war but Buchowski was less fortunate. *The Times* reported that a Polish officer attached to the Polish naval headquarters in London had been acquitted of his murder. It was alleged that he had formed an attachment to the other officer's wife and had been found shot dead in their flat.

Neither officer received an obituary in *The Times*.

5

The Western Mediterranean and Italy

A historian coming fresh to the course of the Second World War might reasonably ask why the American and British allies launched their first joint offensive against the neutral, Vichy French-controlled countries of North Africa. The answer lies in their realization that they were not yet prepared, nor yet strong enough, to attack Hitler's 'Atlantic Wall' of defence across the English Channel, while the 'soft underbelly' of Greece, Italy and unoccupied southern France presented a choice of easier targets. An amphibious assault on any one of these with matching air support required that the Mediterranean's southern littoral should be entirely under Allied control.

To the east, Libya was fast falling to the British Eighth Army by the autumn of 1942 but Morocco, Algeria and Tunisia were under the aegis of the French, who had been defeated and driven to an armistice with Nazi Germany and were – at least on the outward face of things – jealously guarding the consequent neutrality. In the Allies' camp, opinions varied on whether the Vichy authorities in Africa would spring to the Allies' side or would actually fight to defend their neutrality. When the time came, the latter course was initially adopted but, as the Allies became established, the French found a leader of courage and principle in General Henri Giraud. From then on the French worked with the Allies, but the result was a slow and lumbering victory rather than a spectacular one.

The principal role of SOE was the execution of Operation *Brandon*, under which – so it was intended – SOE officers would raise a force from anti-Axis groups to the rear of the German forward defences for purposes of raiding and sabotage. It turned out that such groups as were found were largely anti-French in their sympathies, so any help they were likely to provide would be to the

98

German and Italian armies fighting the allies of the French. In this instance, therefore, SOE met with instructive failure.

From the outset, it was apparent that the SOE operation could not by directed from London, and Gibraltar became the local headquarters during the launching phase of the Allied invasion, codenamed Operation *Torch*. Subsequently, under the codename *Massingham*, it moved to Algiers and remained in control of SOE operations in the western Mediterranean until the invasion of Italy in September 1943 permitted an advance to Bari. A man much involved in the *Massingham* phase was:

Sir Douglas Dodds-Parker
(Obituary *The Times* September 14, 2008)

Although Douglas Dodds-Parker was a Conservative MP from 1945 to 1959 and again from 1964 to 1974, and held junior office under Sir Anthony Eden during the Suez Crisis, he was not really a political animal. He was particularly unhappy over the secret collusion between Britain, France and Israel over the Suez affair, and his career progressed no further when it was over. His knighthood came late in his career, in 1973, when Edward Heath sent this ardent pro-European off to Strasbourg as a member of the Parliamentary Delegation to the European Parliament.

Paradoxically, he received no official honours from Britain (though he did from France) for what was actually the much more interesting and constructive phase of his life – his wartime period with the Special Operations Executive. As first an intelligence officer, then as a mission planner and finally as commander of SOE operations in the western and central Mediterranean, he was involved successively in organising 'dirty tricks', running agents into occupied Europe and eventually large-scale guerrilla warfare.

He had begun his war as a Grenadier Guards officer with aspirations to a regimental career and perhaps command of a battalion. But it was not to be. His pre-war career in the Sudan Political Service and his knowledge of the international political situation gained from extensive travels on leave made him too valuable to be risked as cannon fodder. Thereafter, first under Orde Wingate in the Horn of Africa, then under Colin Gubbins in London and finally in the Mediterranean, he wielded increasing influence on the conduct of irregular

operations in support of Resistance movements in territories
occupied by the Axis powers.

Arthur Douglas Dodds-Parker was educated at Winchester
and Magdalen College, Oxford, where he graduated
in modern history. In 1930 he entered the Sudan Political
Service and in 1934 became Assistant Private Secretary to the
Governor-General, Sir Stewart Symes, in Khartoum. From
this standpoint he gained an insider's knowledge of relations
with neighbouring French, Belgian and Italian colonies.

Symes also sent him on a number of diplomatic missions
on behalf of Sudan. At the League of Nations in Geneva he
met the British Foreign Secretary Anthony Eden, and the
French and Italian Foreign Ministers. On leave periods taken
in Rome, Vienna, Prague, Warsaw and Germany he formed a
clear notion of impending disaster for Europe, while Italy's
invasion of Ethiopia in 1935 gave him contact with irregular
warfare and subversion at first hand.

When war broke out he resigned from government service
and was commissioned into the Grenadier Guards. He was soon
taken off regimental duties and seconded to military intelligence
and, after its formation in July 1940, to SOE. With the Italian
threat to Sudan he was sent to that theatre to engage in the
'ungentlemanly warfare' (Churchill's words) for which the nature
of the conflict – massive Italian numerical superiority but terrain
and a native population both favouring clandestine operations
– seemed to call. In this, his relationship with the volatile Orde
Wingate was not always an easy one, but he acknowledged the
genius of Wingate's leadership of a guerrilla campaign which
contributed so much to the defeat of the Italians.

In May 1941 Dodds-Parker returned to London, where he
was put in charge of organising transport for the insertion by
aircraft and boat of SOE agents into occupied Europe from
Norway to southern France. It was after one such operation,
an abortive drop in the Namur area of Belgium that Dodds-
Parker was compelled to report to the Belgian Foreign
Minister-in-Exile, Paul-Henri Spaak. The Belgian statesman's words on that occasion were to remain with him and
shape his outlook. "When we have won this war," Spaak told
him over dinner "we must unite Europe. We cannot afford
any more civil wars among our nations or we will destroy
civilisation."

With the Allied landings in French North Africa in November 1942, Dodds-Parker was sent to this new theatre where, from Algiers, he had to cope with the difficult problem of sorting out Vichy from Free French sympathisers. The British position in the area was made doubly invidious by the resistance of many local tribesmen to the re-establishment of French authority of any kind over them.

After the clearing of all Axis forces from North Africa the SOE facility in Algiers became the base for operations throughout the western half of the Mediterranean. The SOE played a major role in Operation *Monkey*, the negotiations for the Italian Armistice in September 1943. Throughout, Dodds-Parker, as SOE's area commander, was in constant touch with Eisenhower about the timing of this, a delicate matter as it was to coincide with the American seaborne landings at Salerno, knowledge of which had to be kept from the Germans.

Thereafter, from a base in Apulia, SOE trained thousands of Italian partisans. In the wake of the Franco-American landings in the South of France in August 1944, SOE was active in this theatre, too, aiding French resistance movements. This was not always the self-evidently logical task it seemed from the outside, since one powerful group of anti-German partisans in the South was committedly Marxist and as likely to fight against other Resistance groups as with them.

One of Dodds-Parker's last missions was in December 1944 when he was sent to Athens at a time of tension between communist and government forces in Greece. But the expected shootout on Constitution Square never materialised. After leaving the Mediterranean theatre, Dodds-Parker saw out the war at Supreme Headquarters Allied Expeditionary Force in Paris.

Dodds-Parker, who reached the rank of colonel, was awarded the French Legion of Honour and the *Croix de Guerre*, and was mentioned in dispatches for his SOE services. (He kept up his SOE connections, becoming a valued and popular member of the Special Forces Club in Knightsbridge, where in later years he would often play host to those historians who sought his help as a valued witness to important events).

At the end of the war he decided to go into politics. At the Labour landslide of 1945 he held Banbury for the Conservatives, albeit with a much reduced majority. He came to be recognised in the Commons as an authority on foreign and Commonwealth affairs and when the Conservatives returned to power in 1951 was asked by Churchill to be his PPS. Dodds-Parker declined (a somewhat strange decision), preferring to retain his chairmanship of the party's Commonwealth Affairs Committee.

From 1951 to 1953 he was on the executive of the 1922 Committee. In November 1953 he was given his first ministerial appointment as Joint Parliamentary Under-Secretary of State for Foreign Affairs. In October 1954 he was transferred to the Commonwealth Relations Office as Parliamentary Under-Secretary of State. From December 1955, by which time Eden had succeeded Churchill as Prime Minister, he was again Parliamentary Under-Secretary of State for Foreign Affairs.

In this capacity he was prominent among those who hosted the famous visit of Bulganin and Khrushchev to Great Britain in April 1956. As such he participated in an unlikely conversation with Khrushchev about the purpose of Russian boarding schools, and was greatly amused when the Soviet leader told the assembled company that the schools were Russia's equivalent of maids. "We have no domestic help at home and need to get the children out of the house!"

Dodds-Parker was still holding that office in October 1956 when the nationalisation of the Suez canal by Egypt's ruler, Gamal Abdel Nasser, prompted the governments of Israel, Britain and France to agree to attack Egypt, while pretending to the outside world that the action of the two European powers was coincidental with that of Israel. Before news of the military action broke, Dodds-Parker was firmly against any such thing happening. He was in a doubly difficult position since in the weeks before the action took place he had been put in charge of a committee which was to make recommendations about possible moves against Egypt and Nasser personally. He could not know that a task force was already arming.

When he became aware of the British and French preparations he briefly considered resignation but, with the country in armed conflict with an enemy, he decided that loyalty to the Government was the only course. With the Foreign Secretary, Selwyn Lloyd, absent at the UN, it fell to him and other junior ministers to face the storm in the Commons.

It was a wretched time for Dodds-Parker. Relations with his American friends (his wife was American) were particularly strained. And when Harold Macmillan succeeded Eden as Prime Minister he was not forgiven for what was perceived as his lack of loyalty over Suez. Selwyn Lloyd, who had lied to the nation and to Parliament over the Suez collusion, was re-employed as Foreign Secretary, Dodds-Parker was discarded.

He retired from Parliament at the general election of 1959 and applied himself to the various company directorships that were offered to him. But it was not to be the end of his political career. When the Cheltenham seat fell vacant his name was put forward and he returned to Parliament in the general election of 1964. Of his last ten years in Parliament six were to be in Opposition. But Macmillan's successor, Sir Alec Douglas-Home, was replaced a year after the Conservatives' 1964 defeat by the pro-European Edward Heath. Dodds-Parker found such a leadership much more congenial and served from 1965 as a delegate to the Council of Europe, and to the North Atlantic and Western European Assemblies.

His most celebrated moment in the political limelight came on live television shortly after 11pm on June 18, 1970, when his Cheltenham result in the general election, the second of the night after the declaration at Guildford, showed a 6 per cent swing to the Conservatives. Raising his arms above his shoulders like a champion boxer, he shouted exultantly, 'This means a Tory Government at Westminster.' Although only two results were then in, the electoral pundits in the television studios agreed with him and the Conservatives, against all previous expectations, were returned with a comfortable majority.

The scene of Dodds-Parker's unabashed delight became a much-replayed film clip and, in later years, he wryly commented that despite all the things he had done in his military and political career, if anyone did remember him, it would be for those words in Cheltenham Town Hall. After Heath took Britain into Europe Dodds-Parker was a member of the British delegation to the Strasbourg parliament. He retired from Parliament at the second of the two general elections of 1974.

In retirement he published two memoirs: *Setting Europe Ablaze* (1983), an account of his war with SOE, and *Political Eunuch* (1986). In 1997 he donated his copious political and personal papers to Magdalen College, Oxford, where they were soon appreciated by historians as a uniquely varied source, especially for the light they threw on some of the murkier corners of the Suez operation he had so despised.

Dodds-Parker married in 1946, Aileen, widow of a second cousin, Ellison Woods, who had been killed in Normandy, the daughter of American parents. His wife and a son and stepson survive him.

(He died on September 13, 2006, aged 97).

A colleague in the Mediterranean and earlier, when Dodds-Parker was involved in running agents into Brittany, also had a distinguished later career in public life.

Sir Brooks Richards, KCMG, DSC and Bar
(Obituary *The Times* September 17, 2002)

Brooks Richards joined the Royal Naval Volunteer Reserve on the outbreak of war and had the minesweeper *Sevra* sunk under him by a German acoustic mine off Falmouth in November 1940. He was mentioned in dispatches for getting his crew safely ashore. While in hospital recovering from a leg injury sustained in the incident, he and his friend George Luard, a former naval officer with an intimate knowledge of the Breton coast, wrote a paper on the potential use of fishing boats to carry arms to the French Resistance. This led to Richards spending the rest of the war with the Special Operations Executive (SOE).

Following the fall of France in June 1940, the SOE section responsible for fostering partisan activity in Brittany had several types of craft under trial for the secret shipment of agents and arms. It was in one of these, the 60-ton yawl *Mutin*, built to resemble a French tunnyman, that Richards first sailed for SOE. The vessel was actually a French naval training ship but, once equipped with two diesel engines, she had both the power and appearance for her cross-Channel tasks which continued until 1942, when she was switched to Gibraltar for use in SOE operations in Sardinia, Corsica and Southern France.

Richards was sent to the Mediterranean for the Allied landings in French North Africa in November 1942. He took part in Operation *Brandon* which, owing to lack of reliable intelligence of the situation ashore, succeeded only through his dash and improvisation.

The aim was to find and arm pro-Allied elements in French North Africa, then train them for a role similar to that of the Long Range Desert Group in the Western Desert. Richards disembarked from the coastal vessel *Minna* in command of a group of French irregulars, some of whom were actually Republican Spaniards. Working eastwards along the coast from Bone, he seized the lighthouse at Cap Serrat on December 2. His party held this position on the left flank of the Allied advance on Tunis until the end of January, deceiving the enemy into believing that a much larger Allied force was present. He was awarded the DSC for his enterprise and gallantry.

Although the Allied invasion of southern France was eventually postponed to August 1944, Richards began liaison work with the French Resistance there in early 1943. On one occasion his small vessel was blown up under him. He received a Bar to his DSC in 1943, and for his service as Head of the French Section of SOE in Algiers was awarded the *Legion d'Honneur* and the *Croix de Guerre*.

In early 1944 he was selected to take charge of a Resistance group in Corsica, with whom he kept in contact by submarine. He was again mentioned in dispatches in March 1945. By then, however, he had transferred to the Naval Reserve and was sent to the newly opened British Embassy in Paris to help wind up the SOE structure in France, to which General de Gaulle had taken exception.

Francis Brooks Richards was the son of Francis B. Richards, a civil engineer. He was educated at Stowe and won an open scholarship to Magdalene College, Cambridge, where he read history and took first-class honours in 1939. He found the Paris Embassy in the closing months of the war highly congenial and made many friends through his engaging personality and fast-developing aptitude for reporting on the internal political scene. In 1948 he was transferred to the German Political department in the Foreign Office and in December that year won high praise for his work as Secretary to the Ruhr Conference.

He was transferred to Athens as First Secretary

(Information) in 1952 and two years later to Bahrain where he was Head of Chancery. In both posts he did first-class liaison work, and proved himself a sound Head of Chancery, being particularly successful in his dealings with junior staff members and other British services.

In 1956 he transferred to the Security Department in the Foreign Office but in February 1958 he became Assistant Secretary to the Secretary of State, a post in which he also excelled. In 1959 he returned as Counsellor (Information) to Paris, a largely public relations appointment which allowed him to re-establish links with his wartime contacts.

Richards was a highly intelligent and personable man who at the same time combined modesty with a certain imperturbability in difficult circumstances. He was appointed CMG in 1963. He returned to London in 1964 to become Head of the Information Policy Department. In 1966 he was seconded to the Cabinet Office as Secretary of the Joint Intelligence Committee.

After service at the Embassy in Bonn, 1968-71, he was appointed, in 1972, British Ambassador in Saigon, where the increasingly obvious failure of the United States policy of military intervention did not deter him from travelling widely through the war-torn countryside.

He was withdrawn in advance of the American evacuation to serve, from 1974, as Ambassador in Athens, where the regime of the military junta had recently ended. Life in Greece did not immediately settle down. In January 1975 the Embassy was under siege by students protesting about what they felt was the British Government's ambivalent attitude to the situation in Cyprus. A happier period of Anglo-Greek relations was to follow, and Richards enjoyed the four years of his appointment. He was appointed KCMG in 1976.

Richards retired from the Foreign Service in 1978 to take up the appointment of Intelligence Co-ordinator in the Cabinet Office, a post he held until 1980. For the next two years he served with the Northern Ireland Office as Security Co-ordinator for the Province. In his final retirement he was Chairman of the Friends of the Imperial War Museum, 1989-91, and Vice-President, 1991-97, as well as being Chairman of the Anglo-Hellenic League, 1990-93, and of the charity Paintings in Hospitals, 1990-96.

After the war he kept in touch with survivors of the French Resistance organisations with whom he had come into contact while with SOE. He wrote an immensely readable history of the clandestine sea lanes to France and French North Africa which was published under the title of *Secret Flotillas* in 1996. It was translated into French in 2000.

Brooks Richards married, in 1941, Hazel, daughter of Lieutenant-Colonel Stanley Price Williams of the Indian Army, who had been born on the North-West Frontier of India and had also served with the Special Operations Executive.

His wife died two years ago. He is survived by their son and daughter.

(He died on September 13, 2002, aged 84).

Another naval officer involved in SOE operations in the Mediterranean had previous experience in the Arctic.

Lieutenant 'Paddy' Davies, RN
(Obituary *The Times* November 2, 2010)

Christened Denis but universally known as 'Paddy' Davies was born in Brazil and educated at Stowe, Buckinghamshire. While he was in Rio de Janeiro awaiting his place at Cambridge, the outbreak of war with Germany caused him to volunteer for the Navy. But although dressed in the uniform of a sub-lieutenant RNVR and working for the British naval attaché, his knowledge of the sea was nil.

Becoming dissatisfied after a year, he renounced his rank, wangled a passage home on a tramp steamer and was by mid-1942 an ordinary seaman on board the destroyer *Ashanti*, escorting convoys to Russia. *Ashanti*'s captain was the renowned 'Dickie' Onslow, the only destroyer captain to be awarded three Bars to his DSO for gallantry in action. Davies had the duty of 'captain of the heads', naval jargon for he who keeps the lavatories clean. During an inspection, Onslow recognised that Davies was officer material and advised that he should volunteer for 'special – i.e. dangerous – service to speed the selection process.

Davies did so, and found himself appointed to No 14 (Arctic) Commando which had been formed in late 1942 to attack shipping and German bases in Norway, being transported there with their canoes in motor torpedo boats. Training conditions in the Scottish Highlands were harsh; Davies's team was destined to sabotage the battleship *Tirpitz* near Trondheim but he was fortunate that this suicidal operation never came off. Among 14 Commando's operations was the sinking of several ships at Haugesund with limpet mines, but the seven men were captured, turned over to the SS and eventually, as a consequence of Hitler's directive concerning commandos, shot at Sachsenhausen concentration camp near Berlin.

When 14 Commando was disbanded, Davies was sent to the Mediterranean as intelligence officer for a little known organisation based at Bastia in Corsica, which landed and recovered agents over the Italian and French coasts. The Italians had recently surrendered and were ostensibly on the side of the Allies. Davies had to deal with the needs of the British Secret Intelligence Service and Special Operations Executive, the American Office of Strategic Services, the French Bataillons de Choc and Deuxième Bureau and the Italian OTTO organisation.

Of the variety of vessels used, perhaps the most suitable were the fast and low-profile Italian MAS craft, but it was sometimes uncertain whether the crews had fully changed sides; two British officers were murdered by a crew that reverted. Clandestine approaches in darkness to coastlines where the reception committees were sometimes unreliable demanded accurate intelligence of German movements.

Some 80 agents were landed or recovered in 52 sorties. Davies himself landed in Sicily three days before the Allied invasion. It was an amusing coincidence that the Sicilian invasion was made easier by the deception known as Operation *Mincemeat*, 'the man who never was', run by Commander Ewen Montagu, on whose team was Paddy Davies's future wife Patricia Trehearne.

She was always proud that the address of one of the important deceptive letters in the briefcase attached to the body of the supposed Royal Marine officer that drifted ashore at Huelva in southern Spain was in her handwriting. Davies proposed to Patricia on VE Day and they were married in July 1945. Shortly afterwards Davies met Arthur Hurlestone, a doyen of British perfumery who had founded Lentheric in 1937. When asked what he proposed to do after the war, Davies replied: 'I'll do any job that pays over a thousand a year.' Hurlestone took Davies on and it is a measure of Davies's acumen that by 1958 he was chairman of Lenthéric and subsequently Morny and Germaine Monteil. He retired in 1970.

He is survived by his wife, their son and two daughters. (He died on September 3, 2010, aged 89).

A stalwart character whom we first met in Chapter 1 reappears in our examination of SOE operations in the Mediterranean theatre, in Italy in particular where he made a significant contribution.

Commander Gerard Holdsworth DSO and Bar, OBE
(Obituary *The Times* July 29, 1985)

Commander Gerard Alfred Holdsworth DSO, OBE, one of the pillars of the Special Operations Executive's work during the war in Northwest Europe and in Italy, died at his Suffolk farm on July 24. Born at Stourbridge in 1904 and educated at Tettenhall College, he started a career as a rubber planter in Borneo which did not survive the Great Depression. He returned to England, got work of a kind in film publicity and busied himself with small boats.

He saw early that war with Nazi Germany impended, and was recruited into Section D of the Secret Service. He was working for D in Helsinki when he disappeared for six weeks early in 1940 (the time of the Winter War when the Soviet Union attacked Finland), turning up eventually at Barrow-in-Furness as a merchant seaman after a hazardous escape through the northern Finnish port of Petsamo.

SOE put him in charge of its small-boat operations out of the Helford River into Brittany and further afield. Holdsworth triumphed over countless obstacles both human and material, and organizd an unorthodox travel agency that was both deadly secret and deadly efficient. He received his DSO for gallantry off the Breton cost. After the *Torch* landings in Northwest Africa had succeeded, he sailed three of his small craft to Gibraltar – in those days a feat in itself – and his second DSO was for hazardous work behind the German's western flank in the Tunisian campaign.

When the Allied invasion of mainland Italy began,

Holdsworth was made commander of No. 1 Special Force, SOE's main effort in the new theatre. His rank was only that of Commander RNVR, but rank did not mean much in an organization in which a rear admiral and a full general were taking orders from a squadron leader.

He set up his headquarters at the small port of Monopoli, between Bari and Brindisi, and proceeded to exert a sizeable impact on the war. The only recognition he got for this was an OBE, and much of the credit for the results have been claimed – not always deservedly – by the Italian Communist Party.

Yet it was Holdsworth's special force that arranged drops of arms – particularly arms – for hundreds of thousands on Italian partisans; his special force that helped the partisans to choose targets and coordinate their efforts with Allied strategy; and that continued to arm and assist them until the German military power crumbled.

After the end of the war General Gubbins, the directing genius of SOE, told Holdsworth to set up the Special Forces Club, of which he was the first chairman, later succeeding Lord Selborne, SOE's former Minister-in-charge, as president.

The club's original members, a contentious lot by reason of their wartime profession, were an impossible team to drive and a difficult one to lead. Holdsworth's convivial manner and steely will were admirably fitted to this extra task.

The French at this time awarded him the Croix de Guerre, and he later became a Chevalier of the Legion of Honour. He went back for a short while to publicity, and then into films. He was a director of Rank Screen Services for five years and founded the firm of Gerard Holdsworth Productions, which is still busy filming for industry.

In 1970 he gave up town life so far as he could and managed his own farm near Sudbury. He remained true to the navy's tradition of the silent service and was reluctant to claim that he had been of any importance. His force of personality remained impressive to the end.

He was twice married and leaves a daughter by each marriage.

(He died on July 24, 1985, aged 75).

Prior to the Allied invasion of Sicily in July 1943, Italy had not been high on the SOE's priority list. Although it was known that opposition to Mussolini's fascist dictatorship existed, its ability to challenge the status quo or even to instigate a campaign of sabotage was – at best – uncertain. The situation began to change swiftly, however, following the Allied landings on the mainland in September, and proposals for an armistice were received from representatives of Marshal Pietro Badoglio and other prominent anti-fascists. The problem was how to open negotiations without alerting Hitler and the German Mediterranean command based in Italy. This was where SOE's *Massingham* headquarters in Algiers became closely involved in what became known as Operation *Monkey*, in which Major Peter Murray Lee became a key player.

Major Peter Murray Lee
(Obituary *The Times* February 23, 2010)

When, after the fall of France, the SOE was established in July 1940 in response to Winston Churchill's directive to 'set Europe ablaze', the Secret Intelligence Service (MI6) became concerned lest the amateurs recruited to conduct subversion and sabotage might upset the delicate task of gathering intelligence in enemy-occupied territory.

The paramount importance of the secrecy of SOE operations, in both the planning stages and once agents were deployed, led to the formation of a security department into which Peter Murray Lee was transferred from Intelligence Corps duties in 1941. Initially conducted from SOE's Baker Street headquarters, his work later took him to Algeria and then to Italy.

After Operation *Torch*, the Allied invasion of French North Africa in November 1942, an SOE regional headquarters codenamed *Massingham* was established at Le Club des Pins outside Algiers. Murray Lee was responsible for the security there and also for operations that SOE launched and subsequently controlled in southern France, Italy and the western Mediterranean.

He became involved in SOE's part in the armistice negotiations with Italy in August 1943, which were essentially kept secret as long as possible. Under the codename Operation *Monkey*, the Italian delegates to the negotiations were provided with radio sets, instructed in their use and reminded that they already had an SOE radio operator at their disposal,

Lieutenant Mallaby, recently captured after he had been
parachuted accidentally into a lake near Milan. The Italians
quietly brought Mallaby to Rome and the radio link between
General Eisenhower and Marshal Badoglio greatly facilitated
the exchange of information that led to the conclusion of
hostilities between the Allies and Italy.

As the Allies began their advance up the Italian mainland,
an SOE advanced base was set up at Monopoli near Bari, from
where operations in Italy and Yugoslavia were controlled,
with Murray Lee extending his influence over increasingly
unreliable territory. He also took over the debriefing of SOE
agents returning from operations in Italy and Yugoslavia,
with regard to enemy efforts to penetrate and so frustrate
SOE operations in both countries.

Finally, after Rome was taken in June 1944, he worked out of
the newly established British Embassy, chairing the security intelligence panel monitoring German penetration of Resistance
work organised by SOE and instituting counter-measures.

Peter Murray Lee was born in 1913 and educated at
Uppingham and Trinity College, Cambridge, where he read
modern languages and economics. On leaving the Army and
SOE in 1945, he was a Third Secretary in the Rome Embassy
before joining Rootes Group, with which he worked in Britain
and Canada. Later he was with a family firm in the UK and
Scandinavia until retiring to Oxfordshire.

His first wife, Rosemary, died in 1974 and he was married
to Bunting Fishburn in 1975, who also predeceased him. He is
survived by a son and two daughters from his first marriage.
(He died on February 4, 2010, aged 96).

A significant number of Italian anti-fascists had been active in the
Allied cause well before the armistice on 1943. Of these, perhaps
one of the most celebrated to join the SOE was Massimo Salvadori.

Massimo 'Max' Salvadori, DSO, MC,
(Obituary *The Times* August 29, 1992)

The opposition of Max Salvadori to the rise of fascism
in Italy began when he was still a teenager. He came of
Italian-British protestant descent and was brought up in Italy,
mainly in Florence. His father, a philosopher and author,
was unimpressed by Mussolini's arrival on the scene. This

distaste was passed on to his son and in 1924 both Salvadoris were beaten up by the Blackshirts. They had to move to Switzerland, where Max stayed five years and graduated at the University of Geneva.

By the time Salvadori completed his education, which included a doctorate in political science at Rome University, he had a profound determination not to submit to the tyranny beginning to rule his country. Unlike many of his fellow students who sat back wringing their hands, Salvadori became an activist. In 1929, when he was 21, he went back into Italy as the secret representative of Alberto Tarchiami, the exiled politician and one of the leaders of the Giustizia e Liberta party. Under the code name of 'Speranza' (Hope) he acted as liaison officer between the party in Italy and the anti-fascists in exile in France. He stirred up trouble for the fascists among the university students in Rome and was an agitator during his military service.

Eventually the OVRA, a police arm of the Ministry of the Interior, caught up with Salvadori. He was first kept in solitary confinement in Regina Coeli, the cynically named prison in Rome. Then he was sentenced to 10 years 'confino' on the island of Ponza, where many political prisoners were held, among them the late Sandro Pertini, who was to become president of Italy. An English cousin with some influence got Salvadori out after a year. He could not stay in Italy and spent three years farming in Kenya before moving to the United States to teach in the economics and sociology departments at St Lawrence University.

He kept close links with Giustizia e Liberta and at the first opportunity volunteered for work with British Intelligence, which realised that he was an ideal person for contacting US-based Italians who were anti-fascist. He also sabotaged German radio transmitters in Central America.

In early 1943 he was delighted to hear that his application to join the British Army had been accepted. In February that year he reported to Colonel Cecil Roseberry, who was running the Italian Country Section for SOE in Baker Street. On July 6, after the usual stint of training, including a parachute course, he arrived at the Club des Pins, SOE's Algerian base west of Algiers, taking on the name of Captain Max Sylvester. Thereafter Captain 'Sylvester's' work was mainly behind enemy lines. Together with colleagues he set up a base in Sorrento and there organised the escape of Benedetto Croce, the leading liberal anti-fascist whom Mussolini did not dare to touch. For a short time Salvadori carried the title of Mayor of Salerno. As the allied line went forward, so did Max Salvadori. He won his MC for infiltrating agents behind the front, frequently crossing over the lines himself.

He spent some time running up and down the Adriatic coast on various subversive para-naval operations as well as being heavily involved with the new Italian political scene. This developed even more strongly after the liberation of Rome in June 1944, so much so that Harold Macmillan asked him to take a leading part in the development of the newly formed Italian government. Salvadori refused as he regarded his resistance work as incomplete until the whole country had been liberated.

His final drop was on February 4, 1945, with the mission to proceed to Milan to make contact with the CLNAI (the Resistance organisation for Northern Italy). He reached Milan on March 5 and from then until the end of the war in Italy he led a remarkable clandestine life, meeting as many as 50 people a day. It was during this phase of his work that his impeccable sense of security stood him in good stead. It was needed: Milan was stiff with Gestapo, OVRA and the fascist Milizia. For this effort he was awarded the DSO. Milan made him an honorary citizen in recognition for his part in liberating the city.

When his work against fascism, which he claimed had lasted 23 years, was over he worked briefly for Unesco and then for Nato in Paris. Thereafter he returned to academic life, at Bennington in Vermont and at Smith College, Northampton, where he acceded to the chair of political economics and taught until his retirement.

Max Salvadori was author or editor of more than 20 books on modern European history and politics. Among his most widely read works in English were *American Capitalism, A Liberal View* (1954), *Liberal Democracy* (1957) and *The Liberal Heresy* (1977). The recurrence of the word 'liberal' was no accident. Max Salvadori was concerned with the significance of liberal-democratic institutions and he was unwavering in his opposition to 'the fascination that dictatorialism absolutist and inquisitorial Nazi-Fascist and Leninist in the 20th century exercises over sectors of the so-called educated classes'. His own memoir of the many years he spent fighting fascism appeared in English as *The Labour and the Wounds*, a personal chronicle of one man's fight for freedom (1954).

Salvadori was an assiduous attender at reunions commemorating anti-fascist struggles in Italy. But he was not able to go to one in honour of himself, 'A Day of Study' held earlier this year at his family's home town of Porto San Giorgio. The editor of the local paper declared: 'Count Salvadori belonged to a privileged family but his sympathies were always for exploited peasants and workers, for the oppressed.' He himself put it slightly differently, claiming to be just 'an old-fashioned Radical in the British sense'.

(He died at his home in Massachusetts on August 6, 1992, aged 84)

While not an obituary in the usual sense, the following report published in *The Times* on May 10, 2007, throws some light on the life of someone who served with SOE on the Italian island of Sardinia, which German intelligence was encouraged to believe would be the site of an Allied invasion. But the suggestion that SOE intended Adler and his companion to be captured with documents leading to that conclusion is fanciful.

Gabor Adler
(*The Times* May 10, 2007)

An 'Unknown Englishman' murdered outside Rome by fleeing Nazis was a secret agent who had been landed by submarine to organise anti-Fascist resistance on Sardinia, a historian claimed yesterday.

The officer, whose anonymous grave lay in a wood dedicated to victims of a 1943 massacre, was named last month by Second World War veterans as 'Captain John Armstrong'. But they cautioned this could have been an alias and appealed for those who knew the truth to come forward.

Yesterday it was claimed that 'John Armstrong' was Gabor Adler, a Special Operations Executive (SOE) agent codenamed *Gabriel*, who was landed in January 1943 at Cape Sferracavallo, in German-occupied Sardinia. He was captured almost immediately however, together with Salvatore Serra, a carabinieri (Italian paramilitary police) officer who had defected to British forces while serving in Eritrea. The pair were found to be carrying a list of Sardinian anti-Fascist activists whom they hoped to recruit for sabotage operations, including Salvatore Mannironi, a Catholic anti-Fascist, who was arrested and interned.

Mannironi's son, Domenico Mannironi, a lawyer in Nuoro, Sardinia, said that he had tracked down 'Captain Armstrong's' identity in SOE papers held in the National Archives, at Kew. "After the war my father became a Christian Democratic deputy and served as minister of the Merchant Navy before his death in 1971," he told *The Times*. "He spoke little about his wartime experiences."

He said that SOE files on his father and on Emilio Lussu, a leading Sardinian anti-Fascist partisan who died in 1975, identified Captain Armstrong as Gabor Adler, described by SOE as "a man of astonishing courage" who had swiftly become a first-class radio operator.

Colonel Tom Huggan, a retired army officer and historical consultant to the British Embassy in Rome, said that the embassy was now trying to track down Adler's birthplace and any living relatives. He said the name suggested Hungarian origins, although SOE records indicated his mother was either British or Italian and that his father was a naturalised British subject of Italian origin.

The capture of 'Armstrong' and Serra with a list of partisan recruits may have been an SOE 'double bluff' designed to fool German intelligence into believing that forces gathering in North Africa were preparing to land in Sardinia. Instead, the Allies invaded Sicily in July 1943.

Mr Mannironi said radio messages between Captain Armstrong and SOE supported this theory, as did the fact that the submarine from which he and Serra disembarked had sailed from Algeria. At the end of the war Serra, who survived the conflict and died in 1974, told SOE interrogators that he and Captain Armstrong had pretended to collaborate with their captors to avoid being executed.

After his capture 'Captain Armstrong' was transferred to a Regina Coeli prison in Rome and then to Gestapo headquarters in Via Tasso. When Allied forces entered the capital on June 4, 1944, he and 13 other prisoners were taken in a lorry by German forces retreating northwards up the Via Cassia. Near the Rome suburb of La Storta, the fleeing Germans offloaded their prisoners, herded them into a wood, forced them to kneel and then shot them in the back of the neck. A monument on the Via Cassia records the massacre, and trees planted at the site carry plaques bearing their names – except for one, which simply reads, 'The Unknown Englishman'.

Harry Shindler, spokesman for the Italy Star Association representing veterans who fought in the Italian campaigns, said that Father Hugh O'Flaherty, a Vatican priest who ran a network supporting escaping Allied POWs, had bargained Captain Armstrong's freedom in exchange for protecting the family of Pietro Koch, an Italian Fascist leader who was preparing to flee Rome. The deal had fallen through because, fearing a trap, 'Armstrong' had to the last refused to reveal his true identity.

SOE was always on the lookout for new recruits who had experience or special knowledge of the countryside and conditions where partisans were known to be operating. Following the Armistice of September 1943, Italy became a useful source of new talent in this field as – initially at least – many hundreds of prisoners of war took the opportunity to escape from their camps when the Italian guards left and before the Germans arrived.

Subsequently a number of these men spent the winter of 1943/44 with Italian partisans in the mountains, taking part in sabotage operations against German lines of communications and installations before finally attempting to make their way to the Allied lines in the following spring. Many were recaptured but a significant number reached freedom and were screened for returning to work with the partisans as directed by SOE.

Frederick Rippingale, MBE
(Obituary *The Times* February 24, 2011)

In the early years of the Second World War Italy did not prove susceptible to acts of sabotage and subversion, such as the Special Operations Executive was able to orchestrate in the German-occupied countries of north-west Europe and Scandinavia. Although never universally popular, the fascists maintained widespread control until the September 1943 Armistice, when partisan groups of varied allegiance began to spring up north of the Allied-German battlefronts snaking across the peninsula.

'Rip' Rippingale was able to familiarize himself with the

strengths and limitations of several such groups while hiding in the mountains after his escape from a prisoner of war camp. Having eventually reached the Allied lines, he was asked by SOE to volunteer to return to act as a link with them during the final stages of the war in Europe.

He had joined the RAF Volunteer Reserve in 1939 and commissioned following training as an observer-navigator. While serving with No. 45 Squadron equipped with Mark IV Blenheim light bombers in the Western Desert in November 1941, his aircraft was shot down by a German ME 109 while returning from a bombing mission near El Adem. Injured in the arm and shoulder and badly burned, he spent four months in hospital before being sent to a prison camp at Fontenallato west of Parma in northern Italy.

On hearing of the September 1943 armistice, the Italian guards left the camp allowing Rippingale and several companions to escape before German guards arrived. Anxious to quit the open plain of the River Po, they made for the hills and joined a group of partisans near Borgo Val di Taro. It was there that he met Maria Berni, a local partisan, who was to become his wife two years later.

He accompanied the partisans on operations against German lines of communication and military installations until the autumn of 1944, then took the opportunity of a general lull in the fighting to head south for the forward areas of the 5th (US) Army short of Bologna, where the Americans had paused for the winter in line with the British 8th Army to the east. He finally crossed the lines to safety in November 1944.

On repatriation to England he was invited to join SOE's No. 1 Special Force in Italy, possibly with a view to rejoining his future fiancée still with the partisans around Borgo Val di Taro. After parachute training, indoctrination into SOE techniques of sabotage and subversion – and promotion to flight lieutenant – he returned to Italy in time to be dropped near Piacenza, some twenty miles north-west of Parma, in February 1945.

As part of SOE's Operation *Insulin*, his mission was to arrange for the air-supply of the partisans in the region and, rather than allow them to waste lives attacking German installations, set them to work clearing obstacles and preparing landing strips for Dakota DC 3 aircraft for the possible landing of troops as part of the Allied spring offensive.

This activity brought an energetic German reaction and difficulties of dropping supplies to the partisans due to the winter weather conditions led to deterioration in their morale and motivation. Communism, already the driving force in some partisan groups of the so-called 'Garibaldi Brigades', was also filtering westwards from north-eastern Italy, where the locally settled Slovenes were coming under increasing pressure to spread the communist creed from Tito's partisans across the frontier.

As political considerations began to predominate as the end of the war came in sight, Rippingale and his companions of No. 1 Special Force in the north-west of Italy were kept busy monitoring communist influence in the partisan groups to which they were attached until the Allies push into the valley of the Po in April 1945 concluded the campaign. In consequence he remained in Italy until July 1945. His appointment as MBE in the military division was gazetted on June 1st, 1945, in recognition of his services since escaping from captivity in September 1943.

Frederick Lionel Rippingale was born in London and educated at Erith County School. After SOE debriefing and demobilization in December 1945 he returned to his pre-war employment with the Royal Dutch Shell Group, eventually joining the board before his retirement in 1975. He travelled widely in the company's interest but never lost his love of all things Italian, opera in particular.

In 1945 he married Maria Berni, who he had met with the partisans at Borgo Val di Taro during the war. She predeceased him and in 1982 he married Claudia Maddocks. He is survived by his second wife, two sons from his first marriage and a stepson.

(He died on January 6, 2011 aged 94).

When the end came in Italy with the German unconditional surrender on 27 April 1945, there was no doubt that it was the 5th (US) and British 8th Armies and their supporting air forces who had earned the victory. The principal contribution of the Italian partisans, encouraged by SOE and the American Office of Strategic Services, had been to ensure that the Allies advanced into areas that were welcoming and with a framework on which a civil administration could be rebuilt. Politically, the partisans were important for their contribution to Italy regaining its freedom from fascism.

6

Greece and Albania

The switch of 50,000 Commonwealth troops and all but one squadron of the aircraft supporting them from North Africa to Greece in February 1941 was a strategic error; it was to have lasting implications. Winston Churchill's aim to strike at the Axis through the Balkans, a theme to which he was to return frequently later in the war, was prompted by a pro-Allied coup in Yugoslavia; and new government leadership in Greece favourable to the acceptance of British aid against the invading Italians.

The results were a humiliating defeat at the hands of German armoured divisions in Greece and a small airborne force on Crete, Axis occupation or co-operation by coercion of the whole of the Balkans and Britain's loss of an opportunity to seize control of the Mediterranean southern littoral from Italy at low cost. The post-war contention – rejected by some historians – that diversion of some German armoured divisions to the Balkans delayed the invasion of Russia by three weeks, and so the chances of capturing Moscow before the winter of 1941-42, provides no credit to the British decision, as it was taken in ignorance of that aspiration.

Albania was already occupied by the Italians but the Greeks were still holding their own until the German intervention left them subjugated. In commendable efforts to make the best of a wretched situation, Cairo's SOE staff controlling Force 133 turned its attention to sabotage against German lines of communication through the Balkans and fostering such subversion as might prove helpful; some of the latter proved very tiresome indeed but many of the SOE characters involved were remarkable men.

Lord Terrington, DSO, OBE
(Obituary *The Times* February 15, 2001)

The death of C. M. (Monty) Woodhouse, who became the 5th Lord Terrington in 1998, removes one of that small band of Second World War scholar-soldiers who became legends before they were 30. Woodhouse was an outstanding Classicist, and it was in Greece – a land where legends flourish and abound – that he was catapulted or, more literally, parachuted into the front rank of war heroes. There he helped to transform the Greek Resistance – divided between communists, monarchists, democratic republicans and bandits – into a much more effective fighting force.

His most celebrated success was, as the senior allied officer, to be in charge of the demolition on November 25, 1942, of the Gorgopotamos bridge on the railway line between Athens and Salonika, down which had passed much of the tonnage of supplies and weapons to the German forces in Crete and North Africa.

Though Woodhouse maintained strongly that this guerrilla action had an important direct strategic effect in disrupting German plans, its greatest impact is often seen as psychological. It strikingly contributed to increase the tendency of the German staff to overestimate the power of the guerrillas and to leave large bodies of troops tied up on inactive guard duties at weak points in their long lines of communications.

Not surprisingly, for one who followed so closely in the full Byronic tradition of friends of Greece, Woodhouse wrote years later (in 1969) a sprightly account of the British contribution to Greek independence, entitled *The Philhellenes*. Greece, its struggle for independence and its history after independence, was to be the theme of a postwar career in which he did not pursue the academic course which had seemed likely before the war. In a number of histories and historical biographies published from the early 1950s onwards – beginning with *The Greek War of Independence* (1952) – he charted the conflicts which shaped the Greek experience from the late 18th century onwards.

Christopher Montague Woodhouse was born in 1917, the second son of the 3rd Baron Terrington. Only a few months before the outbreak of war in 1939 Woodhouse had completed his classical education at Winchester and New

College, Oxford, not merely with a double first in Classical
Mods and Greats, but by winning both the Craven and
Hertford and becoming Gaisford Prizeman.

At the age of 23, by dint of a prodigious memory, a dogged
capacity for voracious reading and a keen sense of meticulous
wording, he had laid the foundations for what could always
have been a career of the highest academic distinction, if the
wartime years had not from then channelled his life towards
the world of action.

His wartime career produced at once a new and even more
rapidly constructed string of distinctions: two mentions in
dispatches, a DSO and appointment as OBE, in addition to
decorations from the US and Greece, and a rise in rank from
officer-cadet to commander of the Allied Military Mission to
the Greek guerrillas in German-occupied Greece, all within
four years. He was a colonel at 26.

An early attempt to co-ordinate resistance in Crete failed,
when Woodhouse found himself – at the age of 24 – unable
to handle that most turbulent and thug-like of guerrilla
chieftains, Manoli Bandouvas. But once he had returned
with the Allied Military Mission to mainland Greece and
begun a series of forced marches, secret rendezvous and
other romantic exploits in the full T. E. Lawrence tradition,
his fame quickly spread among a peasantry waiting and
eager to welcome their allies. With the Gorgopotamos bridge
exploit, the momentum to resistance to the Germans gained
strength.

Towards the end of the struggle Woodhouse's main task
was to advise Middle East headquarters on the fighting
capacity and trustworthiness of the different guerrilla groups.
Though he yielded to none in his liking for the Greek peasant,
he was far too shrewd not to foresee the danger to the Western
Allied cause of the predominance of the communist guerrilla
bands in most of Greece.

Criticism of his mission on the grounds that it went on
arming the communists after their takeover seemed probable
is unfair, since, as he often argued, the arms supplied were
only a small fraction of what the communists themselves
captured from the enemy, and an early break with them would
not have helped the West. Woodhouse admitted later that he
underestimated the military resources of the communists,

when they turned upon the British in the December rising in Athens in 1944.

In the immediate post-war years Woodhouse was largely engaged in helping to clear up and record the Balkan mess. He was attached in 1945 to the British Embassy in Athens and was secretary-general to the Allied mission for observing the Greek elections a year later.

Posts in industry and in the Nuffield Foundation and a spell at the Foreign Office were followed by four years from 1955 at Chatham House, where he became Director-General and Director of Studies. Meanwhile, he had published three books on Greek subjects and one on Dostoevsky.

In 1959, later than many of his contemporaries, he entered politics, winning the Oxford seat with a majority of 8,488. But although he reached junior office as Parliamentary Secretary in the Ministry of Aviation from 1961 to 1962 and joint Under-Secretary of State at the Home Office from July 1962 to October 1964, he seemed often too aloof for political life. His book, *British Foreign Policy since the Second World War*, published in 1961, though a careful and precise work, gave little expression of his own views.

It had seemed possible that he might at this stage be given a post at the Foreign Office with a chance ultimately of becoming Foreign Secretary. But when the Conservatives lost office in 1964, the chance was gone. Woodhouse was re-elected himself in 1964, but lost the Oxford seat by a narrow margin in 1966. Although he won it back in 1970 and held it in February 1974, he was defeated in October that year and announced that he would not contest the seat again.

Meanwhile, his books had reverted to dealing with the history of modern Greece rather than current affairs and in 1976 he published his comprehensive work on the Greek war years, *The Struggle for Greece (1941-1949)* – a clear, but scrupulously dispassionate analysis of that passionate theme. Other books dealt with various heroes of the Greek struggle for independence, among them Gemistos Plethon and Rhigas Velestinis. He also wrote about the villains of independence achieved: as in *The Rise and Fall of the Greek Colonels* (1985).

Although he abhorred nostalgia, Woodhouse after so promising an opening to his career could hardly avoid some feeling of anticlimax towards the end of his life. This was a feeling he self-depreciatingly elaborated in his autobiography *Something Ventured*, published in 1983, though in the words of one reviewer 'scoring a century before lunch' did not, in fact, detract from the quality of the stroke play in the afternoon of his life. Indeed, the last task of his life was the monumental venture of translating into English the 13-volume *History of the European Spirit*, by the Greek politician and thinker Panayotis Kanellopoulos. Woodhouse had spent the past eleven years on this task and had completed it just two months before he died.

He had succeeded his brother, a stockbroker and farmer, as 5th Lord Terrington in 1998. In 1945 he married Lady Davina, daughter of the 2nd Earl of Lytton and widow of the 5th Earl of Erne. They had two sons and one daughter. His wife died in 1995 and he is survived by his children and by two stepdaughters and a stepson. The heir to the title is his son, the Hon Christopher Richard James Woodhouse.

(He died on February 13, 2001, aged 83).

The obituarist was mistaken about Woodhouse being the senior Allied officer involved in the Gorgopotamos bridge operation, as revealed by the following letter to *The Times* from Mr Timothy Elliott from Haynes West End, Bedfordshire, on 17 February 2001:

> Sir, My late stepfather, Lieutenant-Colonel D.O.H. Hamson, MC, was one of the six men who laid the charges which blew up Gorgopotamos bridge. I recall him talking with admiration and affection of 'Major Chris' Woodhouse, like him a fine Oxbridge classical linguist, but unlike him not, at the time, a speaker of modern Greek.
>
> Woodhouse was not, as you state, the 'senior Allied officer, present in the gorge on 25 November'. That was Brigadier (then Lieutenant-Colonel) Eddie (E. C. W.) Myers, DSO (obituary, 10 December 1997). Woodhouse was Second in Command.'

A letter received on the same day from Dr Noble Frankland, Director-General of the Imperial War Museum from 1960 to 1982, threw further light on the incident. He wrote:

> 'Sir, Your obituarist of Monty Woodhouse – Lord Terrington – refers to his blowing up the Gorgopotamos bridge in Greece in 1942. After pressing the plunger, he and

his Royal Engineers had to make a rapid withdrawal in the face of swarms of German troops invading the area.

Monty told me that he needed to know whether the operation had been successful but it was impossible to go back and look. Knowing a shepherd boy, whom the Germans ignored as harmless but who was a good artist, Monty asked him to go to the bridge and make a drawing of it. The boy returned with a good line drawing of the bridge in its full glory. Monty was bitterly disappointed. Surely, he told him, there must be some damage. The boy replied that the bridge had gone, but he had drawn it as he remembered it.'

Myers was indeed second in command of the bridge demolition operation and afterwards was obliged, rather against his inclination as he was due some home leave, to remain in Greece, where he was to witness the growing antagonism between the communist and right-wing factions of the local resistance movements.

Brigadier E. C. W. Myers, CBE, DSO,
(Obituary *The Times* December 10, 1997)

In September 1942, a month before the Battle of El Alamein, acting Brigadier Eddie Myers was working in the Combined Operations branch of GHQ, Cairo, when a member of Lord Glenconner's Special Operations Executive came into his office and asked him to lead a demolition team.

This was to be dropped into Greece to blow up the great Gorgopotamos railway viaduct, thus cutting the main German supply line to the Piraeus and thence to Rommel's Africa Korps. Despite being within a fortnight of going home after seven years' service in the Middle East, and with only five training parachute jumps to his credit, the 36-year-old Myers accepted the challenge.

The plan was that he should contact the Greek Resistance bands in the mountains south-west of Lamia. After completing their mission, the team was to be rescued by submarine from the west coast. Despite a difficult drop, Myers managed to link up with General Zervas's right-wing EDES and with their rivals, the left-wing ELAS under 'Aris' – (the Communist, Athanasios Klaras).

Surprisingly, in the light of subsequent events, Myers won the confidence of both Greek commanders and led them in the highly successful combined attack on the Gorgopotamos viaduct, driving off its strong Italian garrison and cutting Rommel's supply line for six critical weeks during his retreat from El Alamein.

Much to the team's disappointment, the submarine rescue had to be cancelled, and Myers was directed to set up a British Military Mission to the Resistance forces in the mountains. He was to expand, arm, train and direct the operations of the *Andarte* (Greek resistance fighters) in harassing the Axis occupation forces. He became aware much sooner than anyone in Cairo or London that Aris's ELAS bands were the military wing of the communist-dominated EAM, a grouping of left-wing political parties in Athens, which was intent on turning Greece into a socialist, if not a communist, republic.

It took all of Myers's very considerable negotiating skills to stop the rival bands fighting each other instead of the Germans. Using his ability to turn off the RAF supply drops to any recalcitrant bands, he proposed and managed to enforce a 'National Bands' agreement, whereby Zervas and Aris accepted the operational direction of C-in-C Middle East and refrained from attacking each other during Myers's time in Greece.

In the spring of 1943 the deception plan for the Allied invasion of Sicily called for a maximum harassing effort in Greece to divert Axis attention eastwards. Myers organised an intensive and widespread sabotage campaign with the willing co-operation of Zervas and Aris, but they were not prepared to tackle the German-held Asopos railway viaduct, which Myers hoped to destroy.

The British members of his team, however, succeeded in blowing the viaduct up themselves by stealth and with the help of local Greek villagers, using an almost impossible approach through the difficult river gorge below the bridge. Such was the severity of the damage that the main Athens railway was closed for four months.

By the summer of 1943 Myers was reporting on the dangers of civil war if the Greek government-in-exile in Cairo was not widened to include representatives of the mountain bands, and if no announcement was made that a national plebiscite on the monarchy would be held before King George II was allowed to return to Greece. Unfortunately, the tenor of Myers's reporting ran counter to strongly held Foreign

Office views, and contrary to Churchill's wish to re-establish the monarchy when the Germans evacuated Athens.

Myers left Greece for Cairo at the beginning of August 1943 in an RAF Dakota from a secretly constructed airstrip, accompanied by four delegates from the mountain bands, to explore the way ahead and to impress upon the British and Greek authorities the dangers of civil war, if more attention was not paid to political feelings within the country as opposed to those of the government-in-exile.

Myers soon found that he was addressing deaf ears. The mountain delegates returned to Greece frustrated and angry, and the civil war that Myers so feared started almost at once. Myers himself was flown back to London for consultations. He had talks with Churchill, Eden and King George VI but, much to his distress, he could not bring about any change of policy. In Whitehall, he was deemed to have helped to precipitate the crisis by being too pro-ELAS. In fact, he had been trying to be realistic about the strength and determination of those Greeks who did not wish to see the return of the monarchy and were prepared to fight for a republic.

Myers was not allowed to return to Greece. Unhappily, his forecasts proved all too accurate when the communist rebellion broke out soon after the liberation of Athens in the autumn of 1944, resulting in the equivalent of three divisions of British troops being diverted from the Italian front to re-establish the authority of the Greek Government.

Edmund Charles Wolf Myers was the son of Dr C. S. Myers, consultant psychologist to the British Expeditionary Force in the First World War and the first Professor of Psychology at Cambridge University. His mother was Edith Seligman, daughter of Isaac Seligman, an eminent Jewish banker. He was educated at Haileybury, the Royal Military Academy, Woolwich, and at Caius College Cambridge; and he was commissioned into the Royal Engineers in 1926. A fine horseman and an amateur pilot as well as being a highly intelligent and forceful personality, he enjoyed his pre-war soldiering in the Middle East, where he first saw active service during the Arab revolt in Palestine. He then commanded the 2nd (Cheshire) Field Company in 7th Armoured Division in the Western Desert during Wavell's 1941 offensive, which drove the Italians out of Cyrenaica.

After attending the Staff College, Haifa, he was employed in Combined Operations until he went to Greece.

Back in England, after his year in the Greek mountains, he continued to work for the Special Operations Executive in preparation for Overlord, but as soon as the Normandy invasion took place he was appointed Commander Royal Engineers of 1st Airborne Division and dropped at Arnhem, where he organised the rescue of the survivors across the Lower Rhine. He also took part in the Airborne Division's liberation of Norway.

In the aftermath of the war, he was Mountbatten's Deputy Director of Intelligence in the Far East, dealing with the problems of the re-occupation of the British, French and Dutch territories. He seemed destined to become an intelligence specialist when he was appointed Senior Military Representative on the Joint Intelligence Bureau in London, but soon after the Korean War began, he found himself Commander Royal Engineers in the Commonwealth Division on the Imjin River in 1951-52.

His last three appointments in the Army were: senior Army Instructor at the RAF Staff College, Bracknell, 1952-55; Chief Engineer, British Troops Egypt, 1955-56; and Deputy Director of Personnel Administration in the War Office, 1957-59.

After he retired in 1959 he had a successful second career in the civil engineering industry. He found time to publish in 1955 an account of his exploits in Greece in his book, *Greek Entanglement*. On his return from Greece in 1943, he married Louisa Sweet-Escott, who had been working for SOE in Cairo. She died in 1995. He is survived by their daughter.

(He died on December 6, 1997, aged 91).

Working diligently, the Germans were able to repair the Gorgopotamas bridge in a matter of weeks, which called for a new attack on the same railway line, this time on the bridge over the Asopos gorge. One of three Royal Engineer officers taking part in this operation was:

Lieutenent-Colonel Kenneth Scott, MC and Bar
(Obituary *The Times* February 11, 2008)
Ken Scott won his first Military Cross with the Special Operations Executive (SOE) in Axis-occupied Greece in 1943.

The single-track railway through northern Greece to the port of Piraeus was carrying 40 trains per day with supplies for the German and Italian forces in North Africa. The line was cut in November 1942 when an SOE team under Brigadier Edward Myers assisted by Greek partisans blew up the Gorgopotamos Viaduct. It was repaired after six weeks, and an attack was ordered on the viaduct on the same line over the precipitous Asopos gorge. Three Royal Engineer officers, Scott among them, were parachuted into the mountains north of Athens for the task.

The viaduct was 175 metres long, supported by three towers on the shoulder of the gorge and a 100-metre steel arch over the river. The SOE party calculated that cutting one of the two legs of the arch with an explosive charge would collapse it completely and drag down the adjacent trusses, creating a 100-metre gap. The viaduct was patrolled from end to end between two tunnels, leaving only the course of the Asopos river 100-metres below as a line of approach.

The communist leadership refused partisan support, so the SOE group resolved on a stealth attack by five British officers, a Greek officer as an interpreter for any locals encountered and a British lance corporal, an escaped prisoner-of-war. Having shaped the explosives in the mountains, the party started down the icy and fast-flowing Asopos river, occasionally carrying the charges on their heads to keep them dry. After three days and nights they reached a 7-metre waterfall across the width of the gorge that barred further progress.

Leaving the explosives under cover on a shingle beach, the party returned to the mountain base to radio to Cairo for an airdrop of more rope. This duly received, they returned to the waterfall, negotiated it and on the night of June 20 reached the point where the northern leg of the arch was embedded in the side of the gorge.

To their surprise, German engineers maintaining the arch had left a ladder to a platform partway up the span. Scott and Captain Harry McIntyre scaled the ladder, hauled the explosives to the platform, fitted them into the girders and having set the time pencils withdrew with their two companions up the previously unknown track used by the German maintenance party. Two hours later the viaduct arch was destroyed.

The line was not reopened until September 1943, by which

time the North African campaign was over. Scott won a Bar to his MC for undercover work with the Greek partisans in support of a deception plan to create the impression that the Allied invasion of southern Europe would be made in Greece, rather than in Italy.

After the war, he joined the consulting engineers Sir Alexander Gibb & Partners, but kept his military connections through his membership of the Engineer and Logistic Staff Corps Royal Engineers, a body of experienced and highly qualified individuals who became Territorial Army officers to give advice on engineering and logistics.

In his capacity as chairman of the Military Engineering Committee of the MoD in 1982, he was able to save the Exchequer a great deal of money by recommending that the construction of a new airfield on the recaptured Falkland Islands be undertaken by the private sector, rather than by the Royal Engineers over a matter of years.

His wife, Betty, died on Christmas Day, 2004, and he is survived by a son and daughter.

(He died on December 25, 2007, aged 89)

The situation between the two main political factions in Greece became an increasing hindrance to Allied efforts to liberate the country and guide it towards a peaceful future. The Italian armistice of September 1943 put the Italian forces in Greece in a difficult position, adding to the problems SOE agents faced. Those faced by Major Philip Worrall were bizarre.

Philip Worrall, OBE
(Obituary *The Times* December 14, 2006)

Philip Worrall's adventures in Greece in the winter of 1943-44 highlight the predicament facing Italian troops serving abroad when Marshal Badoglio negotiated a separate armistice with the Allies, and Italy changed sides. Louis de Bernières's novel *Captain Corelli's Mandolin* (1994) illustrates the grim fate of Italians garrisoning the Greek islands at the hands of their resolute and better armed former *Wehrmacht* allies. As the Special Operations Executive (SOE) liaison officer to the Italian troops of the Pinerolo Division in central Greece, Worrall was on hand to try to avert a similar disaster overtaking them.

His induction into SOE had been informal. Sent to French North Africa with the 56th Divisional Reconnaissance Regiment for Operation *Torch* in November 1942, he was diverted to lead a small group of Frenchmen and Spaniards on an intelligence-gathering sortie between Beja and Medjez el Bab in early 1943. This led to his joining SOE and parachuting into German-occupied Greece.

Italy became a co-belligerent of the Allies on October 13, 1943, just a month after Worrall had dropped into Greece with a small group of SOE reinforcement officers. An SOE mission was already established there, its primary aim to persuade the Greek guerrillas in the mountains to sabotage airfields and installations used by the Germans. Italy's assumption of co-belligerency made the Italian units formerly occupying Greece available as additional resources for this enterprise. But as liaison officer to the Pinerolo Division Worrall found it a struggle to keep his new allies alive.

The SOE's task was complicated by the attitude of ELAS, the military arm of the communist-controlled National Liberation Front, which was itching to seize control of the country after a German withdrawal. The Italian troops offered the ELAS guerrillas a new source of weapons, and their leadership refused to countenance their operating as complete units, insisting that they were scattered to isolated regions. There they were surrounded, disarmed and stripped of their uniforms by the ELAS. Thus instead of a homogeneous force of 7,000 troops, Worrall had that number of near-naked and starving men in his care.

Although he had a copious supply of gold sovereigns with which to pay for food, clothing and shelter, Worrall was dependent on good relations with the local ELAS in order to obtain them. The only real card he held was control of a tiny airstrip, manned by his Italians, through which he could receive supplies from Cairo. To add to his tribulations, the ELAS began a civil war against the non-communist guerrillas who supported the Greek King and Government-in-exile.

After prodigious wrangling with ELAS leaders, Worrall got the bulk of the Italians billeted at Neraida, a village in the Pindus mountains by late October 1943. But when about 2,000 German troops launched an operation to clear them out, he was compelled to send them deeper into the mountains before the snow came. Neraida was burnt down, but after the Germans had withdrawn to the plains ELAS insisted the Italians returned to rebuild it. Later he was able get his Italians housed and fed in other villages.

In May 1944 he was evacuated by air to Bari in Apulia, with suspected appendicitis. He returned with a number of Greek ministers in September when British and Indian troops landed in Greece to restore some semblance of order after the German retreat.

He was flown home from the Mediterranean in early 1945, to join the Special Allied Airborne Reconnaissance Force (SAARF). This was to be parachuted into Germany to obtain information on prisoner of war camps in the hope of avoiding last-ditch massacres by their guards. He was in charge of six three-man SAARF teams that were dropped near Stalag XIA between Berlin and Magdeburg on April 26, 1945.

They first fell into German hands, but with the end of the war in Europe in view, he was able to take control of the situation. "Colonel," he told the German prison camp commander, "if you touch one hair of my head or allow the conditions of the prisoners to deteriorate you will be put on trial as a war criminal."

The camp was liberated by the US Army on May 4 and that afternoon the Red Army arrived to join them. After an inter-allied argument as to where the various nationalities of prisoners were to be sent, Worrall left with his teams next day after arranging for 500 prisoners to be handed over to the care of the US 83rd Division.

He was advanced to OBE for his work in Germany, having already been appointed MBE for his efforts in Greece. By the time the latter was gazetted he was in Ceylon waiting to be parachuted into Borneo or the Celebes. The end of the war against Japan in August 1945 rendered either unnecessary. He was appointed a Commander of the Order of the Crown of Italy for his work on behalf of Italian soldiers in Greece.

Philip Anthony Worrall was educated at Wellington and RMC Sandhurst, from where he was commissioned into The South Wales Borderers in 1938. In April 1940 he sailed for Norway with the 2nd Battalion as part of the Allied Force sent too late to prevent German occupation. After landing near Bodø and engaging German forces, the battalion was evacuated when the Allied situation was judged hopeless.

On return to his regiment after the war, he served as assistant military attaché in Prague and later with the 1st South Wales Borderers during the communist insurrection in Malaya.

He left the Army in 1958 to work for the Central Office of Information, and later with the Government Hospitality Fund. Among the many trips he organised and escorted was one for Raisa Gorbachev, wife of the last Communist leader of the Soviet Union.

He married Nancy Clair Whelan in 1947. She predeceased him. He is survived by three sons, the elder two twins.

(He died on November 1, 2006, aged 88)

It would be neglectful to leave Greece without mention of two stalwart adventurers who spent some months in the latter years of the war doing what they could to liberate some of the Greek islands. They were Earl Jellicoe, son of the commander of the British fleet at the Battle of Jutland in 1916, who was not a member of SOE but commanded the Special Raiding Squadron formed from the Long Range Desert Group of North Africa repute, and Count Julian Dobrski.

Count Julian Dobrski, OBE, MC
(Obituary *The Times* February 8, 1968)

An unusually wide circle of friends in this country, Western Europe and the United States will be saddened by the death of Julian Dobrski.

Julian was a true citizen of Europe for his father came from an old Polish family settled for many years in France, and his mother was an Italian lady. Educated in Paris, where his contemporaries and friends included Jean Monet and René Plevan, he came to London between the wars to represent a celebrated silk house. Here he soon acquired a firm if objective affection for this country, and applied for British nationality, his passport arriving a few days before the outbreak of war in 1939.

His knowledge of Europe and of foreign languages, and the Torquemada-like intricacy of his powerful and well-trained mind soon caught the eye of Lawrence Grand, and within a short time he found himself a commissioned officer in the British Army with the *nom de guerre* of Dolby and one of the founder members of the Special Operations Executive.

Posted to Cairo to help with the infiltration of Italians into Southern Europe, he was parachuted into Rhodes with Earl Jellicoe of the Special Boat Section after the Italian armistice in September, 1943, to obtain a surrender of the Italian commander. Julian was no longer young. He landed, alone with a broken leg, in the no-man's-land of a battle between Italian and German troops. Hiding himself away, he managed in the end to cross the lines and get himself to General Campione. But the Germans had overpowered the Italian forces and all Campione could do was to secure a safe conduct for Julian and Lord Jellicoe back to Cairo, where he spent the rest of the war in charge of SOE's operations in the Aegean, eventually liquidating SOE's exceedingly involved operations in Greece.

For nearly 20 years, in London, in Brussels and then in Geneva, he was the Eastern Hemisphere representative of a vast American concern in the field of electronic communications, in which his charm and unequalled knowledge of Western Europe stood his employers in good stead.

(He died in February 1968).

Albania, occupied by Italy in April 1939, never took on a significance of a critical nature during the Second World War but it attracted a number of SOE officers of outstanding energy and talent. The only economic target worth the effort deployed against it were the Albanian oilfields at Patos-Marinza and the first SOE Mission parachuted into the country in April 1943 had an attack on this facility high on its priority list. The Mission was under command of Lieutenant-Colonel 'Billy' Maclean.

Lieutenant-Colonel Neil 'Billy' McLean, DSO
(Obituary *The Times* November 19, 1986)

Neil Loudon Desmond McLean was born on November 28, 1918, into a distinguished Highland family with extensive connexions in the Far East, and was educated at Eton and Sandhurst. Commissioned into the Royal Scots Greys, he was sent out to Palestine with his regiment still mounted.

His love of adventure, however, inherited perhaps from a

great-uncle, the Kaid Sir Harry McLean – who deserted the British Army to become Commander-in-Chief in Morocco – led him to abandon regular soldiering for guerrilla warfare. He served under Wingate in 1941 in the Abyssinian campaign, commanding a mixed force of Ethiopian guerrillas and Sudanese regulars.

Back in Cairo he joined SOE and after a spell in their office in Istanbul was dropped by parachute into Greece to lead the first British mission to the Albanian resistance movement. With the fall of Italy, the Resistance expanded rapidly and a more senior mission was sent in. The brigadier commanding was captured by the Germans and different factions of the Resistence began to fight each other. McLean was sent back to Albania to attempt a reconciliation between the factions in 1944 but this proved impossible.

McLean was next posted by SOE to the Far East and became military adviser to the British consul-general in Kashgar, in Chinese Turkestan. After the war he travelled extensively in China, India, Iran and the Middle East. He also spent some time studying guerrilla operations in Vietnam and Algeria, and in 1949 was deeply involved in the attempt to win back Albania for the West – an attempt tragically foiled by Philby's treason.

On his return to England he twice contested the constituency of Preston South, in the Conservative interest. This was a highly marginal seat which on the first occasion he lost by only sixteen votes. In 1954 he won Inverness at a by-election and held that seat until 1964. In Parliament he was active behind the scenes rather than in the Chamber, and he was a strong member of the Suez Group.

In 1962 the Egyptians invaded the North Yemen to instal a Republican president in place of the Imam. At the suggestion of King Hussein of Jordan and King Saud of Saudi Arabia, McLean volunteered to reconnoitre the situation, crossing the whole of Yemen from Saudi Arabia to Aden and back on foot, by truck and on camel. He reported to London that at least half the country remained in royalist hands. Thanks to this report the Cabinet turned down a proposal that Britain should recognize the Republic as the United States had already done.

For the next five years McLean spent much of his time in

the Yemen as principal military adviser to the Imam and his supporters. In so doing he rendered decisive service to Britain in the Middle East generally and in Aden in particular. His constituents in Inverness, however, failed to appreciate the importance of his work, and in 1964 he lost his seat.

He continued his interest in the Yemen until after the 1967 war, when Nasser withdrew his forces and royalists and republicans arrived at a compromise peace. Thereafter McLean travelled extensively in North Africa and the Middle East, China and Pakistan.In recent years he spent much time making notes for a possible autobiography. Yet, though he achieved a reputation in the Yemen little short of Lawrence's, he lacked the diligence to put this experience on paper.

The dashing cavalry officer of the late 1930s broke many hearts, but in 1949 he married Dashka Ivanovic whose striking beauty led to her being known as 'the pearl of Dubrovnik'.

(He died on November 17, 1986 aged 67).

His obituary reveals very little about 'Billy' McLean's efforts in Albania or his plans for an attack on the oil-fields, which were well advanced when the group of partisans he was with refused to participate without Allied air support. As this proved impossible to arrange, the plan was abandoned. He was succeeded in 1943 as Mission commander by Brigadier E. F. 'Trotsky' Davies who, as we have seen, was wounded and captured by the Germans who occupied the country after the 1943 Italian armistice.

Another SOE agent already known to McLean accompanied him on his first Mission to Albania and remained associated with him for many years after the end of the war, including his support for the Royalist cause in Yemen.

Colonel David Smiley, LVO, OBE, MC and Bar
(Obituary *The Times* January 26, 2006)

When Lieutenant David Smiley was ordered to Palestine with the 1st Cavalry Division in January 1940 his immediate concern was how to dispose of his private aeroplane, two racehorses and a Bentley. The next five years were to bring him more exacting problems, but he completed the war as a three times decorated lieutenant-colonel.

The Life Guards and Smiley's regiment, the Royal Horse Guards (The Blues), each provided two squadrons to form the

1st Household Cavalry Regiment (HCR), which, together with two other horsed cavalry regiments in Palestine and several Yeomanry regiments, furnished the 1st Cavalry Division with the capability to relieve an infantry division in Palestine for service in the Western Desert. Smiley found Palestine interesting but, seeking more active duty, he volunteered to join No 52 (Middle East) Commando under training at Geneifa, Egypt, in November 1940.

Operations against the Italians in Abyssinia in the early months of 1941 gave him his first taste of action, but when 52 Commando was withdrawn to Egypt, after Haile Selassie had been restored to his throne, he heard that 1st HCR had been motorised and was about to go to the Western Desert, so he hastened to rejoin. Diversions of the regiment – to Iraq, during the Rashid Ali anti-British revolt, Syria and then Persia with the force assembled to oppose any German thrust from the Caucasus towards the oilfields – intervened. But Smiley eventually reached the desert in time for El Alamein. Afterwards, while in Cairo under orders for return to Syria, he snapped up an invitation to join the Special Operations Executive (SOE) mission about to be sent to Albania.

Although there was little reliable information on the situation in Albania, SOE hoped to orchestrate partisan attacks on the occupying Italians. A team comprising Major N. L. D. 'Billy' McLean, Smiley, Lieutenant Garry Duffy – a demolitions expert – and a radio operator was parachuted into Axis-occupied Greece, where an SOE mission was already established.

The team crossed the Albanian frontier to find that the communist and royalist guerrilla groups were principally engaged in outmanoeuvring each other in readiness to take control of the country once the Axis forces had been evicted. However, Smiley and Duffy were able to make contact with a group of communist partisans intent on attacking the Italian garrison in the town of Leshovik. Surprise was achieved, and despite the partisans' failure to press home their advantage, the Italians burnt down their barracks and withdrew.

Impressed by this success, Smiley called for an airdrop of explosives and destroyed a bridge used by the arriving German troops. The encouraging report he sent to SOE headquarters in Cairo as soon as he rejoined McLean and the radio operator elicited news of the imminent despatch of a brigadier to take control of the Albanian mission. On arrival, the brigadier sent McLean and Smiley – whom he suspected of 'going native' – to the coast for collection by the Royal Navy and some leave.

They were recalled from London after news that the brigadier and his staff had been betrayed to the Germans, who had taken over the occupation following the Italian armistice of September 1943. In Cairo they met up with Captain Julian Amery – late of the British Embassy in Belgrade – and all three were dropped directly into Albania.

This second mission began well, as initially the two partisan factions agreed to act jointly against the Germans, but the communist leader Enver Hoxha, Stalinist Prime Minister 1944-54 and in effect his country's leader until his death in 1985, was to renege on this. Even so, damage was inflicted on German lines of communication and supply convoys. After return from Albania, Smiley was awarded the Military Cross for his first mission and a bar for his second.

While on leave in Cairo in early 1945 he received an invitation from the Thai Prince Subha Svasti, whose family had lived near his in Surrey, to join SOE's Force 136 in the Far East. Siam – as the country was then known – was supposedly at war with Britain under Japanese pressure, but SOE was active in promoting anti-Japanese activity in the country. Smiley accepted and was instrumental in organising the repatriation of former Commonwealth prisoners held by the Japanese in Thailand. But in French Indo-China he met obstruction from communist partisans interested only in resisting the return of the French colonial authorities. He was appointed OBE for his work in South-East Asia.

On return to England he was seconded to MI 6 to work on proposals for the SAS to assume the SOE role in future conflicts and then, as part of an Anglo-US project, he went to Malta to brief agents being sent to Albania.

He commanded The Blues with the Army of the Rhine and then in Windsor from 1952 to 1955. This included command of the Sovereign's Escort at the Coronation, for which he was appointed MVO (later LVO). Stockholm as military attaché followed on promotion to colonel and as this assignment drew to a close, he and his wife were on the point of buying a farm in Kenya when Julian Amery, by then Secretary of State for War, offered Smiley command of the Sultan of Oman's Armed Forces.

The Sultan's forces – then of limited capability – were unable to deal with a rebellion mounted from the hinterland plateau of the 8,000ft-high Jebel Akhdar. At Smiley's request, two squadrons of 22nd SAS Regiment, a Life Guards squadron and RAF ground-attack aircraft were put at his disposal and the rebels were dispersed, after a heroic scaling of the Jebel by the SAS. Modernisation, expansion and better training of the Sultan's forces were subsequently instituted. The rebels were finally defeated after a heroic scaling of the Jebel by the SAS

On leaving Oman in 1961, he was offered command of the SAS Group in England but not promotion to brigadier. By his own admission, he left the Army in a huff and tried to settle down as a restaurants inspector for the Good Food Guide. He was rescued from this by Billy McLean, his friend from the Albanian missions – then MP for Inverness – who asked him to go to Yemen. There he was to act on behalf of the Saudi Arabian government as military adviser to the Imam commanding the force fighting the republican movement supported by President Nasser of Egypt.

Over the next four years Smiley visited Yemen, travelling the areas controlled by the Imam, on foot or by donkey, offering his advice on operations, organisation and training until the Israel-Arab War of 1967 obliged Nasser to withdraw from Yemen and the Saudi Government brokered a compromise truce between the two sides.

Smiley and his wife then farmed in the Alicante province of Spain for 20 years, but he maintained his Albanian contacts. When a coalition came to power in Tirana in 1991, Amery and Smiley were invited to visit as guests.

At a reunion in the Bixha Valley, site of the wartime parachute drops, they met their former interpreter, who had endured seventeen years' hard labour for his help to the Allies during the war.

David De Crespigny Smiley was the third son of Major-General Sir John Smiley, Bt, and was educated at Pangbourne Nautical College and RMC Sandhurst, from where he was commissioned into The Blues in 1936. He recorded his adventures in three volumes, *Arabian Assignment*, *Albanian Assignment* and *Irregular Regular* published in 1975, 1984 and 1994 respectively.

He was married in 1947 to Moya (Moy), the second daughter of Lieutenant-Colonel Lord Francis Montagu Douglas Scott, the youngest son of the 6th Duke of Buccleuch. She survives him with two sons, a stepson and a stepdaughter. (He died on January 8, 2009, aged 92)

Scarcely surprisingly, given the primitive nature of the country and its constantly feuding factions, the conditions under which the SOE Missions were obliged to exist left much to be desired. The circumstances are well illustrated by the obituary for Doctor Jack Dumoulin.

Doctor Jack Dumoulin
(Obituary *The Times* January 11, 2008)

Jack Dumoulin was one of a small group of young British Army doctors recruited during by the Special Operations Executive for work in enemy-occupied territory. He later enjoyed a distinguished peacetime career as a consultant obstetrician and gynaecologist based in Plymouth.

He joined SOE in the summer of 1943 and was parachuted into German-occupied Albania as medical officer with an SOE mission commanded by Lieutenant-Colonel (later Major-General) Norman Wheeler. There, in appalling conditions, the group worked with partisans led by the country's future dictator, the communist Enver Hoxha.

Dumoulin's task was to do what he could, with the scarce and basic resources he had to hand, to treat sick and wounded guerrillas and the shared sufferings of his colleagues. A fellow SOE officer, Captain Marcus Lyon remembered Dumoulin as an excellent doctor who remained utterly calm and controlled in the most testing of circumstances.

The struggle in the Albanian mountains between the occupying Axis forces and the local partisans was harsh, with no quarter given by either side. Ruthless reprisals were inflicted on villages suspected of harbouring partisans and bitter rivalries between partisan groups often led them to fight each other as well as the Germans.

Brought out from Albania in December 1944, Dumoulin

volunteered for further SOE service. He was assigned to Force 136, the arm of SOE operating in the Far East, and parachuted into Malaya. There the task of SOE was to organise local guerrilla groups, mostly comprising Straits Chinese. After the end of the war in the Far East, he was appointed MBE for his medical work with SOE.

In Albania, he had been assisted by a young local nurse, Drita Kosturi. When a card marked 'Captain J. G. Dumoulin, RAMC' was found in her possession after the war, she was accused by Hoxha's regime of spying for the British. She was sent to a labour camp where she remained for 40 years. As Albania was a closed country under Hoxha, Dumoulin did not learn of her experiences until he met her again on his first return visit in 1990 and arranged for her to be flown to Plymouth for medical treatment.

John Geoffrey Dumoulin was born in Ferriby, near Hull. After school at Malvern College, he studied at St Thomas' Hospital and qualified in 1942. Post-war he worked at Hammersmith and University College hospitals, specialising in obstetrics and gynaecology, before being appointed as a consultant in Plymouth, where he practised until retirement in 1984.

He had a wide interest in the management of obstetrics and gynaecology at national, local hospital and speciality level, and particularly in research and training. A member of the Royal College of Obstetrics and Gynaecology in 1949, he became a Fellow in 1960. He subsequently served on the council of the college, where he was able to influence both training and the maintenance and improvement of standards of care.

He contributed numerous papers to specialist journals, including in 1953 a seminal paper on the use of intravenous ergometrine (a drug that makes the womb contract) to prevent postpartum haemorrhage, which was then the fourth-commonest cause of maternal death.

His wife, Enid, predeceased him. He is survived by two daughters.

(He died on December 10, 2007, aged 88).

The Lieutenant-Colonel Norman Wheeler and Captain Marcus Lyon mentioned in the Dumoulin obituary both endured frustrating times in Albania, as their own obituaries reveal.

Major General T N S Wheeler CB, CBE
(Extract from *The Times* obituary of October 2, 1990)

Norman Wheeler was first and foremost a Royal Ulster Rifleman, dedicated to soldiering and devoted to his regiment, and yet equally successful in business after he retired from the army in 1971. The attribute which made for success in both careers was his regard for and understanding of people and his ability to get on well with everybody military and civilian at all levels. He invariably saw the brighter side of life, however discouraging the circumstances might seem to others at the time, and his optimism could be infectious.

His father, Thomas Henry Wheeler, served in the 3rd Hussars in the Boer war, and later in the Worcestershire Regiment before joining the South African police. His strong Irish connections came from his mother. He was educated at St Helen's College, Southsea, and at Sandhurst before being commissioned into the Royal Ulster Rifles in 1935.

He first saw active service with his regiment during the Arab revolt in Palestine in the late 1930s, being mentioned in dispatches. He showed his administrative and business abilities when as a second lieutenant he took over and successfully carried out the duties of the regimental quarter-master, who had been invalided home.

When war broke out he was adjutant to the RUR depot in Ulster, and after going to the staff college in 1941 he became the brigade major of 38th (Irish) Brigade. He then held a number of 'Q' staff appointments in the Middle East before volunteering for parachute training in 1943.

He first came to military prominence after being parachuted into the Balkans as a lieutenant-colonel in Brigadier 'Trotsky' Davies's Special Operations Executive mission to the Albanian partisans. His drop was continually delayed by bad weather, and before he could reach the SOE base and hideout in the Germanika mountains north east of Tirana, 'Trotsky' had been wounded and captured in a German encircling operation, designed to catch Enver Hoxha and the partisan general staff. Hoxha and his closest associates escaped to set up a new headquarters for the winter in the fastnesses of the southern mountains where Wheeler managed to join them and take over Davies's role as senior British officer with the partisans.

Wheeler witnessed and shared the grave crises through which the partisans passed during the winter of 1943-44, and their extraordinary recovery in the following spring. He had just as much difficulty in getting out of Albania to report to SOE at Bari as he had in making his original drop. It was due to no fault of his reporting that Britain failed to catch the partisan tide in Albania (unlike Yugoslavia), and became over-committed, and ineffectually so, to the losing nationalist side.

He returned from Albania just in time to rejoin the 2nd Royal Ulster Rifles in the 3rd Division in Normandy in July 1944, first as support company commander and then as second in command, fighting with them for the rest of the war in north west Europe. After the war he held a series of staff appointments, including assistant adjutant general and quartermaster general to the 6th Airborne Division and military assistant to the adjutant general in the War Office. By 1957 he was on the general staff in HQ Northern Army Group, grappling with the reorganisation of BAOR resulting from the Duncan Sandys defence review, which ended national service.

He commanded the Royal Ulster Rifles in Cyprus during the EOKA terrorist campaign, and had the personal excitement during the ``battle'' of Liopetri of climbing onto the roof of a defended terrorist farm hideout and flushing out the gang by pouring burning petrol down the chimney. At the end of his regimental command in 1960 he was delighted to be given command of the 39th Brigade, Ulster's regular garrison.

The last 10 important years of his military career were on the continent, and after a number of senior staff posts and a divisional command he became chief of staff, BAOR, from 1969 to 1971.

(He died on September 21, 1990 aged 75)

Marcus Lyon, TD
(Obituary *The Times* March 12, 2007)

Marcus Lyon was one of the last surviving officers of the Special Operations Executive to have worked behind the lines in wartime Albania. This wild and mountainous country had been occupied by the Axis since 1939. Small SOE missions, given the task of blowing bridges, ambushing convoys and encouraging locals to resist, started arriving in April 1943. Lyon was dropped by parachute in December.

Guerrilla warfare in Albania was a ruthless, difficult business. Prisoners were shot out of hand and terrible reprisals inflicted on villages suspected of harbouring guerrillas. SOE casualties were appalling and the privations extreme. Lyon, brought out from the coast in June 1944, parachuted back in July and stayed until December. In his final weeks he was acting senior SOE officer with Enver Hoxha's partisans and, when the Germans withdrew, the only officer to accompany Hoxha when the partisans marched into Tirana.

Back in Britain and promoted to major, Lyon joined the Special Allied Airborne Reconnaissance Force, an unusual unit, thick with SOE officers, given the hazardous job of parachuting into POW camps in Germany. The intention was to stop German guards from massacring the inmates, but the war ended when only a handful of teams had been sent. Lyon was not among them. He and other SAARF officers were then sent anyway to Germany where they were put to work catching war criminals. In October 1945 he returned to Albania, to spend six months on the staff of the official British Military Mission.

The son of a cavalry officer from whom he inherited his artist's eye, James Marcus Lyon was born in York in 1919. Double pneumonia three times as a child upset his early schooling and he was taken for three years to Switzerland. Then he went to Stowe. Still treated as a delicate child and anxious to do something tough, on leaving he took a deckhand's job on a tanker to Texas and back.

With a territorial commission in the Warwickshire Yeomanry he was mobilised immediately war broke out and shipped to Palestine. In 1941 he volunteered for the Libyan Arab Force, a mobile unit working with tribes in the desert. In 1942 he joined the Yorkshire Dragoons and pushed through to Tunis. When the Dragoons went into reserve Lyon found himself in Cairo just as SOE was looking for volunteers.

Returning to London in 1946, Lyon resumed his pre-war studies at the Architectural Association. With his heart now set on painting, however, he decided to switch to Chelsea School of Art. After some film illustration work and a period painting murals and designing London nightclubs, he married, moved to Crowborough and began teaching, finally becoming director of art and art history at Eastbourne College.

His wife, the sculptress Marion Danziger, whom he had met in Palestine during the war, died in 2003. He is survived by his stepson.

(He died on February 1, 2007, aged 87)

As succinctly expressed by William Mackenzie in *The Secret History of the SOE*, the endemic brigandage in Albania critically inhibited the early SOE attempts to direct such resistance groups as they found into any coherent strategy of sabotage against the occupying Italian forces. It was only after 1942 and more particularly the Italian Armistice of September 1943 that any remotely reliable guerrilla movement could be established.

The change of sides by Italy brought German troops into Albania to take over defence of key points on their lines of communication. The Nazis skilfully played the nationalist card by giving support to Albania's aspirations to acquiring territory at the expense of Greece and Yugoslavia. The most cohesive opposition coalesced around the National Liberation Front (FNC), the left-wing opposition to return of ex-King Zog of Albania, largely manipulated by the local communists, to which the SOE Mission was inevitably drawn, despite its strong communist affiliations.

Once the Germans began to withdraw from Greece and Albania in the autumn of 1944, the FNC expanded quickly, receiving arms and supplies delivered by the Allied Balkan Air Force based in Italy. FNC guerrillas, advised and aided by SOE and American OSS agents, inflicted casualties on the Germans estimated to be in the region of 6-7,000 men. One SOE party sabotaged the chrome mines at Kan, which the Germans had been using, and another under David Smiley sabotaged the bridge at Gjolos as a German convoy was crossing it. What had originally looked like a lost cause could be said to have ended tolerably well from the Allies' point of view, albeit leaving Albania under hardline communist control that was to persist for forty years.

7

Yugoslavia

SOE operations in Yugoslavia during the Second World War received a good deal of publicity at the time. This was chiefly due to the two resistance groups – nationalist and communist – breaking into open conflict while still under Axis occupation. Elsewhere this fundamental divide was constrained as each faction armed and prepared to confront and defeat the other once the enemy had withdrawn.

An additional factor in publicizing Yugoslavia was the high profile of some of the participants. Of these, the communist leader Josip Broz, or 'Tito', as he became known, was the most prominent, while Sir Fitzroy Maclean, Randoph Churchill – the Prime Minister's son – and the novelist Evelyn Waugh added contemporary weight and colour – principally colour in the case of the latter two.

The first name to emerge after the German invasion and occupation of 1941 was that of the nationalist guerrilla leader General Dragolub 'Draza' Mihailovic, whose obituary in *The Times* neatly encapsulates the entire political and military drama from 1941 until the end of the war.

General Draza Mihailovic – Leader of the Chetniks
(Obituary *The Times* July 18, 1946)

The rise, decline and final downfall of General Draza Mihailovic, who was shot by firing squad in Belgrade yesterday morning, illustrated vividly the ideological trend of the past few years. He himself felt this. He was expressing the same thought when he said in a singularly moving last speech, "the gale of the world has carried me away."

Mihailovic was a regular officer of the Serbian and, later, Yugoslav army. He served with distinction in the war of 1914 to 1918. The German invasion of Yugoslavia in the spring of 1941 found him holding a command in the field. It was at this juncture that he took a historic decision. When the Germans overran Yugoslavia, Mihailovic, instead of capitulating, took to the woods and continued to resist the enemy.

The (Monarchist) Yugoslav Government in exile appointed him commander-in-chief of the Yugoslav army in the Fatherland, and gave him the post of Minister of Defence. He was also recognized by the British military authorities in the Middle East, who attached liaison officers to his forces and, as soon as it became possible, dropped him small quantities of supplies by parachute. Such were the origins of the Chetnik movement.

Meanwhile in the summer of 1941 a new resistance force had entered the field – the communist-led Partisans of Marshal Tito. Meetings took place between Tito and Mihailovic and an effort was made to unite the two forces under one command. But it was found impossible to reach agreement; clashes occurred between Partisans and Chetniks; each accused the other of bad faith, and there followed a breach between them which was never healed.

The differences between the two movements were military as well as ideological. Mihailovic's early operations led to savage enemy reprisals against the civilian population. He came to the conclusion that the results achieved did not justify such sacrifices. Thenceforward he grew less and less active. His main objective was to preserve his strength. He was encouraged in this policy by the British military authorities, who urged him to hold his hand. Meanwhile Allied propaganda continued to represent him as an active leader of resistance.

The (communist) Partisans, on the other hand, with ruthless determination typical of their communist leaders, allowed nothing to deter them. As the fame of their successes spread, their numbers increased. Mihailovic soon found himself outstripped. As a loyal Monarchist and strong Serbian nationalist, he was appalled by the meteoric rise of a communist-inspired movement. To him communism seemed no less of a menace than Nazism. More than ever, he was convinced of the need to preserve his strength in order that in the ultimate analysis he should hold the decisive cards.

While there was a falling off in his operations against the Germans and Italians, his operations against the Partisans were intensified. The fact that these operations often coincided with attacks by the Axis forces lent substance to the charges of collaboration with the enemy brought against him by the Partisans. However this may have been, there can be little doubt that 'accommodations' with the enemy were reached by many of his commanders, but Chetnik discipline seems to have been so bad and Mihailovic's control over them so loose, that it is not impossible for this to have happened without his approval.

Once on this slippery slope the Chetnik movement went fast downhill. Allied support was transferred to the militarily more effective forces of Tito and the allied missions withdrawn. Thousands of Chetniks went over to the Partisans, others finally threw in their lot with the Germans.

Milhailovitch's fate was henceforward a foregone conclusion. An allied victory was now assured, and there could be no doubt that the withdrawal of the Germans would leave the Partisans in control of the country. The incredible bitterness of the struggle which for nearly four years had ravaged Yugoslavia meant that there could be no quarter for the vanquished. Past services to Yugoslavia, good intentions for the future would not be taken into account. Mihailovic knew this but made no attempt to escape his fate. He preferred to face certain death for ideals which had long since become unattainable.

(He was executed by the communist regime on February 17, 1946)

The first British agent to be sent into German-occupied Yugoslavia was an individual of extraordinary courage and resourcefulness. His obituary, like that of Mihailovic, also sheds much light on the course of a war that left much bitterness and, seemingly, him with personal remorse.

Colonel D T 'Bill' Hudson, DSO, OBE
(Obituary *The Times* November 10, 1995)

Of all the agents recruited into the wartime secret services, Duane Tyrrel Hudson 'Bill' to his friends was one of the most effective. His physical strength, intellectual subtlety and moral courage all found ample scope in intelligence gathering, sabotage and liaison with guerrilla forces. When Ian Fleming created James Bond, one of his models was Hudson, who was tall and handsome, enjoyed an active social life and charmed the women of many nations.

Hudson played a key role in the controversial history of British intervention in Yugoslavia. He was the first agent to penetrate the country after it was occupied by the Axis powers in 1941, and for 11 months was the only one there. He was the only agent who met both the rival leaders of resistance Tito and Mihailovic.

Born into a South African family, Bill Hudson went to St Andrew's College, Grahamstown, and then to the Royal School of Mines in London. He was an outstanding athlete, playing rugby for London University and boxing as a heavyweight in student and ABA championships. He always reckoned his fists were better in close combat than a revolver.

In 1935 he took a job in Yugoslavia as manager of an antimony mine and travelled widely on prospecting expeditions. He became devoted to the Serbs, especially the peasants from whom he learnt his fluent Serbo-Croat. Many were veterans of the Salonika front in the First World War, grateful admirers of their British allies. In 1936 Hudson married a prima ballerina, Ada Proskurnikova, one of many White Russians who had fled the Soviet Union. Unhappily she found it impossible to adapt to life in his mountain home, and they agreed to divorce. He never remarried.

When Britain went to war in 1939 Hudson was asked to work for Section D, the secret service branch set up to wage 'ungentlemanly warfare''. He was posted to Zagreb, where the struggle with the Gestapo in a still-neutral Yugoslavia was most dangerous. One British agent was murdered, and Hudson had a narrow escape when pro-German Croat extremists planted a bomb beneath his office. Hudson recruited a network to carry out sabotage against Axis shipping in Dalmatian ports, and in February 1941, blew up an Italian cargo ship.

By now Hudson had been incorporated into the Special Operations Executive (SOE). In June 1941 the Soviet Union was forced into the war by the German invasion and in July SOE's Yugoslav section in the Middle East received vague reports about guerrilla groups in Yugoslavia, some nationalist, some communist. SOE discussed with its Soviet counterpart, the NKVD, the possibility of flying a joint British-Soviet-Yugoslav mission into the country, and Hudson volunteered to be its British member.

This fell through, but another came to fruition and Hudson was landed by submarine on the coast of Montenegro in September 1941. Hudson's orders were to 'discover who is fighting the enemy' and to 'co-ordinate all elements of resistance'. Within five weeks of landing Hudson reported most of the basic facts, and met most of the personalities on the ground who were to feature for the next few years in the convoluted deliberations of the British authorities.

He met a guerrilla force known as the Partisans and led by the hitherto unknown Josip Broz Tito, and Draza Mihailovic, leader of a force of Royalist Serbs known as the Chetniks. Though both fighting against the Germans in Serbia these were already at odds with each other. Mihailovic had been appointed by the Yugoslav government-in-exile in London to exercise sole authority in its name; Tito had set up a Soviet-style People's Republic as a first stage in a revolution against that government.

Hudson warned SOE that civil war between the two groups was imminent, and when it broke out in November 1941, the Partisans got the upper hand. Mihailovic asked for a truce but while this was being negotiated a German punitive expedition drove Tito into headlong rout into Montenegro and forced Mihailovic and his men to go underground.

Mihailovic abandoned Hudson, who happened to be with him, resentful of his having told SOE to drop no more arms to be used against fellow Yugoslavs. As a result, Hudson was left for the next six months in an area where the Germans were taking reprisals by burning villages and hanging 100 Serbs for every German killed. He was ambushed and his horse was shot under him; he was twice captured, once by Quislings, and once by bandits, but managed to escape. He lost his radio set, all his money, and most of his belongings. He survived thanks to the hospitality of ordinary Serbs who gave him shelter, regardless of reprisals, and shared their meagre food with him. Even so, by April 1942 he was nearly starving and in mental anguish as a result of his isolation.

By that time Mihailovic was back in radio contact with SOE. Having assured it that he had ended the civil war, Mihailovic was again receiving drops of money, supplies and Yugoslav personnel. In May he allowed Hudson to rejoin the Chetniks. In June Mihailovic moved his HQ to Italian-occupied Montenegro but refused to resume active warfare against the Axis, pointing to the appalling losses suffered by the Serbs in German reprisals and in massacres carried out by the Croats in Bosnia.

In fact, in spite of Mihailovic's earlier assurances the civil war was continuing; Mihailovic was effectively a guest of Montenegrin Chetnik leaders who were clearing their country of Partisans in co-operation with the Italians. Although Mihailovic was not a party to these transactions, he was not opposing them and risked the taint of collaboration.

Meanwhile Tito's Partisans were vigorously fighting the Axis and Hudson, who could see that they were militarily stronger than the Chetniks, became convinced that they could usefully work with the British. But when he reported these facts to SOE, the British authorities, who were backing Mihailovic, refused to believe them. Hudson was variously accused of being unhinged by his ordeal, politically naive, a leftist and of being under duress when he wrote his reports.

But when, in late 1942, Colonel Bailey was sent out to check on Hudson he confirmed every detail and quickly found himself in the same frustrating impasse with Mihailovic. Hudson was allowed to stay on as political adviser, first to Bailey and then to Brigadier Armstrong, who became head of the mission to Mihailovic in late 1943. By now the Deakin and Maclean missions to the Partisans had confirmed what Hudson had been saying for more than two years and, in December 1943, Churchill took the decision to drop Mihailovic and support Tito.

Hudson had just toured Serbia and knew that the Partisans were predominant in Bosnia and Montenegro. But they were barely present in Serbia where the mass of the population was anti-communist and there were at least 100,000 Chetniks under arms. To save these men from being wasted in a final round of fratricidal fighting with the Partisans, Hudson proposed to SOE that the two movements should be merged into a single army for the final campaign against the Germans.

Mihailovic would have to stand aside, but Tito, too, would have to make concessions.

In May 1944 Hudson was flown to London to expound his view to Churchill and Eden. They were much impressed and his plan for the Chetniks became Foreign Office policy. But by then Tito, enjoying British and Soviet support, was not prepared to make any concessions. He knew that to control Yugoslavia he had to conquer Serbia. In the violent struggle that followed the Chetniks were totally destroyed.

Hudson's last SOE operation was to command a mission to the Home Army in Poland. This was a hazardous operation which involved him in being arrested by the NKVD and spending time in Moscow's Lubianka jail, before the mission was released. For his war services Hudson was awarded the DSO, appointed OBE and mentioned in dispatches.

After the war Hudson thought of going back to mining in Yugoslavia, but was told he was a war criminal because of his association with the Chetniks. When Mihailovic was put on trial as a traitor in 1946 he offered to testify in his defence, but was turned down. Mihailovic was sentenced to death and executed.

Hudson went back to South Africa, where he discovered a deposit of tungsten and mined it for a while. He then sold out so profitably that he was able thereafter to lead a life of leisure. He divided his time between his flat in St James's and one in Durban. He became a member of the Hurlingham Club and a keen tennis player. Inside Hudson's rugged frame was a generous, gentle and romantic spirit. He suffered from bouts of depression; in particular he was always haunted by his failure to mediate between the Partisans and the Chetniks. (He died in South Africa on November 1st, 1995, aged 85).

Another early participant in the Yugoslav drama joined SOE on account of his linguistic rather than diplomatic skill. Despite the hesitancy of the nationalist Chetniks to risk further German reprisals for acts of sabotage, by sheer determination he was able to achieve some success in that field.

Erik Greenwood
(Obituary *The Times* October 14, 2009)

Erik Greenwood was recruited into the Special Operations

Executive (SOE) in 1942 when a Russian speaker was required to accompany a party of Royal Engineer demolition experts being sent to the South Caucasus. The purpose of the mission was to inflict damage on the local oilfields in case of their capture by the swiftly advancing German Army, but on reaching Azerbaijan it was discovered the Russians had plans of their own. On return to Cairo, he was assigned to lead a small SOE team into Axis-occupied Yugoslavia.

The spring of 1943 found Winston Churchill pondering whether to continue to support the Serbian guerrillas led by General Draza Mihailovic, the Chetniks, who were proving difficult to stir into action against the occupiers, or switch to the communist partisans fighting under Marshal Tito. Accompanied by a royalist Serbian officer and a sergeant, a radio operator, Greenwood parachuted into north-eastern Serbia on April 18, 1943. Despite bringing only a dozen rifles, they were welcomed by the Chetniks, who regarded their arrival as evidence of British support.

The head of the SOE mission to Mihailovic was Colonel 'Bill' Bailey, a metallurgist who had worked in Yugoslavia before the war. He told Greenwood to urge acts of sabotage on the group to which he was assigned. Greenwood proposed two targets: sabotage of the copper mines at Bor and blocking the Danube to the barge traffic supplying the Axis forces in Yugoslavia and Greece. The Chetniks were unwilling to tackle either, stating that they had insufficient strength to hold Bor long enough to sabotage the mines and, as with disruption of the Danube traffic, such action would bring down unacceptably heavy German reprisals on Serbian civilians.

It soon became clear to Greenwood that Mihailovic's guerrillas were essentially a Serbian national organisation dedicated to the restoration of the monarchy with Serbian domination of the country – after the Axis withdrawal – rather than attacking their German and Italian occupiers.

Exasperated by his lack of progress, in October 1943 he persuaded the Chetnik leader of the area close to the Danube to co-operate in an attack on the barge traffic. Taking a handful of Chetniks who knew the river region well and appeared ready to take aggressive action, he ambushed a convoy of barges causing the tug to run aground and the barges to pile up in confusion behind, blocking the river for some days.

His exultation at this success was soon curtailed as the Germans announced the execution of 100 civilian hostages in Belgrade as a reprisal. Strangely, this did not appear to damage his good relations with Chetniks, but when the British Government declared its support for Tito's partisans in early 1944 and abandoned Mihailovic, he began to wonder whether he and his radio operator would be able to withdraw. Eventually a plane was sent to extract them and four other British officers of the SOE mission, the Chetniks accepting the matter as a decision of war.

Greenwood was mentioned in dispatches for his service in Serbia, arguably a surprisingly modest recognition of the efforts he had made and the risks he had run.

Erik Spencer Greenwood was born in 1916 in Halifax, Yorkshire, where his father prospered in the wool trade. He was educated at The Leys, Cambridge, from where his marked facility for foreign languages led to him to begin a career in the Consular Service. On the outbreak of war he was living in Estonia studying Russian but returned home to enlist in the Corps of Military Police in October 1939. After the invasion of Finland by the Soviet Union in November he volunteered for the 5th (Ski) Battalion Scots Guards, raised largely from officers of other regiments who relinquished their commissions. It was intended that this unit would go the aid of the Finns, but they were overwhelmed before it could arrive.

In April 1940 he went to Norway with the force of special volunteer companies led by Lieutenant-Colonel (later Major-General Sir) Colin Gubbins – who became the Executive Head of SOE from 1943 – with a view to attacking German coastal targets, but with little success. On return to England he served with No 3 Commando before going to the University of Cambridge to train as an interrogator of German PoWs, the role that took him to Cairo and SOE. In the closing months of the war and until the spring of 1946 he was with the Control Commission Germany.

After demobilisation as a major, he worked abroad for Alcan, the producers of aluminium for 25 years, then with Rio Tinto-Zinc in the UK.

He married Catherine Mackinnon, a Canadian, in 1941. She predeceased him, as did their son, killed in a gliding accident in June 2009. He is survived by a daughter.
(He died on September 6, 2009, aged 93).

As the question intensified as to whether the British Government should back Mihailovic and his Chetniks or Tito and his Partisans, Winston Churchill decided to send a senior officer to each to make an assessment based on what they found in the way of aggressive activity against the Axis occupying forces. The man sent to Mahailovitich was a professional soldier of high standing and considerable experience.

Brigadier Charles Armstrong, CBE, DSO, MC
(Obituary *The Times* December 16, 1985)

Charles Armstrong served through both world wars and in 1943-44 commanded the British Military Mission which supported Draza Mihailovic, the leader of the Serbian Cetnik resistance forces in Yugoslavia. The British Mission was withdrawn in May 1944 when the British Government decided to switch its full support to Tito and his Communist Partisans.

Commissioned into the East Surrey Regiment, Armstrong was seconded to the Machine Gun Corps, twice wounded and awarded the MC in 1919.

A dedicated, brilliant, if stubborn, regimental soldier, he eschewed the staff and spent most of his service with the East Surrey Regiment. Tough and resilient, he continually sought action and between the wars fought in North Russia, Mesopotamia and on the North West Frontier.

During the Second World War he commanded three battalions of the East Surrey Regiment and one of the Duke of Wellington's Regiment and was awarded the DSO for his leadership at Dunkirk. While in command of 'the Dukes' he was selected to command the Military Mission to Mihailovic.

His exploits in that confused Balkan war are legendary. Fresh evidence published by the Hoover Archival Documentaries in 1980 indicates that some actions carried out by Mihailovic with Armstrong were erroneously credited to Tito. After the withdrawal of his Mission, Armstrong saw service with the

Polish Parachute Brigade and was appointed CBE in 1946. In 1946 the Tito Government tried and executed Mihailovic. (He died on December 11, 1985, aged 88).

The man sent to make a recommendation regarding Tito and his Partisans was of an altogether different stamp: a former diplomat and politician with first-hand experience – and scepticism – of communism, Fitzroy Maclean had to be rapidly advanced to Brigadier for the assignment.

Sir Fitzroy Maclean of Dunconnel, Bt, KT, CBE
(Obituary *The Times* June 18, 1996)

In an era short of heroes, Fitzroy Maclean came closer than most to filling the role. His life was full of adventure, high drama, danger and diversity. As a diplomat, he witnessed the show trials of Stalin's Russia; as a soldier he fought with David Stirling in the fledgeling SAS; as a traveller, he explored parts of Soviet Central Asia never visited before by a Westerner; and as an author and historian he wrote with passion and authority about his native Scotland.

Above all he was a central figure in one of the crucial episodes of the Second World War when he parachuted into Yugoslavia as Churchill's personal envoy; his favourable assessment of Tito meant that the Allies backed the communist Partisans rather than the Cetniks of General Mihajlovic, a decision that undoubtedly altered the course of post-war European history. In the light of subsequent events in that troubled country, it remains a matter of controversy. But neither Maclean nor Churchill was ever in doubt that it was the right decision, and that Tito's independence of mind made him not only a valuable resistance leader in combating the German occupation of his country, but acted as a buffer against Moscow domination after the war.

Fitzroy Hew Maclean was the son of a distinguished soldier, Major Charles Maclean, of the Queen's Own Cameron Highlanders who had won a DSO in the First World War and had, during an earlier adventure, been shot through the mouth during hostilities in Sierra Leone in the 1890s. The Maclean connections in Argyll could be traced back to the 13th century and a forebear called Gillean of the Battle-Axe, as well as the 15th-century Lachainn Bronnach, or big-bellied

Lachlan of Dowart, a cousin of the Lord of the Isles. Those clan links were always to remain important to him.

Conceived in Inverness, Maclean was born in Cairo and spent his first two years in Scotland. Long spells in India and Italy followed. His mother, who instilled in him a love of languages, taught him French and German (later he was fluent, too, in Russian and Serbo-Croat). She guided him away from Walter Scott to more intellectually challenging works by Thomas Mann and Anatole France.

He was educated first at Heatherdown preparatory school, Ascot, then Eton, where he was described by the Eton Chronicle as having won 'all the prizes for which he was allowed to compete'. He won a scholarship in 1928 to study Modern Langues at King's College, Cambridge, but spent a year in between in Germany where he studied Latin and Greek, thus enabling him to switch to Classics and to win a first in his Classical Tripos. He read History in his third year and got a second in Part Two.

After Cambridge, he joined the Diplomatic Service and was sent, as third secretary in 1934, to the Paris Embassy, where he found himself caught up in the volatile atmosphere of French politics, the riots of 1934, the sit-down strikes of 1936, and the massed demonstrations on the Champs-Elysees, where he listened to the crowds chanting the Internationale.

He was fascinated by the Soviet Union, and in 1937, at his own request, he was posted to Moscow. The next two years, up to the outbreak of war, were, he believed, 'the most horrendous in the whole of Russia's blood stained history,' and few episodes horrified him more than the trial of Nikolai Bukharin, one of Lenin's closest associates, which he attended throughout, and which opened his eyes to the terror of Stalin's regime.

Returning to London in 1939, he listened to Neville Chamberlain's announcement on September 3 that Britain was at war, and decided that he must leave the Diplomatic Service and join the Army. The only way of doing so was to pursue a political career that being the swiftest way out of the Diplomatic Service, which he did by standing successfully for election as Conservative MP for Lancaster. More importantly for him, it allowed him to join the Cameron Highlanders as a private.

Promoted to lieutenant in August 1941, he fell in with David Stirling who had formed the SAS, a fighting force which consisted of no more than half a dozen officers, and was employing guerrilla tactics against Rommel's Afrika Korps in the Western Desert. This involved him in several hair-raising commando raids behind enemy lines, none more so than a raid on Benghazi with the Long Range Desert Group, wearing Arab headdress, and fooling German sentries with a stream of schoolboy Italian.

But it was a subsequent adventure, no less dramatic, that was to plunge Maclean, by now promoted to brigadier, into the mission for which he will always be remembered. On the strength of his experience of irregular warfare, he was chosen by Winston Churchill, in the summer of 1943, to be dropped into German-occupied Yugoslavia as his representative with Tito. Churchill described him as 'a daring ambassador-leader to these hardy and hunted guerrillas'.

Maclean makes it clear in his book, *Eastern Approaches* one of the most gripping and colourful of modern memoirs that his role was not to make a recommendation about whether Britain should back Tito, but rather to pass on his assessment about whether he or Mihajlovic was most effective in fighting the Germans. He was in no doubt that Tito was the right man, and the two formed a strong personal attachment.

But he was also impressed by Tito's robust attitude towards Moscow and when, towards the end of 1943, he passed back to Churchill the comment, "Much will depend on Tito and whether he sees himself in his former role of Comintern agent, or as the potential ruler of an independent Yugoslav state", there was little doubt about what his own view was. On this, he and Churchill saw eye to eye. History may well debate the wisdom of that crucial choice, but no one should doubt Maclean's clear recognition that in Tito Yugoslavia had found a natural leader.

After the war, Maclean resumed his political career, first as MP for Lancaster. But then, to the surprise of some, in 1959 he gave up this seat for Argyll and North Bute, for which he sat until February 1974.

In 1946 he married Veronica Phipps, second daughter of the 16th Lord Lovat, and widow of Lieutenant Alan Phipps,

RN. It was a marriage of two equally strong characters, close but volatile, in which no assertion would be left unchallenged, no opinion unquestioned, but where in the end mutual love and respect underpinned the strongest of unions. They made their home at the Maclean seat of Strachur in Argyll, from where, to the end of his days, and despite growing lameness, Maclean would set off on endless travels, often undertaken in conditions of extreme discomfort.

(He died on June 15, 1996, aged 85).

The partisan leader to whom Maclean was sent was a shrewd guerrilla fighter and a cunning and dynamic politician who used typical communist ruthlessness to establish and maintain his grip over the disparate elements of his Partisans, no matter from which nationalist group they came.

Marshal Tito
(Extract from *The Times* obituary of May 5, 1980)

Whatever judgment historians will pass on the life and significance of Josip Broz Tito, his name will go down as the first communist ruler to have defied Stalin and to have established his country's independence at a time when throughout eastern Europe communist regimes bowed to Soviet supremacy and Moscow was installing, dismissing and purging their governments at its will.

A staunch communist – perhaps one of the few remaining idealists – trained and hardened by the Comintern yet deeply rooted in his own country, Tito never hesitated when the independence of Yugoslavia was at stake. While other European communists, as he so contemptuously used to say, "sat in Kuybishev waiting to be installed in power by Russian bayonets", Tito won his country's independence and emerged from the war himself an internationally recognized figure owing 'gratitude' to nobody. It was this, the wartime struggle for independence, which more than anything else shaped his character and determination to be master in his own house. Once he emerged victorious from the war, once he felt an 'equal', proud of his country's and its people's achievement and courage, he could not agree to accept domination and the tutelage of others even if this meant domination by the 'first country of socialism'.

Whether one agreed or disagreed with his policies – whether one was his zealous admirer or his bitter opponent – one had to recognize that he was one of the most colourful personalities to have stepped on the postwar political scene. He lived ostentatiously – his diamond ring, his exaggerated uniforms, his love for expensive cloth, for flashy cars and speedboats, his island of Brioni – were as much part of his character as his political shrewdness, his courage, his faith in the doctrine and his simplicity and loyalty to that small number of people with whom he shared the hardships of the past. In a country which came out of the war deeply divided, torn by national, religious, and historical antagonisms, he represented the only true Yugoslav.

More than anything else, he saw his role as bringing about a new unity of Yugoslavia's distinct yet associate nations, unity of equal partners, jointly responsible for their common destiny. For a while he believed that all national groups would merge into one Yugoslav nation – and saw the future in a kind of supra-national integration. But he was a realist and though he may have been disillusioned and deeply perturbed by the emotional tensions this idea provoked in later years, he realized that, given the multinational context and historical background, Yugoslavia's future was in a looser federation guaranteeing each nation full equality and recognizing national individuality and cultural distinctiveness.

Early in 1938 Tito returned (from exile in the Soviet Union) to Yugoslavia. He had seen from the beginning the dangers of political exile and so he started to pick new men with practical experience in the country, most of whom he knew from prison. By 1940 communist membership rose to 12,000. In true Stalinist fashion he purged the dissidents and soon achieved complete 'unity', the monolithic party of iron discipline.

When in the summer of 1941 Tito issued a proclamation calling for insurrection against the Germans, it was still as a disciplined communist, obeying the Comintern's orders. Russia had to be assisted and he was responding to her call. It was during the war, however, that Tito first disregarded Moscow's orders and that his disillusionment began. While Moscow, for reasons of its relations with the Allies, wished Tito to give the latter no cause for suspicion, and warned him he was to conduct a fight against the Germans and not engage in civil war with the aim of establishing communist rule, Tito's reply was to send a defiant telegram. "If you cannot help us, do not hinder us", he wrote to Stalin then.

The first strictly military recognition of Tito came from the Allies at Tehran and by the summer of 1943 the first military supplies began to arrive for his Partisans. Feeling considerably strengthened, on November 29, he convened an assembly of the Liberation Council which transferred the powers of the Royal Government in London to the newly formed National Committee of Liberation and banned King Peter from returning to his country until the Yugoslav people were able to decide what form of government they wanted. On that date too the title of Marshal of Yugoslavia was conferred on him, and, for the first time since he left prison 10 years before, his real name was publicly revealed.

So, for the first time since he became Comintern's trusted agent, he confronted Stalin with a fait accompli. In May, 1944, under strong Allied pressure, King Peter finally invited Dr Shubashich, one of the leaders of the Croatian peasant party, to form a government in exile with the task of reaching agreement with Tito. When finally agreement was reached, Tito had all the cards. In August, 1944, resplendent in his new marshal's uniform, Tito arrived in Capri for a meeting with Winston Churchill.

(He died on May 4, 1980, aged 87)

Although Sir Fitzroy Maclean is credited with the recommendation that the British Government should back Tito rather than Mihailovic, his and earlier reports by a young academic named Deakin provided the security cover for the 'Ultra' intelligence that actually caused Churchill to order a change of sides in Yugoslavia.

Sir William Deakin, DSO
(Extract from *The Times* obituary of January 25, 2005)

The first Warden of St Antony's College, Oxford, William Deakin was a distinguished historian who will be remembered for his published work and, especially, for his creation and development of St Antony's as a centre of international graduate studies.

He also had a meritorious war career, leading a hazardous Special Operations Executive mission to Tito's Partisans in Yugoslavia. For this he was awarded the DSO, and his persuasive reporting on the situation on the ground had a decisive influence on British government thinking about which of the Resistance movements to support in Yugoslavia.

Deakin's qualities were such that he might have been successful in many other professions. His independence, courage and intellectual vitality, together with his warm heart and deep loyalties, made him an outstanding personality with a wide circle of friends in many countries. His reputation extended far beyond the academic world where his main work was done.

Frederick William (Bill) Dampier Deakin was born in 1913, the elder son of Albert Witney Deakin. He was educated at Westminster School and Christ Church, Oxford, and already as an undergraduate he was gaining the reputation of being one of the most brilliant and dashing figures of his generation. After being placed in the first class in the modern history school in 1934 and winning the Amy Mary Preston Read scholarship in 1935, he was elected to a fellowship at Wadham College, which he was to hold with periods of absence on war service and other duties until 1950.

He quickly established himself as an outstanding teacher and lecturer, but in his early days as a don he was also employed as a research assistant by Winston Churchill, who was at that time writing his life of Marlborough. Churchill at once appreciated Deakin's qualities, and the professional association became a friendship that was to last until Churchill's death. Even before the outbreak of war in 1939, Deakin had joined The Queen's Own Oxfordshire Hussars, and in 1941 he was transferred to the Special Operations Executive (SOE). He was subsequently sent to Cairo to work on Yugoslav questions.

When reports from British officers attached to General Mihailovic's Cetnik organisation in Yugoslavia, which the British were supporting with arms and supplies, suggested that Mihailovic was a much less effective ally than the Partisans, under their still shadowy leader Tito, Deakin was sent to Yugoslavia to report at first hand on the Partisan movement.

In late May 1943 he was parachuted to the Partisan HQ in Montenegro. With another officer, Captain W. F. Stuart, and two wireless operators, he arrived at the height of a German offensive, and for the next few weeks Deakin shared the hazards and hardships of the partisans during one of their worst ordeals of the war. Within a few days of their arrival Stuart was killed, and Deakin and Tito wounded by fragments of the same bomb.

During this period Deakin's courage and cheerfulness won the confidence and admiration of Tito and the other partisans, and his integrity and his friendly nature did much to overcome the prejudice and suspicion which Tito and his staff felt towards the representative of a government which was still officially supporting their rival Mihailovic. It was largely as a result of Deakin's reports of the Partisans' effectiveness and perhaps, too, of the faith which Churchill personally had in Deakin's judgment, that the British Government decided to withdraw its support from the Cetniks and to concentrate on helping the Partisans.

Deakin left Yugoslavia in December 1943, two months after a formal military mission, under Brigadier Fitzroy Maclean, had been dispatched to Tito's headquarters. But he continued to be responsible for Yugoslav affairs and at the end of the war he served as first secretary at the British Embassy in Belgrade. These experiences gave him a lifelong interest in Balkan and Eastern European history, reinforced by the ties of friendship which now bound him to Tito and other leading figures in Yugoslavia.

In 1946 he returned to Oxford and resumed his teaching at Wadham. But he soon received another summons from Churchill, this time to be one of the leading members of the team which was helping the former Prime Minister in the preparation for his war memoirs. Churchill's temperament and working habits and Deakin's own scholarly scrupulousness and loyalty made this an exacting task. During the next few years Deakin's own creative gifts as an historian were fully absorbed by his work for Churchill, and he was obliged to postpone his own projects.

In 1948 Antonin Besse, a French merchant and shipowner resident in Aden, offered Oxford University one million pounds to found a new college which should keep a proportion of its places for Frenchmen. In 1950 Deakin was asked by the university to become its first warden.

Deakin had to determine the nature of the college from its inception and had, in effect, sole responsibility for assembling a small group of Fellows and selecting the first students. He quickly established excellent relations with the founder and his family, and he won the confidence of the committee under Sir David Maxwell Fyfe (later Lord Kilmuir) which was supervising the affairs of the college until it became fully independent. It was agreed that the college should become an international graduate college, specialising in the first place in the fields which especially interested Deakin – modern history and political studies.

Within a few years St Antony's College was established as an integral and valuable part of the university, and there is no doubt that it was Deakin's personality and imagination which gave it its unique international quality. He enabled it to make a distinctive contribution to the development of European, Russian and, later, other regional studies in Oxford. Although often impatient of administrative detail and sometimes complaining of the provincialism of Oxford, Deakin devoted all his intense nervous energy to the tasks of running and developing St Antony's and raising additional funds for it. In truth the latter was something he never found congenial, and indeed this contributed to his decision to resign the wardenship in 1968.

However, he found time to produce a major work of scholarship, *The Brutal Friendship*, published in 1962. This was a long and detailed study of German-Italian relations during the Second World War, based to a very large extent on unpublished documents. It revealed Deakin not only as a first-rate diplomatic historian, but also, in his account of the end of the Fascist regime in Italy, as a political analyst of a high order.

(He died on January 22, 2005 aged 91)

During the period of the war after the clearance of the Axis powers from North Africa in 1943 and the launch of the liberation of Europe by the invasion of Normandy in June 1944, it became – not to be too light-hearted about the matter – 'fashionable' to be involved with the SOE in Yugoslavia, the strong communist fervour of Tito's Partisans attracting those who in their innocence professed a penchant for that illusion.

Summarizing the value of the SOE missions to the Partisans, Professor William Mackenzie in his acclaimed *The Secret History of the SOE 1940-1945*, (St Ermin's Press 2000), wrote, 'Supplies (of arms) were not sent in any reasonable proportion to the number of Allied Missions, and it is a little doubtful whether the Missions served any purpose except to give adventurous occupation to a number of very tough young men. Their reports were useful, though limited in value, by their ignorance of the general political problem. But they were observers, not leaders.'

Some specialists in guerrilla warfare would contest Mackenzie on this point, not least as Tito did depend on the supply of arms the SOE Missions arranged, but there is an element of truth in his observation. As a scholar renowned for his stringent scrutiny of the facts and motives, it might just be that he had the following military dilettanti in mind, who were certainly not attracted by Tito's political affiliation.

Lord Amery of Lustleigh
(Extract from *The Times* obituary of September 4, 1996)

Amery himself described his wartime service, carried out mainly in the Balkans for the Special Operations Executive, in his memoir *Approach March* (1973).

He told the tale in the manner of John Buchan though, in his case, the hero often failed to triumph. It seemed to him wholly contrary to British interests to lend succour solely to communist Resistance movements in the Balkan countries.

Yet, so far as Yugoslavia was concerned, he had to sever his connections with the royalist Chetniks led by Mihajlovic. This came about when the Special Operations Executive authorised Fitzroy Maclean and others (including Amery's great friend, Randolph Churchill) to throw Britain's full weight behind Tito. In Albania, too, he had to abandon the guerrillas supporting King Zog in November 1944, after having himself fought with them (sustaining a minor wound to the face) for several months. His mission was, in his own words, an "utter failure"; Britain had once again decided to back the communists.

(He died on September 3, 1996, aged 77)

Randolph Churchill, MBE
(Extract from *The Times* obituary of June 7, 1968)
If in the war years he expected a ministerial appointment, he was to be disappointed. He served throughout the war as an Intelligence Officer, first in the Middle East and then in Yugoslavia. On this latter mission he was accompanied by Evelyn Waugh who, in order to stop him talking (always difficult, and usually impossible), induced him to read through the Holy Bible; an arduous, but by no doubt rewarding undertaking. What Tito and his Partisans made of these two unusual officers can only be a matter of speculation.
(He died on June 6, 1968 aged 57).

The obituary of Evelyn Waugh, published in *The Times* on April 11, 1966, focused on his literary achievements and his personal relationships, making only passing reference to his war service with the Royal Marines and the Royal Horse Guards, his part in the battle of Crete but none of his time with SOE in Yugoslavia. He died on April 10, 1966, aged 62.

8

France 1943 and 1944

Despite some setbacks in the early years, SOE was making substantial progress in France by the end of 1942. Around twenty circuits had been set up, ranging in geographical spread from Normandy to Bordeaux, over to the Massif Central and through to Var in the extreme south-east. France is a large country, however, so the spread was undeniably thin – and some of the circuits were in danger of collapsing due to betrayal by locally recruited agents or detection of radio traffic, a hazard greatly increased by German occupation of the entire country following the Allied invasion of French North Africa – Operation *Torch* – in November 1942.

The Allies' strategic planners were soon to turn their attention to the invasion of northern – and subsequently southern – France and the help or possible hindrance that the French Resistance might contribute to this key enterprise became of increasing importance. SOE Headquarters in Baker Street was drawn into this and F Section was soon examining ways in which the weaker circuits could be strengthened and the stronger ones extended in their reach and influence. New men and women were sent to France, together with some already experienced in working there.

Major B H Cowburn, MC and Bar
(Obituary *The Times* February 10, 1994)
Benny Cowburn happened to be one of the few Englishmen who could pass easily for French; he was almost bilingual. He was an oil technician by trade, who had lived in Paris before the war began, and was early picked up as a likely candidate by SOE. He went through the usual courses in paramilitary training, and parachuted into central France with five

companions, four of whom were soon arrested, on the night of September 6-7, 1941.

He had plenty of common sense and a temperament that did not flap easily: ideal qualifications for his early task, which was to sound out likely local heads of sabotage teams and to provide them eventually with explosives. The shortage of available wireless operators soon drove him to Paris, where he made touch with an operator who had been, it turned out, planted on him by the German *Abwehr*. He and two friends had the eerie experience of standing on a north Breton beach, closely watched by the *Abwehr*, while a British torpedo boat failed to rescue them. Cowburn politely and firmly detached himself both from his friends and from his German shadow and returned to England across the Pyrenees.

Though well known to the enemy, he soon parachuted back into France on June 1-2, 1942, for a successful four-month spell organising sabotage around Limoges. He returned quietly by Lysander in October. He made himself useful to his section, lecturing and advising agents under training; and then went back to France again in the spring of 1943.

He set up an unusually efficient rail sabotage circuit, codenamed *Tinker*, round Troyes. This put a dozen locomotives out of action in a single night by a raid on the round house there on July 3-4, 1943. By accident Cowburn left the plan for the raid on the blackboard of the local school where he had trained his sub-agents for the task; the school-master's wife, married to one of the sub-agents, rubbed it out in time. He again got back to England unscathed.

His fourth mission was his least successful. His friend and wireless operator at Troyes named John Barrett, had gone back to France early in 1944 with a different organiser and fell into enemy hands in July. Cowburn parachuted in yet again, on July 30, to attempt the almost impossible task of cutting Barrett out from German captivity; at least he survived himself, though his friend was murdered in a concentration camp. As he was always one for speaking his mind when invited to do so he received no grander decoration than a Military Cross and Bar for a series of exploits of unusual daring.

He wrote a strikingly good book about his war experiences called *No Cloak, No Dagger* (1960). It did not receive the acclaim it deserved for its splendid matter of fact accounts of what a secret agent's life was really like. By the time it appeared he had long gone back to a flat in Paris, and to the decent obscurity of the life of an adviser behind the scenes to oil companies. Everyone who knew him at all well knew that he was a man who could be relied on to keep his eyes open and his mouth shut; and that behind his impassive exterior he concealed a rollicking sense of humour.

He had a long, happy, but childless marriage to a former secretary of Georges Bidault, wartime Resistance leader and, briefly, one of France's post-war prime ministers.

(He died in 1994 aged 85)

Some of the more successful SOE agents came from the country where operations were being planned but it proved important that they received SOE training if they were to achieve their full potential One such agent was Baron Philippe de Gunzbourg, a former Jewish-French playboy.

Baron Philippe de Gunzbourg, MBE
(Obituary *The Times* July 23, 1986)

The son of a Russian banker and a French mother, de Gunzbourg never felt at ease in the cosmopolitan Jewish world of his parents; and, as a young man, he was a playboy and a rebel. When the French Army demobilized in 1940, he rejected all thoughts of emigrating to safety and chose instead to buy a farm near Agen in the unoccupied zone. As early as 1941, he made contact with a British emissary of the SOE's French section and began working for the organization.

By 1943, when the Germans had occupied the whole of France, his involvement had grown and he sent his wife, Antoinette, their two children and English nanny to the safety of Switzerland. Under the command of George Starr, one of the SOE's most successful agents in south-west France, de Gunzbourg assumed responsibility for the area around Sarlat, Bergerac and the northern Lot-et-Garonne. He proved himself an outstanding organizer, welding those around him into an effective fighting force and frustrating German attempts to destroy it.

His achievements bore fruit in June, 1944, at the time of the Normandy landings, when the Germans needed without delay to transfer their 2nd SS Panzer Division (Das Reich), through his fief to the Normandy battlefield. Ordered from the neighbourhood of Toulouse on D+1, the Reich division was scheduled to reach the battle front – where its heavy tanks of the newest type might well have had decisive effect – on D+3.

In the event, the division received such harassment from de Gunzbourg's section, and at the hands of other SOE-organized *Maquis* further north, that the move took seventeen days – a delay of strategic significance at a time when the Allies were fighting fiercely to consolidate and extend their beach-head foothold, and would have regarded with considerable anxiety the addition of another first-class, fully-equipped, armoured division to the German defence.

As it was, by the time the Reich division moved into its lagers close to the battlefield on D+17, it was with fighting qualities and morale much undermined by the attacks of the guerillas.

Many felt that de Gunzbourg's MBE (military) was scant recognition of his role in these events.

After the war, he devoted much time and considerable resources to the problems of those who had been his companions-in-arms; and despite a considerable local standing, he never sought political office. His sister was married to Sir Isaiah Berlin.

(He died on July 10, 1986).

A man of contrasting background and motivation who became one of SOE's most successful circuit leaders in France began the war strongly opposed to the idea of military service.

Francis Cammaerts, DSO
(Obituary *The Times* July 6. 2006)

Registered as a conscientious objector before the Second World War, Francis Cammaerts felt he could no longer stand aside after his brother was killed while serving with the RAF. A fluent French speaker with a deep affection for the country, he became one of the most outstanding agents of the Special Operations Executive (SOE) in France. Curiously for one who was to prove so successful, he was initially assessed as 'lacking in dash' and 'not suitable as a leader'.

Francis Charles Albert Cammaerts was born in London, son of Professor Emile Cammaerts, a Belgian poet and patriot. He became a pacifist in the 1930s while at Cambridge, where he read English and history at St Catharine's College and won a hockey Blue. He began a teaching career at Cabin Hill School, Belfast, in 1937, and became an agricultural labourer in 1940 as an alternative to military service.

He left farming to join SOE in October 1942. After training, he was flown into northern France in March 1943 by a single-engined Lysander monoplane piloted by Squadron Leader Hugh Verity of 161 Squadron RAF. The Westland Lysander, designed for army co-operation and reconnaissance, was vulnerable to German fighter attack in daylight but its short take-off and landing capability and robust undercarriage made it ideal for landing two or sometimes three agents with pinpoint accuracy by night; a feat then impossible by parachute.

More than a dozen SOE circuits were active in France at the time of the German occupation of the area previously under Vichy control in November 1942. Cammaerts was assigned to the *Donkeyman* circuit then operating in the upper Rhône valley, but his SOE reception party drove him first to Paris with a brash disregard for security that alerted him to the risks of such behaviour. Over six feet tall with large feet he felt very conspicuous, so left by the evening train for Annecy to join *Donkeyman*. But his intuitive zeal for security led him to a safe house in Cannes, where he established a cover as a teacher recuperating from jaundice.

This was the first, and last, time that he spent more than four nights in the same place, as security rather than urgency was the SOE watchword at this stage of the war. He spent his early months in France gradually building his own circuit, *Jockey*, of seven or eight reliable individuals who – thoroughly indoctrinated of the importance of security – set about recruiting potential saboteurs for when the time was ripe. His key to individual safety was to insist that his agents always had a credible reason for what they were doing, if stopped by a German patrol.

In the later months of 1943 he established several small and semi-independent groups, all part of his *Jockey* circuit, down the left bank of the Rhône between Vienne and Arles and eastwards through the hinterland to the Isere Valley. He travelled by motorcycle to visit each group, but no one knew his real name, nationality or where he lived. Having established the *Jockey* circuit ready to play its part in sabotaging German lines of communication and routes north when the Allied invasion came, Cammaerts was recalled to London for briefing in November 1943.

While there he raised the problem of the enmity between the agents working in France under the aegis of General de Gaulle's headquarters and those, many of them French citizens, recruited by SOE's French section. There was a strongly held view in the Gaullist camps in London and Algiers that it was unconstitutional for French citizens to be recruited by a foreign power. As Britain and the Free French were fighting for the same cause, including the liberation of France, this may seem a very minor quibble. It was never entirely resolved, however, and De Gaulle insisted that all SOE operations in France ceased soon after the liberation of Paris in August 1944.

Cammaerts's aircraft crashed on landing when he returned to France in February 1944. Fortunately, he was unhurt and hastened to check the readiness of the *Jockey* circuit. He also visited the 3,000-strong group of *Maquisards* – young Frenchmen who had fled to the Vercors plateau to avoid conscription for forced labour in Germany. In April 1944 he informed SOE's London headquarters that the "Vercors has a finely organised army, but they need long-distance and anti-tank weapons".

This was not a request London wished to hear, as the ability of the German Army to deal effectively with guerrillas who tried to stand and fight was already well proven in Yugoslavia. Arms drops were made to the Vercors but did not include heavy weapons.

As soon as the Allied invasion was launched on June 6, 1944, the railway line cutting teams of *Jockey* and other SOE circuits went into action, proving the value of Cammaerts's training. In his book, *SOE in France*, the official historian of the SOE campaign, Professor M. R. D. Foot, records that every train leaving Marseilles for Lyons after D-Day was derailed at least once and in the Indre Department more than 800 lines were cut in June.

But disaster awaited on the Vercors plateau. Cammaerts's warning that the *Maquisards* needed heavy weapons had been disregarded, not through neglect in London but because it was reckoned, on sound precedent, that it was not the role of guerrillas to fight pitched battles.

After the Normandy invasion Cammaerts was appointed head of Allied missions in south-eastern France. Consequently he was present when elements of at least two German divisions with tactical air support attacked the Vercors *Maquisards* in mid-July. The plateau cliff tops were fiercely contested, but the result was a foregone conclusion. When the order was given for the *Maquisards* to seek what hiding they could find, Cammaerts left the region in despair.

Subsequently, he was satisfied to see his *Jockey* and neighbouring SOE teams supporting Operation *Dragoon*, the Allied invasion of southern France launched on August 15, 1944. SOE teams held open the route from Cannes, through Digne and Gap to Grenoble, to allow the Allied armies, comprising American and French divisions, to clear the lower Rhône, although many units of the German 19th Army – already further north – escaped into Alsace.

It was at this point, despite his meticulous care for security, that he and two colleagues were arrested by the Gestapo in Digne. They may not have realised Cammaerts's significance, but it was because of the sheer nerve and resolve of his courier, Christina Skarbek, an alluring and dynamic Polish woman who had avoided arrest, that the three were eventually released. She confronted a French liaison officer to the Gestapo and a Belgian interpreter with the news that the leading US troops would arrive within hours and she would ensure they were handed over to the town's avenging mob unless they co-operated. Terrified, they engineered the three officers' release.

This was the final chapter of a total for Cammaerts of 15 months in occupied France. (Christina Skarbek – by then Granville) was tragically murdered in London by an unwanted suitor in 1952). Cammaerts was awarded the DSO for his leadership and gallantry in France but, as in the case of others who operated in enemy-held territory for prolonged periods, he gave great credit to the ordinary French people who provided him and his companions with safety and comfort. In the BBC TV series *Secret Agent*, broadcast in 2000, he said: "The most important element was the French housewife who fed us, clothed us and kept us cheerful."

He was appointed a Chevalier of the *Legion d'Honneur* and awarded the French *Croix de Guerre* in 1945, the US Medal of Freedom in 1947 and advanced to Officer of the *Legion d'Honneur* in 1991.

After demobilisation he joined the International Reparations Agency in Brussels.

He returned to teaching in 1952 to be headmaster of a school in Stevenage for nine years, Principal of the City of Leicester College of Education, 1961-66, and Professor of Education in Nairobi, 1966-72. He came out of retirement at 65 to go to Botswana to start up a new college for mixed-ability teacher training in 1981. He finally retired in 1987.

Cammaerts married in 1941 Nancy, daughter of James Finlay, architect to the Leeds education committee. She predeceased him, as did one of his daughters. He is survived by a son and two daughters.

(He died on July 3, 2006, aged 90).

As already indicated in many of the foregoing obituaries, the role of the SOE radio operators was vital for the success of arming the Resistance fighters with weapons and providing them with explosives for sabotage. The radio operators were one of the principal chinks in the armour of agent security, particularly when tempted to remain transmitting long enough to allow the German detection service – which was very efficient – to get a geographical 'fix' on the site from which the transmission was being made. Gaston Collin was an example of a reliable operator.

Gaston Collin, MC
(Obituary *The Times* June 11, 2007)

Gaston Armand Collin, born of a French mother and English father in London in 1918, changed his surname from Cohen after the Second World War, during which he distinguished himself as member of the Special Operations Executive. Although bi-lingual, it was not until he had served for three years with a heavy anti-aircraft gun battery in Southampton that he was picked up by SOE and trained for operations in France.

A highly competent and resourceful radio operator, he was twice parachuted into German-occupied France to maintain wireless contact back to SOE headquarters in London. He

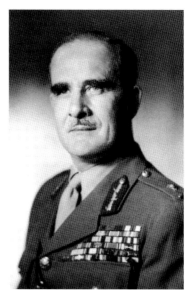

Dr Hugh (later Lord) Dalton   Major-General Sir Colin Gubbins

Pilots of 161 (Special Duties) Squadron RAF: *(left to right)* James McCairns, Hugh Verity, Wing Commander 'Pick' Pickard, Peter Vaughan-Fowler and Frank 'Bunny' Rymills with Verity's Lysander 'J' for Jiminy Cricket.

Wing Commander 'Tommy'
Yeo-Thomas, GC

Odette and Peter Churchill

Anthony Brooks

Colonel Maurice Buckmaster

Einar Skinnarland.

Jos Mulder-Gemmeke

Major-General Albert Guerisse, GC

Commander Gerard Holdsworth

David Smiley (left) with 'Billy' McLean in Albania in 1943

Lord Terrington

Philip Worrall

Sir Fitzroy Maclean

Pearl Witherington

Colonel 'Bill' Hudson (left) and General Drazo Mihailovic (right) with a
Montenegrin guerilla

Jedburgh sixtieth anniversary reunion at Milton Hall on June 12/13 2004.
Left to right: David Stern, Bob Keloe (USA), Ron Brierley, Ken Brown, Major
Richard (Dick) Rubinstein, Donald Gibbs, Frank Bailey, Jack Grinham, Paul
Aussaresses (France), Arthur Brown, Bob Rogers, Jack Singlaub (USA), Glyn
Loosmore, Oswin Craster, Tom Carew, John Sharp, Harry Verlander

Lisa de Baissac

Colonel John Davis

'Troff' Trofimov with Karen fighters in Burma

Peter Dobrée with Lieutenant Mohamed Nor bin Rani in Malaya in 1945

George Fielding

John Coates

Andrew Croft

Peter Kemp

worked first with the SOE *Juggler* circuit east of Paris and later with the *Gardener* circuit near Marseilles. In common with most, but not all, SOE circuits, the task of the *Juggler* team was to organise sabotage, in particular against railways used by the German forces for re-supply, in this instance in the upper Marne around Châlons-en-Champagne.

In no sense due to lack of security on his part, as he was meticulous in avoiding detection when transmitting, the *Juggler* circuit ran into critical difficulties in the summer of 1943, losing a number of key agents through arrest by the Gestapo. Cohen continued to transmit messages for an adjacent circuit, but aware the Gestapo knew his name decided to get out of France as quickly as possible. His request for pick up by a Lysander aircraft from England having failed to elicit any response after six weeks, he resolved to head for the Pyrenees.

By then he had money for his rail fare only so far as Tours. There he entered a restaurant and joined a table of Frenchmen he judged to be friendly and explained his predicament. They passed round a hat and gathered cash for his onward fare to Pau, where he made contact with an organization helping agents and escaped prisoners of war to cross the Pyrenees. He crossed safely only to be imprisoned by the Spanish police until the Embassy in Madrid negotiated his release. As promised to his benefactors in Tours, he arranged for the BBC to broadcast a message telling them of his safe return, but several were arrested as they met in the restaurant to celebrate.

He returned to France by parachute on March 6, 1944, as the radio operator for Robert Boiteux who was to take over the *Gardener* circuit operating around Marseilles. This was a workmanlike and secure organisation and, following Operation *Dragoon* – the invasion of southern France from the Mediterranean by American and French forces in mid-August 1944 – the SOE group took part in the liberation of Marseilles at the end of the month.

The citation for Cohen's Military Cross described how he acted with great dash in establishing radio contact from the Hotel Splendide, in the centre of the city, despite intense German mortar fire. He was also later awarded the *Croix de Guerre* and appointed to the Legion of Honour for his services to the French Resistance in 1943 and 1944.

After his return to England in December 1944, he became a wireless instructor to the SOE teams – known as 'Jedburghs' – under training for operations against the Japanese in the Far East. In civilian life, he worked for many years as a consultant in France and Algeria for the British engineering industry.

He was unmarried.

(He died in France on May 4, 2007, aged 88).

The role of radio operator was often undertaken by women, as they were generally more meticulous in their encoding and security disciplines than men. Women were also valued as couriers, as they were less likely than men to be stopped and questioned by the Vichy police or German patrols when travelling with SOE messages for the Resistance or another circuit.

Many of these women, all quite young, were outstanding personalities, who stepped up to take charge when the leaders of circuits were away, captured or killed. Their resourcefulness and courage were remarkable, even when they fell into the hands of the enemy and were handed over to the Gestapo for interrogation. Pearl Witherington was one such heroine.

Pearl Witherington, CBE,
(Obituary *The Times* February 26, 2008)

'Outstanding. Probably the best shot, male or female, we have yet had,' ran an early report on Pearl Witherington during her training for the Special Operations Executive (SOE) in 1943. Once trained, she was parachuted into German-occupied France as an SOE courier. When the leader of her group was caught by the Gestapo, she took over the organisation of a 2,000-strong band of French *Maquisards,* and conducted herself with great gallantry with them. For this she was appointed MBE (Civil Division) but returned the insignia with an icy note saying that she had done nothing remotely 'civil'.

Born in 1916 in Paris, from where her father travelled widely as the supplier of Swedish paper used in the manufacture of bank notes, she had an instructive childhood. Her father lived very extravagantly and she once returned to their apartment to see the family furniture being piled up in the street by the bailiffs.

At the time of the German *Blitzkrieg* into northern France in May 1940, she was working as an assistant to the Air Attaché in the British Embassy, but due to being 'locally enlisted' was not included in the evacuation scheme and had to make her way to England through the Vichy-controlled zone (which initially avoided German occupation) then via neutral Spain to Portugal, from where she boarded a coaster to Gibraltar.

She arrived in England in July 1941. Yet although burning with zeal to do something seriously worthwhile for the war effort, it took two years before she found her niche in SOE. At the end of her training, her final report assessed, 'This student, although a woman, has got leader's qualities. Cool, resourceful and extremely determined. Very capable, completely brave.' She completed parachute training without hesitation or difficulty; only Morse code gave her problems but she was to be a courier between SOE groups, not a radio operator.

Parachuted into the Châteauroux district on the night of September 22-23, 1943, after failed attempts on the two previous nights when the pilot could not find the dropping zone, she was blown by a high wind away from the DZ but eventually found by Squadron Leader Maurice Southgate, leader of SOE's *Stationer* circuit operating between Perigueux and Montluçon. Three weeks later Southgate was recalled to London for an expected two weeks consultation which ran into three months. Pitched in at the deep end, Witherington took over the handling of the circuit, aided only by her radio operator and another courier, Jacqueline Nearne.

A sabotage attack on the Michelin tyre factory at Clemont-Ferrand, in which 40,000 tyres for the German army were destroyed, was carried out by *Maquisards* working on her guidance. She judged it less than ideally successful, however, reporting to London, "If they had been better trained they would certainly have done better." At this stage, she was still without a reasonably safe base and so spent her time travelling about the region at night, when German or Vichy police checks were less frequent, using a first-class season ticket.

Her first narrow escape was not from the enemy, but from a French Resistance group with whom she was unable to establish her SOE credentials until she gave the name of the farmer into whose field she had parachuted. The second occasion was more nerve-racking. After his return in January 1944, Southgate sent her to check out a supposed contact in Poitiers from whom he had received a letter. Warned by a concierge in Poitiers that the house she was to visit was full of Gestapo and the owners arrested, she returned immediately to report to Southgate.

The most urgent task for the *Stationer* circuit in the spring of 1944 was preparation to receive the three-man groups of 'Jedburghs' – SOE officers to be dropped in uniform on or soon after D-Day in June, to guide the various factions and groups of the French Resistance on acts of sabotage helpful, rather than a hindrance, to the Allied landings and subsequent breakout in Normandy.

Southgate was arrested by the Gestapo in Montluçon at the beginning of May, and London gave instructions for the *Stationer* circuit to be divided into two, with Witherington in charge of the northern one – *Wrestler* – operating between the Cher and the Creuse. Her job was to call for air delivery of arms to four Resistance groups and give them weapons training. By this point Pearl had been joined by her pre-war fiancé, Henri Cornioley, who had escaped from a German prisoner of war camp and linked up with the *Stationer* circuit. The pair established themselves in the empty gatehouse of a château belonging to a strongly Petainiste family, close to the woods where the four Resistance groups had taken refuge.

On June 11, five days after the Allied landings in Normandy, a German military unit attacked the area of their base, probably after spotting the *Maquis* activity by air reconnaissance. While Henri Cornioley and the 40 men near the base tried to fight off their attackers, Witherington grabbed the cash reserves and crawled into a cornfield, knowing her role was to avoid capture.

She found refuge with a farmer and his wife some miles away, from where she was able to re-establish contact with her main *Maquis* group and arrange an arms drop. These continued intermittently until the group was well armed and provided with demolitions. (The group attacked near the gatehouse suffered 24 casualties, but Cornioley and the remainder escaped). From early July, her group regularly attacked German convoys moving north, delaying them with felled trees, then ambushing the stationary vehicles. In one attack on a convoy on Route National 20, the Germans admitted the loss of 76 men killed and 125 wounded.

In her final report she wrote: 'It is important to remember

that most of France south of the Loire was liberated by the Resistance.' German losses in the area of the *Wrestler* circuit under her control exceeded 1,000 killed and many more wounded. She was appointed MBE (Military Division) but her recommendation for the Croix de Guerre for Henri Cornioley, whom she married in London in October 1944, was rejected.

She settled down to live with her husband in the area where they had worked together with the *Maquisards*. She later played a leading role in setting up the SOE memorial at Valençay. In 1996, with the help of a journalist, Herve Larroque, she published a memoir, *Pauline*, whose title recalled her wartime codename.

In 2004 she was advanced to CBE, the insignia being presented to her in Paris by the Queen during a state visit to France. One acknowledgement still eluded her – the award of her parachute wings (which she regarded as more important than her appointments in the Order of the British Empire). This was eventually rectified after an RAF parachute instructor went to interview her at her home in France about her wartime experiences, and in 2006 she was presented with the coveted wings.

Her husband died in 1999. There were no children.
(She died on February 24, 2008, aged 93)

The obituary is at fault about 'no children', as Pearl had a daughter – still alive at the time of this publication – by her husband Henri.

Pearl's courier with the *Stationer* circuit, Jacqueline Nearne, had a brother Francis who served in France with SOE and also a sister Eileen, who proved equally resolute, even after capture.

Eileen Nearne, MBE
(Obituary *The Times* September 15, 2010)

Eileen Nearne, known as 'Didi' to her family and friends, was brought up and educated in Grenoble, where her parents were living at the outbreak of war. She and her older sister Jacqueline were bilingual in English and French and, after reaching England, responded to a call for volunteers familiar with France and the language. This led to their joining the SOE, to which both gave valuable service after the fall of France in 1940. But Eileen was captured, interrogated and sent to Ravensbrück.

After enrolment in the First Aid Nursing Yeomanry (FANY) that provided uniformed cover for women SOE agents, she was trained for signals duties, then retrained as an agent in 1943 and flown into France by RAF Lysander aircraft in March 1944. She and her accompanying agent – 35-year-old French lawyer, Maître Savy, brought back to England by another SOE agent – were landed near Châteauroux in order to establish a circuit of French supply and finance experts around Paris.

Soon after arriving in France, Savy received information about a stock of German V1 missiles concealed in a quarry near Creil. Appreciating the crucial importance of this intelligence, he returned by the next Lysander flight to England to report it and sent Nearne and another radio operator to Paris. This resourceful pair attached themselves to the *Spiritualist* circuit working on plans for railway sabotage and in urgent need of their services and radios.

The ensuing weeks were taken up by transmitting economic and military intelligence gathered by the *Spiritualist* circuit to London. Nearne sent 105 messages in all, including a number for arms drops. On one occasion she transmitted just long enough from the same site to fall victim to the German radio detectors and was arrested in July 1944. Fortunately, hearing German voices and insistent knocking at the house next door while transmitting, she had time to burn her messages and hide the radio.

A thorough search of the house brought the set to light, together with an unused one-time-code pad and her pistol, so she was taken to Paris for interrogation at the Gestapo headquarters.

Despite the incriminating evidence found in the house from where she had been transmitting, with remarkable sang-froid she maintained she was just a French shop assistant called Jacqueline du Tertre who had been sending messages on behalf of her employer with no idea that they went to England. Telling her interrogators she had met her employer in a coffee shop, that she had been working for him for only three months and that he had supplied the one-time pad, she made up a name and address for him when pressed. This bought her only such time as it took for the Gestapo to discover both were false.

She was then subjected to 'strong interrogation' including

being repeatedly plunged into cold water until her lungs were bursting. She stuck to her explanation, revealing nothing about the SOE or her true role but finally 'admitted' to a planned meeting with the imaginary employer at Gare St Lazare at 7pm that evening. She was taken to the rendezvous and won another respite by the sounding of the air-raid warning at 7.15. Next day, to avoid further *baignoire* immersions, she offered to take the chief Gestapo interrogator to the addresses she had given. This offer was not tested and she was sent to Fresnes prison, then to the notorious women's concentration camp at Ravensbrück.

There she met Violete Szabo, later executed together with two other women SOE agents in early 1945. Nearne managed to escape while being marched with a group of prisoners through a forest at night to another camp at Markelberg on April 5, 1945. She slipped out of the line into the trees to be joined by two other women. The rest of the escape involved considerable hardship. After sheltering for two nights in a bombed house, the three women began walking westwards only to be stopped by SS troops demanding their identity cards. Having none, Nearne explained that they were French volunteers working in a German factory and were allowed to pass.

On reaching Leipzig on foot, they persuaded a German priest to shelter them until Allied troops arrived. On April 15, the three rushed out to greet American units entering the city only to be subjected to questioning yet again. Nearne, suspected for some reason of being a German agent, was put in a camp with Nazi women until identified and taken to safety by a British officer. She was later appointed MBE for her SOE services and bravery under intense and ruthless interrogation.

Eileen Nearne was the third child and second daughter of John Nearne and his Parisian-born wife, Marie, née de Plazoala. Throughout her life she remained steadfastly reluctant to discuss her wartime experiences. She was unmarried.

(She died on September 2, 2010, aged 89)

A number of SOE agents had already distinguished themselves in other fields during the early years of the war, only turning to the SOE due to meeting with a friend already working with the organization or some other coincidence. George Millar was one such very successful agent.

George Millar, DSO, MC
(Obituary *The Times* January 20, 2005)

Having planned to become an architect and then turned his hand to journalism, George Millar made his name as an officer of the Special Operations Executive (SOE). His French was embellished by a distinct Scottish accent, which proved no hindrance as he was not engaged in the clandestine activities of SOE in the early years of the war, but parachuted into the French Jura to work with the local Resistance groups.

Millar had begun the Second World War by being commissioned into the Rifle Brigade in 1940, and he served with the 2nd Motor Battalion in the 7th Armoured Division in the Western Desert. He was wounded and captured in the fighting around Gazala in June 1942 and shipped to Italy. In a prisoner-of-war camp near Taranto, he organised the buying of black-market food from outside the camp, played female parts in prisoners' theatricals and, as a fellow inmate was to relate, "while others were forming escape committees and drawing up rotas for tunnelling parties, Millar was planning to climb over the wire, dressed as a nun".

His opportunity to escape came when the prisoners were being sent to Germany by rail after the collapse of Italy in 1943. Jumping from the train at night near Münich, he made an extraordinary journey via Strasbourg to Paris – his command of French and German enabled him to pass as a migrant worker. There, the former administrator of the Daily Express office, Mara Scherbatov, a White Russian princess, gave him money to complete his journey across France and then through Spain to Gibraltar and safety. On being flown back to England, he was shattered to find that his marriage had not survived his absence. Declining an offer to stay in London to help to organise escape routes for other British fugitives, he volunteered for the SOE.

After training, he was parachuted into France, near Besançon, on June 1, 1944, to work with the *Maquis* in delaying the movement of German reinforcements from the South of France to the Normandy battlefield after the Allied invasion which was to begin five days later. He established the SOE *Chancellor* network in the region and embarked on a series of sabotage operations in conjunction with the *Maquis,* once he had won their confidence.

He began by a night operation against the Besançon railway marshalling yards, blowing up the turntables for shifting rolling stock from one line to another. Enthused by their success, the *Maquis* were easily persuaded to return in strength the following night – relying on the Germans not expecting lightning to strike twice in the same place – to put charges on each set of points. These caused such disruption to rail traffic that Millar advised SOE's headquarters in Baker Street against an RAF bombing attack on the marshalling yards – this had the welcome side-effect of preserving the city's 17th-century architecture from destruction.

Millar's courage in the Western Desert and subsequent escape from the train carrying him to prison camp in Germany had already been recognised by the award of the Military Cross. His quick thinking and reactions were again put to the test when he was with the *Maquis.*

Challenged by an enemy sentry, he shot the man dead with a pistol fired through his overcoat pocket. A measure of his achievement during the months he spent in France in 1944 was the award of the DSO, the *Legion d'Honneur* and the *Croix de Guerre.*

George Reid Millar was born in 1910, into a prosperous Scottish family. The second son of Thomas A. Millar and Mary Reid Morton, he inherited his parents' good looks. Beneath the charm, however, there was a great determination, occasionally amounting to ruthlessness. This was demonstrated when as a 12-year-old boy at Loretto, he turned on two bullies with such ferocity that it was he who was beaten by the housemaster.

Millar, destined to follow his father's profession as an architect, trained at St John's College, Cambridge, where he was a contemporary of Sir Hugh Casson. He started well but both men enjoyed rowing and, while Casson was a cox and had only to keep his weight down, Millar was an oar and undertook rigorous training, so falling behind in his work – so far indeed, that he decided to abandon architecture in favour of journalism. He proved himself on The Daily Telegraph and then on the Daily Express, whose editor,

Arthur Christiansen, sent him to Paris in 1939 to relieve Alan Moorehead as assistant to the senior correspondent Geoffrey (later Sir Geoffrey) Cox. It was Christiansen who coined the nickname 'Golden Millar', after the racehorse, prompted by Millar's looks and fair hair.

Shortly before the war, he had married Annette Stockwell but both he and Cox decided that they should fight, resigned from the Daily Express, and enlisted in the Army. Returning to London before the end of the war in Europe, he wrote a book about his experiences, *Maquis*, which told the public that British officers had been fighting with the French Resistance.

In 1945 he married the half-Spanish Isabel Paske-Smith and, after writing a second book about his war experiences, *Horned Pigeon* – the title referred to the ending of his first marriage – he found himself a successful and relatively affluent author. The Millars bought a yacht and cruised in the Mediterranean, an experience which he put to practical use by writing his first book about sailing, *Isabel and the Sea*.

Soon after their early cruises in the Mediterranean, Millar decided to farm, for he came from farming stock and wanted to live in the country. He bought Sydling Court, a beautiful old house near Dorchester, and leased a thousand acres adjoining it from Winchester College and began many years of successful sheep and cattle farming. He hunted in winter and sailed in summer, becoming a member of the Royal Yacht Squadron.

Half a dozen more books followed, including A *White Boat from England*, *The Bruneval Raid* and his autobiography, *Road to Resistance*, published in 1979. He was for a spell the principal book critic for his old newspaper, the Daily Express. Latterly, he gave up hunting – but not sailing – and reduced his farm to 600 acres, although he and his wife actively worked it, often with the help of only one farm worker.

Charming and witty as he was, Millar was regarded as something of a recluse by his neighbours in Dorset, seldom being seen beyond the belts of trees and Elizabethan topiary hedge that surrounded his house, or outside his secluded farm. However, he valued a number of close friends elsewhere in the county, in London, Scotland and in Spain and will be remembered by them for his warmth and his skill as a raconteur. He and his wife were a devoted couple, although different in temperament. She predeceased him; there were no children.

(He died on January 15, 2005, aged 94)

It was undeniably frustrating for the French Resistance – and their SOE mentors – to see their carefully planned and executed acts of sabotage all too quickly repaired under efficient German super-vision, particularly damage to railway lines and marshalling yards. The targeting of specific industrial facilities, although usually more difficult to attack, guaranteed longer-lasting effects, as an operation conducted by Major George Hiller and Captain Cyril Watney, indicates in the latter's obituary.

Captain Cyril A. Watney, MC
(Obituary *The Times* March 31, 2009)

Cyril Watney was recruited into the wartime Special Operations Executive (SOE) for his knowledge of French and France, having been born there, and his expertise as a radio operator acquired with the Royal Corps of Signals before being commissioned into the Middlesex Regiment in 1943. Together with Major George Hiller, he was to be responsible for one of the most successful – and lasting – acts of indus-trial sabotage in France during the war.

On the night of January 7, 1944, Hiller and Watney were dropped by parachute to set up SOE's *Footman* circuit in the Lot and find out what the local French Resistance could do to assist in sabotaging the Retier factory at Figeac, east of Cahors, that was turning out variable-pitch propellers for the *Luftwaffe*. One of their first contacts was a foreman at the factory who confirmed that some 300 propellers were being produced each week. Further, he had made a plan to wreck the factory – given a few fuses and explosive charges.

Hiller and Watney made up the demolitions, and by the end of January the Retier factory was out of action and remained so until the end of the war.

The pair had also been instructed to track down an elusive member of the French Resistance operating under the name of 'Colonel Véni' and known to have a large following but, as a dedicated socialist, suspected of supporting the communist element of the Resistance that was planning to seize power in France after the liberation.

Véni was eventually located and, moving his radio from place to place in a requisitioned van to avoid detection, Watney called for airdrops of weapons to arm his followers, Hiller having extracted a guarantee that they would support de Gaulle – a promise later honoured more in the word than the deed (Véni's group made little attempt to interfere with the move north of the 2nd SS Panzer (Das Reich) Division to Normandy after the Allied invasion in June.)

In July Hiller was wounded during an encounter with the enemy and taken prisoner. Watney took over command of the circuit and carried out a daring and successful action to rescue his chief, breaking through a German road block with a handful of Resistance volunteers. After Hiller had been evacuated to a hospital under Resistance control, Watney organised an attack on a German supply column passing through the Lot. He was later awarded the Military Cross for these actions.

During Hiller's absence in hospital, he managed to hold the various Resistance groups in the vicinity together, among other ventures arranging for acts of sabotage farther south, around Toulouse, for which he was awarded the *Croix de Guerre*.

Cyril Arthur Watney was born in 1922 in Calais where his father was engaged in the lace business. The family moved to Nottingham in the depression of the early Thirties, and Watney went to school there before going to Cambridge to take a degree in electric and magnetic sciences. After demobilization in 1945 he worked as an interpreter for Whitbread Brewers and later in Canada for the Canadian Government.

He was twice married and is survived by his second wife, Peggy (née Vaughan), a stepson and stepdaughter from his first marriage and two stepsons from his second.

(He died on January 23, 2009, aged 86).

A few SOE agents were recruited into the organization after acquiring significant experience of undercover work in occupied Europe. These were especially valuable, as they had demonstrated their ability to work under constant risk of discovery and – by their survival – indicated a sure sense of personal and organizational security. André Hue was such a man.

André Hue, DSO
(Obituary *The Times* January 14, 2005)

André Hue entered the Second World War while having a shower aboard the French liner *Champlain*, which struck a mine off La Rochelle on June 18, 1940. The ship sank in 15 minutes but he and his half-brother, also a crew member, were picked up and taken to Casablanca. Despite the restrictions of the Franco-German armistice, he eventually reached the small Brittany town of Guer, west of Rennes, where his widowed Welsh mother was living, having been evacuated from Le Havre. Aged 17, Hue had been a trainee purser aboard the *Champlain* but, in the circumstances, was glad of a low profile job at Guer railway station.

Cleaning the station office and lighting the fire was his lot until the arrival of a German stationmaster provided a new interest. Guer had become a terminus for the rail re-supply of the German army of occupation in northern France. He was approached by a member of the Special Operations Executive (SOE), established on Winston Churchill's order to 'set German-occupied Europe ablaze'. The individual concerned was François Vallée, organiser of the SOE circuit codenamed *Parson* operating around Rennes.

Although in contact with several groups in the French Resistance, Vallée restrained them from acts of sabotage for fear of savage reprisals against the civilian population. Hue's position in the railway office provided an alternative method of harassing the German lines of communication. He handed to Vallée copies of the load manifests of trains passing through Guer, and London was informed by radio of the freight concentrations the RAF should bomb. But when Hue set about forming his own Resistance group, with a view to receiving air drops of arms, someone talked carelessly and he fell under German suspicion. Warning of a Gestapo raid on the siding where he was working reached him just in time to make his escape.

Taking refuge within the Resistance, he worked in Brittany and along the Normandy coast as a courier between the groups, and collecting Allied pilots who had been shot down and avoided capture. By 1943 there was a well-established system for airmen to be taken off certain beaches in northern France by vessels of the Royal Navy's 15th MGB Flotilla or trans-shipped at sea from French trawlers. Having established his reliability and personal courage, Hue was himself collected by MGB 502 in February 1944 and taken to England for training by the SOE.

He received a commission and, with the acting rank of captain, was parachuted into Brittany with a party of French SAS in the early hours of D-Day. It was his responsibility to guide the party, but having landed a considerable distance from the rest he had to bluff his way through several groups of the enemy to reach them. The SAS orders were to organise local Resistance groups into small parties to cut the railway lines, blow up bridges and mine roads that the four German divisions in the peninsula would use to join the Normandy battle. As it was, the Germans had been ordered to man the coastal defences, so when the American VIII Corps swept along the roads towards Brest they found the main road junctions already under control of *Les Forces Francaises de l'Interieur* (FFI), armed by airdrop and operating largely on SOE instructions.

They did not act with impunity. Although the FFI had more than 20,000 men in Brittany, the group Hue had joined lost 60 in a pitched battle with an 800 strong German battalion near Saint-Marçel in mid-June. The FFI eventually managed to break off the action and withdraw. Later, Hue took over command of the French SAS party when their commander was killed and continued organising and arming the FFI without pause. Once the remaining German force in Brittany had formed a perimeter round Brest, Hue was ordered back to England.

He was again parachuted into France on August 30 to join the Resistance in the Nievre, west of Dijon. His principal task was to instruct the *maquisards* working with the SOE *Gondolier* circuit in use of the arms and sabotage equipment being dropped to them. While there he supervised the destruction of three bridges to be used by German units moving from the south of France to the Normandy battlefield, and the lifting of mines left by the enemy around the town of Luzy.

Aged only 20 during these exploits, he was one of the youngest officers to be awarded the DSO during the Second World War. He was also appointed a Chevalier of the French Legion of Honour and awarded the *Croix de Guerre* with palm in January 1946.

André Hunter Alfred Hue was born in Swansea of a Welsh

mother and French father. He went to school at Le Havre but when he was 14 his father died, leaving little money. He lied about his age and joined the French merchant marine, where his half-brother was already serving.

After the end of the war in Europe, he was granted the acting rank of major and sent to join the SOE in Ceylon. He was parachuted into Burma at the end of January 1945, to gather intelligence on Japanese troop dispositions and to try to direct the activities of Burmese guerrilla groups.

Either by chance or warning, the Japanese attacked the landing zone. Narrowly avoiding capture, he managed to subsist in the jungle for 29 days without re-supply and, hardly surprisingly, wrote a critical report of the operational planning when he reached safety.

He served for several years in the British Army, first in Palestine during the final years of the British Mandate, then in Cyprus. His fluency in French made him the ideal choice for the post of British military attaché in Cambodia in 1954-55. He met his future wife in Phnom Penh, where she was a secretary attached to the British Embassy. Subsequently, after leaving the Army, he served with the Special Intelligence Service, MI6, in the Far East.

He resigned in 1967 to begin a business career. He worked for British American Tobacco in Paraguay and Senegal, with another business concern in Malawi and then for various companies in France. He retired in 1980 to Chichester, where he became a local councillor. He married Maureen Taylor in 1957. He is survived by her and by their daughter.

(He died on January 11, 2004, aged 81)

Mention has already been made in the obituary for Francis Cammaerts of Christina Skarbeck, later Granville, a Polish countess who served with SOE with special distinction and success, only to be murdered soon after the war by a rejected suitor. In the manner of the day her obituary had a named author, in her case no less than Major-General Sir Colin Gubbins who wrote the following in *The Times* of June 21, 1952:

Christine Granville, OBE, GM

To the many who knew and served with 'Christine' as she was known throughout Special Forces, her untimely death has come as a terrible shock. In the earlier part of the war, based in Budapest, she and her small team performed prodigies of courage and endurance to help her compatriots in occupied Poland. Eventually forced to leave due to German pressure, they withdrew to Palestine and finally Cairo, where she came directly under the aegis of the Middle East branch of the Special Forces.

She was to spend the rest of the war in the Mediterranean theatre; it was from Algiers that she was parachuted into France to join the rising of the French Resistance behind the German lines, timed to assist the allied invasion of Southern France.

The decorations awarded her were well-earned, but she never spoke of these things. Physically strong, an expert ski-runner and of strong, independent personality and high intelligence, she was well suited for action. With her people suffering dreadful horrors under Nazi oppression oppression, the ease of life in Cairo and forced periods of inaction often irked her spirit; she was impatient of authority that kept for long periods in relative safety and comfort, and that frequently turned down operations she proffered as the risks seemed disproportionate to the possible fruits; she was happy only in action.

Like many other gallant men and women of her country who fought for the Allied cause, she could not return to a Russian-dominated Poland and like them had to make a new life in exile, which she was courageously facing in her independent way when she died.

(She was murdered in London on June 16, 1952, aged 37).

Constraints on what could be published about SOE's wartime activities in force in the early 1950s severely limited General Gubbins' tribute. Her rescue of Francis Cammaerts and Xan Fielding from execution by the Gestapo owed something to bribery as well as bluff (see page 173.) Her go-between with the Gestapo demanded 2 million French francs for his services – and she got them delivered by air drop within 48 hours.

The life of Christine Granville, born Krystyna Skarbek, before, during and after the Second World War is admirably covered in the chapter about her in the book *The Women Who Lived For Danger* (2002) by Marcus Binney, stepson of Sir George Binney whom we met in Chapter 3, but her courage, idealism, romantic personality and sheer beauty of body and spirit have been portrayed in other publications.

Men found her irresistible – for her vitality as much as for her physical qualities – while she took or rejected lovers instinctively. She met her murderer, George Muldowney, a ship's steward, while working for the Shaw Savill shipping line. His infatuation with her – which she neither sought nor welcomed – became so tiresome that she decided to leave London in an attempt to shake him off, but her flight to Brussels on the day of her planned departure was delayed. Returning to her hotel after an impromptu dinner with friends, she was stabbed by him on the stairs. He made no effort to avoid arrest or responsibility for her death.

There were almost fifty SOE undercover circuits active in France by the spring of 1944, half of them north of the Loire. All their leaders knew that the Allied invasion would come that year but none knew precisely when or where the principal blow would fall. Their plans for directing or urging Resistance activity towards acts of sabotage that would assist the Allies' liberation campaign were close to completion, yet they were to be joined shortly after the landings by an SOE group of a new kind. These were not to be undercover agents, but officers in uniform, to demonstrate that the long-awaited invasion had begun, to reinforce the circuits where required, cover gaps in co-operation with the Resistance and – as far as possible – avoid any actions by the Resistance detrimental to the Allied cause.

9

The Jedburghs

There is a myth that the codename 'Jedburgh' occurred to Major-General Colin Gubbins while on a train passing through the small Scottish town of that name. The prosaic truth is that it was allotted by the Inter-Services Security Board for the three-man teams SOE was planning to parachute into France after D-Day. But the Jedburgh concept had a broader Genesis. It was brought into being through collaboration between SOE, the United States' Office of Strategic Services (OSS) – formed in 1942 primarily as an intelligence gathering agency – and the Free French *Bureau Central de Renseignements et d'Action* in London.

The purpose of the Jedburgh teams was to provide some organization and direction to groups of the French Resistance, where these were yet to be firmly established by an SOE circuit in the region and, where the strength and motivation of a group appeared justified, to call for an air drop of arms and explosives. In essence, they were complementary to the SOE circuits, not an alternative. The fact that they dropped in uniform also shifted the level of action from clandestine activity to open warfare.

Each team comprised three men: two officers of different nationality – one at least being French-speaking – and a radio operator, sometimes a junior officer or more usually a sergeant. Having trained together for this role, the individuals were allowed to choose with whom they would form a team. None of the three nationalities dominated the structure or had a monopoly of the team leader appointments. Each team had a codename and each member had an individual codename.

The speed with which the liberation of France progressed – Paris was freed on August 25 – resulted in many of the Jedburgh teams being overrun on the ground by advancing Allied troops, rendering their further activities largely redundant, other than where they had assumed positions relevant to local security or help in the return to French administration – something to which General de Gaulle took a strong personal objection despite the welcome the teams received from the local population.

Once withdrawn to England, the teams were offered – usually on an individual basis – opportunities to deploy their experience and skills in the continuing fight against the Japanese in the Far East. Many Jedburgh members accepted this challenge and, especially in Burma, went on to make valuable contributions to the defeat of Japan in occupied territories. Indeed the scale of their successes in forming and motivating guerilla groups, in Burma in particular, exceeded what some teams had chieved in Europe. As the following obituaries suggest, many Jedburgh team members were at least the equal in terms of post-war accomplishment as their comrades who worked under cover in the SOE circuits.

Baron Albert de Schonen
(Obituary *The Times* March 27, 2007)

Albert de Schonen was destined for a career in French national administration but the outbreak of the war interposed with military service.

When the *Blitzkrieg* was unleashed in May 1940, his company formed part of the defence of the Passe d'Anor facing the German breakthrough at Sedan. De Schonen was awarded the *Croix de Guerre* for gallantry but taken prisoner. After two escapes followed by recapture he was eventually released from prison camp due to ill-health in January 1941. Determined to get to Britain to join General de Gaulle's Free French, he attempted to cross the Pyrenees into Spain only to be apprehended again. His alias as a wool buyer saw him through, however, and he finally reached England via Portugal.

His resolve to see further action and his fluent English soon led to him to be recruited by the Special Operation Executive (SOE). Together with the British Captain 'Ed' Bennett and Sergeant Ron Brierley forming a team codenamed *Daniel*, de Schonen was parachuted into the Côtes-du-Nord region on the night of August 4-5, 1944.

Although the Allied invasion of Normandy was well under way, the German Army was holding out in Brest, while thousands of French Resistance fighters were clamouring for action throughout Brittany. The task of the *Daniel* team was to provide arms for the Resistance, by parachute delivery, and to help to co-ordinate subsequent action against the common enemy.

Arms drops were duly called for and the *Daniel* team took part with the Resistance fighters in attacks on German vehicle convoys in Brittany. In his post-operation report, General Eisenhower remarked: "By their ceaseless harassing activities, the French forces surrounded the enemy with a terrible atmosphere of danger and hatred that ate into the confidence of the leaders and the courage of the soldiers."

This episode was but one example of the missions of the three-man SOE teams known as 'Jedburghs' to establish contact with the Resistance all over France after D-Day on June 6, 1944, ensuring that action against the German forces and facilities – including the French railway system – would help rather than hinder the Allied campaign of liberation.

Recalled to England from Brittany, de Schonen and the other members of the team were rebriefed and, under the new codename *Gregory*, parachuted into the Vosges at Pont-de-Roide in September 1944. Contact with the Resistance was no sooner established than their combined party was ambushed by a German patrol. Bennett and de Schonen were wounded, but de Schonen succeeded in dragging his injured comrade clear of danger and drove him to a field hospital with the US 7th Army advancing from the Mediterranean coast.

After recovering in a US military hospital in Naples, de Schonen avoided further evacuation to Algiers by boarding a ship bound for England. On arrival, he was directed back to France, where he served for a while as an instructor for French Resistance fighters seeking incorporation into the French Army. During this time he argued against the dispatch of French former Jedburgh officers to the Far East for operations against the Japanese, pointing out that they were trained to work with organised groups of Resistance fighters, unlikely to be available there to any significant extent. He was to be proved largely correct in Indo-China.

Pierre Etienne Albert de Schonen was born in Paris in 1912. On completion of his military service in 1945, he began a career with the French Ministry of Foreign Affairs. He served with the French embassies in Dublin and Rome before becoming ambassador to the Central African Republic at the time of the self-proclaimed Emperor Bokassa, a task which President Pompidou characterised as a 'mission impossible'.

He was subsequently ambassador in Lusaka and Wellington and advanced from the rank of Officer of the Legion of Honour, to which he was appointed in 1945, to that of Commander for his diplomatic services. He was later elected a councillor of the Eure-et-Loire département.

In addition to his diplomatic work, de Schonen was instrumental in founding the French Association of Jedburgh members and concerned himself for many years with reunions and the welfare of the families of those killed in action.

He married first Valdetta Grifeo di Partanna from the family of Prince Ruffo di Calabria, by whom he had three daughters, then Yolaine de La Rochefoucauld, who survives him with two sons.

(He died on March 8, 2007, aged 94)

The radio operator who accompanied de Schonen with team *Daniel* on the operation into Brittany and later into the Vosges mountains was one of the Jedburghs who volunteered for service in the Far East, to which de Schonen was opposed, adding the Military Medal to the Croix de Guerre he had received for his service in France. His obituary throws a little extra light on the operation into Brittany and his experience in the Vosges.

Ronald Brierley, OBE, MM
(Obituary *The Times* August 15, 2005)

Ron Brierley was the radio operator of the three-man team codenamed *Daniel* dropped by parachute into the Departement Côtes-du-Nord on the night of August 4, 1944. The role of the *Daniel* team was to assist the Inter-Allied Mission, *Aloes*, in its task of making contact with the *Forces Françaises de l'Interieur* (FFI) resistance group in Brittany, then overseeing the return of the region to civilian control once the German Army had been driven out. Brierley and his two companions were dropped in the wrong place because a party of French teenage would-be partisans lit a fire in hope of receiving a consignment of arms. When they received the Jedburgh team instead they led them to the rendezvous with

Aloes, but by that time most of Brittany was already under FFI control and *Daniel* was recalled to England.

After rebriefing, the same team – renamed *Gregory* – was flown to an improvised strip in the Vosges on September 5, together with the eight-man liaison mission, *Etoile*. Next day, Brierley's two companions were wounded in a clash with German troops and evacuated. He became the radio operator for the survivors of *Etoile*, until the mission was recalled in November. Brierley was twice mentioned in dispatches for his part in these missions and also awarded the *Croix de Guerre*.

Next he volunteered for service with Force 136, the SOE arm in the Far East. He took part in Operation *Nation* in the Burmese Pego Yomas range of hills between the valleys of the Irrawaddy and the Sittang rivers. The group for which Brierley was the radio operator, codenamed *Reindeer* and led by Major D. J. C. Britton, parachuted into the jungle west of Toungoo on the night of March 30-31, 1945.

Britton's task was to raise a guerilla force from the Burmese Anti-Fascist Organisation (AFO). Within two weeks he had 300 men armed who were so eager for action that he had to restrain them from a premature attack. As the enemy was using the Sittang valley railway to reinforce Toungoo, which General Slim's 14th Army was about to attack, Brierley's radio link became the vital means of directing RAF air attacks, causing significant disruption and forcing many of the reinforcements to abandon the railway and make their way into the hills. There they were ambushed by the AFO guerrillas and an estimated 400 killed.

Reindeer suffered a serious setback on June 3 when Britton was killed, but the other two members joined up with the Jedburgh team, *Chimp*, led by Major Dick Rubinstein nearby. During July, large concentrations of Japanese troops gathered in the Pegu Yomas in preparation for an attempted break out across the Sittang and escape into Thailand. The *Chimp/Reindeer* team identified likely river crossing points and informed the 19th Indian Division covering the river between Pyinmana in the north to south of Toungoo. AFO guerrillas led by the joint team accounted for over 1,000 Japanese; many more were killed by the regular units of 19th Division as they attempted to break out across the river.

Rubenstein was awarded the Military Cross for his leadership of *Chimp/Reindeer*; Brierley was promoted to

Warrant Officer, awarded the Military Medal and mentioned in dispatches a third time for his part in the earlier operations around Toungoo.

Ronald Brierley was born in Oldham, Lancashire, and left school early to begin a career with the Alliance Assurance Company in Manchester. He enlisted in the 70th (Young Soldiers) Battalion of The Border Regiment in 1940, but transferred to the Royal Tank Regiment in 1942 to serve with the 34th Tank Brigade. The demand for expert radio operators led to him joining SOE and becoming the operator for the *Daniel* Jedburgh team. When SOE operations in South-East Asia ended, he reverted to the RAC to join 146 Regiment then serving in Sumatra after the surrender of the Japanese forces occupying the Dutch East Indies.

On demobilisation, he returned to Alliance until opening his own insurance broking company in 1948. He eventually became deputy chairman of Sedgwick UK. He was appointed OBE for his services to Manchester in 1984. His wife Mary survives him with a son and daughter.

(He died on July 11, 2005, aged 83).

Geoffrey Hallowes became a Jedburgh quite a bit later in course of the war and would laughingly explain that he was better known for being married to a heroine, rather than for anything he had achieved. The earlier part of the war was, however, not without eventful moments.

Geoffrey Hallowes
(Obituary *The Times* September 27, 2006)

Geoffrey Hallowes served in the latter part of the war with the Special Operations Executive in Europe. But before then he had endured a testing time on the run from the Japanese in the Far East immediately after the surrender of Singapore in February 1942. In the 1950s he married, as her third husband, the celebrated wartime SOE heroine *Odette* (see Chapter 2). She had survived capture, torture in Fresnes prison and incarceration in Ravensbrück concentration camp, and was awarded the George Cross.

Hallowes had served with the 2nd Battalion The Gordon Highlanders in the final stage of the unsuccessful struggle to establish a defence of Malaya against the Japanese offensive.

Despite the numerical superiority of General Percival's British, Australian, Indian and Malay troops, the Japanese prevailed. The 2nd Gordons and 2nd Argyll and Sutherland Highlanders were the last units to cross into Singapore before the causeway was blown. When the island surrendered on February 15, 1942, he was one of four officers sent in pairs to carry the ceasefire order to the garrisons of the outlying islands of Balang Mati and Pulau Brani. The officers were told that, after delivering the order, they were at liberty to try to escape if they could avoid the Japanese.

Hallowes and Major 'Nick' Nicholson, of the Royal Engineers, found a 14-foot dinghy with two paddles. Their progress was slow, especially after Nicholson's paddle snapped, but they found four British soldiers on a nearby island with a barely serviceable boat and two oars. After they had rowed for five days with loops of rope deputising for the missing rowlocks, the dinghy ran aground on a reef off the east coast of Sumatra and sank. Unaware that the Japanese had landed on the south west of the island, the six men followed a river bed and crossed the western range of hills to the small port of Padang on the west coast.

There they spent a week in a fruitless search for another boat, but rescue came in the form of a Royal Navy destroyer calling to refuel, after having taken part in the Battle of the Java Sea. This took them to Ceylon (now Sri Lanka), from where they were flown to India. On reaching Bombay in May 1942, Hallowes was employed as a staff captain dealing with administrative matters in the local headquarters. He escaped this by volunteering for the Special Operations Executive and attending the special forces training school at Haifa. He then joined the Yugoslav section of SOE's Force 133, based in Cairo.

It is uncertain whether it was owing to his being surplus to requirements in Yugoslavia or his ability to speak French that resulted in his move to Peterborough, where the 'Jedburgh' SOE teams were training. Each team comprised one British or American officer, a French officer and a radio operator. In all, 94 such teams were dropped by parachute into France in the days and weeks after D-Day. With few exceptions, their role was to try to guide the sabotage carried out by the various factions of the French Resistance, along lines helpful to Allied plans.

The Jedburgh led by Hallowes, codenamed *Jeremy*, comprised himself, Lieutenant Henri-Charles Giese and their radio operator, Sergeant Roger Leney. Fifteen such teams were sent by sea to Algiers and flown from there to parts of southern France beyond the range of aircraft from Britain. Team *Jeremy* was dropped on the night of August 24, 1944. It was met on the dropping zone by the remarkable Virginia Hall, nicknamed 'La dame qui boite' (the limping lady).

Hall was a highly respected SOE operator. An American citizen who had lost the lower part of her left leg in a shooting accident, she had entered the Vichy-controlled zone of France by boat in 1941 and established the SOE network in the Haute-Loire. Leaving Leney with her to establish a radio link with London, Hallowes and Giese set out for Le Puy, the local headquarters of the Gaullist *Forces Francaises de l'Interieur* (FFI). He called for an arms drop for this group, estimated to be some 1,500-strong. But when the drop took place there were weapons for only 100 men, giving Hallowes some difficulties over their distribution.

With the FFI concentrating their efforts on liberating towns and villages already vacated by the Germans, Hallowes turned his attention to delaying the escape of German units across the Rhône that were trying to head eastwards for home. In this he was partially successful, persuading the Haute-Loire FFI commander to move those of his men who were armed, by this time the majority, northwards to Vichy.

On return to England in late September 1944, Hallowes was sent to join SOE's Special Planning Unit 22, examining the feasibility of infiltrating German-speaking Poles and selected former German prisoners of war into German held territory and Germany itself. He was responsible for the German ex-prisoners part of the operation, working from liberated Brussels and later from Hamburg.

Some useful work was achieved in the form of short-range intelligence gathering on behalf of the British 21st Army Group as it advanced into Germany in early 1945 and, later, investigating the activities of the Soviet Army in occupied Germany. Hallowes was awarded the *Croix de Guerre* for his services in France in 1944 and was mentioned in dispatches on his return from Germany in 1945.

Geoffrey MacLeod Hallowes was born in 1918, the son

of Edward P. Hallowes of the Dry Monopole champagne importers Twiss, Browning & Hallowes of London. He was educated at the Lyceum Alpinum Zuoz in Switzerland and Jesus College, Cambridge, although he did not take a degree. Joining the family company on demobilisation after the war, he became a founder director of International Distillers and Vinters in 1962 and was the first chairman of IDV Europe on its formation in 1972. He remained on the IDV board until his retirement in 1983.

He married, in 1956, Odette Sansom, GC, MBE, née Brailly, who had also been appointed to the *Legion d'honneur* by France. She was the former wife of Captain Peter Churchill, also of SOE. Odette died in 1995. There were no children of their marriage.

(He died on September 25, 2006, aged 88).

Geoffrey Hallowes's radio operator in Jedburgh team *Jeremy*, Roger Leney, was another volunteer for service in the Far East after return from operations in France.

Roger Leney, MM
(Extract from obituary *The Times* May 27, 2008)

A trained radio operator with the Royal Armoured Corps in England in July 1943, Roger Leney volunteered for – as advertised on squadron orders – 'special duties of a hazardous nature'. The duties became clear after reaching the signals training school of the SOE at Henley-on-Thames two months later, and the hazards on transfer to Milton Hall, near Peterborough, in February 1944. He was to be a member of a three-man team parachuted into German-occupied France after the start of the Allied invasion of Normandy in June that year.

On March 15, 1945, Leney was parachuted into Burma with a team from Force 136, an arm of SOE operating in South East Asia, as the radio operator for a group raising local Karen guerrillas. After training, the guerrillas were deployed to assist General Slim's 14th Army in preventing the escape of the Japanese 28th Army over the Irrawaddy into Thailand. The operation, in which Leney took part, codenamed *Character*, proved highly successful, the Karen guerrillas fighting tenaciously in their native hills. Leney was awarded the Military Medal for his service in Burma and also mentioned in dispatches. In 1946 he received the *Croix de Guerre* with Silver Star for his work with SOE in occupied France.

After demobilisation, he became engaged in the agricultural engineering industry and, after retirement, acted as a voluntary conservation warden for the National Trust and Dorset Wildlife Trust.

He married, in 1950, Shirley Rollett, who survives him with three sons and a daughter.

(He died on his 85th birthday on May 4, 2008).

An officer who achieved striking success in command of Jedburgh teams in France and again in Burma was awarded the DSO for his leadership and resolution in both campaigns. Reading his obituary, the thought arises that his decoration was especially well deserved.

Lieutenant-Colonel Thomas Carew, DSO
(Obituary *The Times* February 26, 2009)

Tom Carew parachuted into France on the night of August 26, 1944, as a member of the Special Operations Executive Jedburgh team *Basil* His companions were Captain Robert Rivière of France and Technical Sergeant John L. Stoyka of the US Army. Dropped south of Besançon, close to the Swiss frontier, their task was to make contact with the local Resistance groups and help to arm and organise them. His personal motto was 'Luck comes to the prepared mind', but his first Jedburgh operation had an inauspicious start.

Their pilot had difficulty finding and identifying the drop-zone recognition letter but eventually dropped them at low altitude after six circuits. Rivière broke a finger, none of their personal kit was dropped with them and the vital radio set was lost. They made almost immediate contact with the local Resistance, however, and were taken to the nearby Château de Grange-Maillot where, according to Carew, they suffered from excessive hospitality. Discovery of a radio – not their own – the following day allowed contact with London to be established and a request dispatched for arms for the 500 members of the local Resistance.

Having established contact with London, Carew's *Basil* team and another, which dropped on August 28, were instructed to prepare an attack by the Resistance *Groupement Frontière* and a regular French battalion on the German garrison at Mouthe. The town was taken after two days fierce fighting. Carew then left for Salins to concentrate on organising what became the partisan *Régiment Franche-Comté*. After the liberation of Paris on August 25, he was withdrawn from France, mentioned in dispatches and awarded the *Croix de Geurre*.

Thomas Arthur Carew was born in Dublin, the son of a former officer of the Royal Navy who had served at the Dardenelles. He was educated at the Perse School, Cambridge, and RMA Woolwich, from where he was commissioned into the Royal Artillery in 1938.

He took part in the ill-starred campaign in Norway and volunteered for service with SOE after serving for a while in Gibraltar. On return from France in the autumn of 1944, he and the other retuned British Jedburghs were given the option of going back to their parent units or volunteering for service with the SOE Force 136 against the Japanese in the Far East. Carew chose the latter and sailed for Bombay in early November.

Promoted to major to lead a Jedburgh team comprising Captain John Cox and Sergeant John Sharp, who had served with Jedburgh teams in France, and an officer familiar with the people and language of Arakan, he was parachuted into western Burma two days after Christmas 1944. There had been no time for any jungle training – they had been in the South-East Asian theatre for barely a week. His team's task was to make contact with local partisans and report back on the movement and concentration of Japanese troops to assist in the 14th Army and RAF operations against them.

After making contact with a local guerrilla group, Carew called for an air attack on a concentration of Japanese troops at Minzegyang, which inflicted about 200 casualties on January 4, 1945. Subsequently, he organised a series of ambushes by the guerrilla groups, inflicting more than 100 casualties and, rather more importantly, disrupting the enemy's logistic support at the time of General Slim's third and decisive campaign to clear Arakan of Japanese troops.

The success of this operation, codenamed *Camel*, was attributed very largely to Carew's personal courage, coolness and resourcefulness, for which he was awarded the DSO. By the time the citation for this award was submitted, he had been withdrawn from Arakan and parachuted in to the Pegu Yomas. This broad strip of territory, between the Irrawaddy river and the Rangoon-Mandalay railway, was the obvious refuge for the bulk of the Japanese 28th Army withdrawing southwards as General Slim advanced south from Meiktila into central Burma.

Carew attributed his success in working with the Burmese resistance and other groups to his 'Irishness' and belief in a new independent Burma, in sharp contrast to the British civil servants of the pre-war regime who, isolated in northern India for the duration, persisted in the view that restoration of the old colonial structure was an essential precursor to any form of political advance.

The most significant event of his second Jedburgh operation in Burma was his meeting with the commander of the Burma Defence Army, General Aung San, father of Aung San Suu Kyi, today's leader of the Burmese National League for Democracy. Slim was suspicious of Aung San, because of his pre-war anti-British stance and co-operation with the Japanese, but was interested to meet and persuade him to operate under Allied command.

Carew had a hand in facilitating safe conduct for Aung San to 14th Army headquarters in April 1945, when Slim decided he could do business with him and subsequently arranged for their co-operation in the final defeat of the Japanese in Burma.

At the end of the war in the Far East, Carew returned to the Royal Artillery and served with 6th Airborne Division in Palestine. He was later an instructor at the Mons Officer Cadet School in Aldershot and an intelligence officer in Trieste. He retired as a lieutenant-colonel in 1958 to begin a new career as a boat builder. He also set up his own management consultancy and was a pioneer of employee outplacement.

He later built a house in France and lived there.

His wartime marriage to Margot Goodchild was dissolved soon after the war and he married Jane Suckling in 1953. This was also dissolved and in 1975 he married his business partner Jill Strahan, who predeceased him. He is survived by two sons and two daughters of his second marriage.

(He died on February 16, 2009, aged 89).

Another successful Jedburgh team leader who operated in both France and Burma came to SOE from an academic background and later became the Principal Inspector of Ancient Monuments for England.

Oswin Craster
(Obituary *The Times* February 3, 2006)

Os Craster, as he was more usually known, had what he liked to describe as 'a varied war'. It certainly went from low to high points of activity, the latter a distinct contrast with his work for the Ancient Monuments Inspectorate, which he had begun on leaving university. He learnt his French in Lausanne before the war, and spoke it with a style that made him a natural recruit for the Special Operations Executive, which he joined in January 1944.

Oswin Edmund Craster was educated at Stowe and New College, Oxford, where he was a member of the horsed cavalry section of the Officers' Training Corps. When war threatened in 1938 he enlisted in the 5th (Territorial Army) Battalion of The Oxfordshire and Buckinghamshire Light Infantry and was called up on the outbreak of war. Commissioned in 1940, he served with the same battalion during the invasion scare after Dunkirk, but in 1943, with no active service in prospect, he put his name forward in response to a letter to units stationed in England calling for French speakers willing to undertake 'tasks of particular danger'.

The demand was for about 100 volunteers to form the British element of three man teams to be dropped by parachute into occupied France on, or soon after, the Allied invasion of Normandy on June 6, 1944. Principally, their purpose was to establish contact with the local French Resistance groups, where necessary arrange for weapons to be dropped to them and, above all, to ensure that acts of sabotage that the Resistance undertook helped rather than hindered the Allied operational plans following the breakout from the Normandy beachhead. The three-man teams usually comprised one British and one American or French officer and an experienced sergeant radio operator.

Craster dropped into the Haute-Marne departement on September 1, 1944, in charge of the Jedburgh team *Stanley* The other two members were Lieutenant Robert Cantais, of

France, and Sergeant Jack Grinham, a former Coventry Police constable, of the Royal Armoured Corps. The parachute descent on to the Plateau de Langres was made from above the usual height, but all members of the team landed safely. Contact was quickly established with the local *Forces Francais de l'Interieur*, the element of the Resistance aligning themselves with General de Gaulle, but the FFI commander suggested Craster should take his team 15 miles north to the area of Bussieres, where a group of the *Maquis* was believed to be in need of weapons and operational guidance.

There he found about 400 men, some from the *Premier Regiment de France,* which had been kept in being after the 1940 armistice, a group of gendarmes from Langres and 45 enthusiastic railway workers. He radioed to SOE headquarters requesting a weapons drop on a drop zone (DZ) of his selection, only to be told one would be made at another location which was close to a German garrison.

Thanks to a clever diversionary tactic of lighting fires near the first DZ, the *Maquis* were able to collect the arms and other supplies from the designated alternative and begin a campaign of harassment of German troops already in the area and others passing through.

Before being recalled to England via Paris, which had been liberated by the Allies on August 25, Craster and his team organised a spectacularly successful air strike by four US Air Force fighters on a German battalion stubbornly resisting the *Maquis* group in the villages of Belmont, Grenant and Saulles. Troops from the French 7th Army advancing from the south arrived soon afterwards, so he left the *Maquis* to mop up the German survivors in the three villages. He was mentioned in dispatches for his services and awarded the French *Croix de Guerre.*

On return to England, he was posted to the 2nd (glider-borne) Battalion of his regiment, which had acquitted itself so well in the D-Day landings, but he volunteered for further service with SOE, this time in the Far East, and sailed for India in February 1945. Little time was allowed for acclimatisation and he was dropped into Burma on All Fools' Day.

The SOE had been operating against the Japanese occupation forces in the Far East since 1942, from March 1944 under the title of Force 136. Former Jedburgh team members redeployed from northwest Europe played a significant part in Force 136's Operation *Nation*. Their instructions were to harass the Japanese, wherever found, working with the local anti-fascist organisation (AFO) Burmese guerrillas and the Burmese National Army, under General Aung San (father of the leader of the human rights and democratic movement in Burma and Nobel Peace Prize winner Aung San Suu Kyi). This had originally been formed under Japanese auspices but had switched to the Allied cause in early 1945.

Craster's group, code-named *Zebra*, dropped into central Burma, but found working with the head of the local AFO, Than Tun, extremely difficult. The group therefore made a 95-mile march westwards across the Pegu Yomas to Tharrawaddy, itself a considerable feat of endurance and determination.

Operations against Japanese forces in the area, who were waiting their chance to fight their way eastwards across the Sittang river in an attempt to escape into Thailand, began at the end of April. Together with another Force 136 team, *Jackal*, the group Craster was with had accounted for 800 of the enemy by the end of May. He was mentioned in dispatches for a second time.

After what he regarded as a relatively slow start to his wartime experiences, he could reasonably claim that he had finished on a high note, although he would be the last person to do so. On demobilisation he returned to his work with the Ancient Monuments Inspectorate and was Principal Inspector for England on his retirement in 1976.

In 1944 he married Mary, née Molony, whom he met in Dover when she was with the WRNS. She survives him, with one son and two daughters.

(He died on January 29, 2006, aged 89).

The subject of the next obituary had the misfortune to see both his team members seriously injured by the parachute drop into France and was thrown on his own resources.

Glyn Loosmore, MM

(Obituary December 5, 2007)

Glyn Loosmore's change of career from the Midland Bank eventually to become a district commissioner in Tanganyika was largely the result of his wartime experiences with the Special Operations Executive (SOE) in German-occupied France and later against the Japanese in Burma. He enlisted in the Royal Armoured Corps in July 1942 for training as a radio operator. Once qualified, he volunteered for 'special operations of a hazardous nature' and went to Milton Hall, near Peterborough, to train as a radio operator with one of the SOE teams to be dropped into occupied France on or shortly after the Normandy invasion.

Codenamed 'Jedburghs', the majority of these three-man teams were used to establish contact with the French Resistance and call by radio for airdrops of arms and explosives for such groups to undertake sabotage helpful to the Allies' campaign to liberate France.

Loosmore was assigned to the team codenamed *Andy* that was dropped in the wrong place and too low, as a result of which both officers were injured on landing and had to be evacuated. Loosmore was instructed to join Team *Ivor* whose radio operator had been killed when his parachute failed to open. This was not a matter of a few miles' walk but a journey across central France by taxi, provided by the Resistance.

The *Ivor* team leader contacted the main Resistance group in the Morvan *departement* led by the previous commanding officer of the 1st *Régiment d'Infanterie*, disbanded when Germany occupied the Vichy Zone in late 1942. By persuading other Resistance groups in the Morvan to unite under a French Colonel Bertrand, a force of 1,700 was assembled but only half of them armed. Loosmore was kept hard at work calling for airdrops of arms and ammunition. But only one supply of small arms was received and these were unsuitable for harassing the large number of German troops moving through the Morvan en route for Germany.

The *Ivor* team dispersed to other duties on recall to England. Loosmore sailed for the Far East in November and was dropped into Burma to join already deployed units of Force 136 in March 1945. Although the war in Europe was all but over by then, the Japanese were still fighting stubbornly. In Burma, the former Jedburghs were employed to supply the local anti-Japanese guerrilla forces with arms and direct their operations on lines set by General Sir William Slim's 14th Army advancing from the north.

Loosmore worked with the *Mongoose* team commanded by Lieutenant-Colonel Ronald Critchley, in the Karen tribal area, where some 7,000 local levies were raised. Attacks on the Japanese were mounted but *Mongoose* was driven into the hills by retaliatory attacks and the burning of Karen villages.

Loosmore was awarded the Military Medal and the *Croix de Guerre* for his work with Team *Ivor* in France – and mentioned in dispatches for his time with *Mongoose* in Burma. On demobilization in 1947 he returned to his job with the Midland Bank but left to attend the University of Wales, graduating with a first in 1951. He joined the Colonial Administrative Service, and served in Northern Rhodesia until, opposed to the imposition of the Central African Federation, he transferred to Tanganyika and became district commissioner, Shinyanga. He retired in 1963 to take up a lectureship in English at the University of Leicester.

He is survived by his wife, Elizabeth, nee Goldsworthy, and a son and daughter.

(He died on November 29, 2007, aged 84)

The final three obituaries of this chapter record the achievements of three officers of extraordinary resourcefulness and judgement.

Richard A. Rubinstein, MC
(Obituary *The Times* February 28, 2005)

Dick Rubinstein was parachuted into Brittany on the night of August 6 and 7, 1944, as leader of the SOE 'Jedburgh' team *Douglas I*. His companions were Lieutenant Jean Roblot of France and a British radio operator, Sergeant John Raven. Their Stirling aircraft met ground fire as it ran into the dropping zone, yet the SOE team and a 15-strong SAS group with them all landed safely. For Rubinstein, this was a useful apprenticeship for future operations against the Japanese in Burma.

Rubinstein had joined SOE from Anti-Aircraft Command, which was both dangerous and demanding work during the London Blitz, during which he was in charge of a search-light detachment. He found it insufficiently adventurous, however, once the *Luftwaffe* ceased its mass bombing offensives. Disappointed not to be accepted for either commando training or as an artillery air-observation pilot, he volunteered for unspecified 'tasks of particular danger' advertised by letter to units in the United Kingdom in October 1943. This led him to the SOE, possibly because he had a Higher School Certificate qualification in physics, which provided a useful basis for learning demolition work. Shortly afterwards, he joined the 300 or so individuals at Milton Hall being trained to form the Jedburgh teams.

The task of his *Douglas I* team was to establish contact with a 25-strong SOE Inter-Allied Mission code-named *Aloes*, sent to the area on August 4, and provide liaison between the mission and the French Resistance in the Morbihan *Departement*. Having been unable to make radio contact with *Aloes*, Rubinstein decided to gather what information he could on German dispositions around Lorient, before his team was withdrawn to England two weeks later. After a pause for re-briefing, the team returned to France as *Douglas II*, this time to Le Doubs in eastern France close to the Swiss frontier on September 16. This operation was able to collect intelligence in the Montbeliard area before Rubinstein was again ordered to return to England, this time via Paris following liberation of the city on August 25. Rubinstein was mentioned in dispatches for his services in France and awarded the *Croix de Guerre*. He and other surviving British 'Jed' members were then given the option of going back to their parent units or volunteering for service with the SOE Force 136 against the Japanese in the Far East. He chose the latter, and sailed for Bombay with other volunteers in November.

His first operation in Burma, leading a group codenamed *Cheetah*, began in January 1945 with the aim of raising local levies among the Kachins sympathetic to the Allied cause in the upper Irrawaddy valley, where an attempt had been made to establish an SOE network in 1943. Despite his parachuting experience in France, Rubinstein had some qualms about the prospects in Burma. In his book *SOE in the Far East*, Charles Cruickshank recounts Rubinstein's feelings before the jump: "Felt rotten all afternoon and very frightened. Annoyed at the offhand manner of the non-operational types saying, 'Don't worry, old boy, the 'chute won't open anyway', all very funny! When take-off came I felt much better. Quite easy run. The moon was bright and even colours showed up. A grand reception, all fear gone and glad to have arrived. One never notices the fear going; it just does".

Cheetah produced useful intelligence on Japanese dispositions and supply lines. Rubinstein's next operation, leading group *Chimp*, was also judged successful. His party was parachuted into a jungle clearing near Pyinmana, around 100 miles east of the Irrawaddy, in early April 1945 with the aim of raising a guerrilla force from the local anti-Japanese militia, the Anti-Fascist Organisation or AFO. He quickly raised a force of 200 guerrillas who operated against the Japanese under their own leaders but on his guidance, until the area was overrun by the advancing Fourteenth Army. Rubinstein then moved his SOE team southwards to Toungoo to join *Reindeer*, another team operating against trains ferrying Japanese reinforcements through the Sittang valley.

He was awarded the Military Cross for his gallantry and leadership with the SOE in Burma. Operations with *Reindeer*, which concluded using AFO guerrillas to help to mop up Japanese troops who had avoided the Fourteenth Army and escaped into the Karen Hills, marked the end of his adventures in the Far East.

He returned home to read mechanical engineering at Imperial College, University of London, taking up a place he had been allocated in 1939. He graduated with a first and began work with ICI on Merseyside. He joined a Territorial Army battalion of The Parachute Regiment. When De Havillands offered him a post in its sales engineering division, however, he returned to the south in 1956.

After an enjoyable and successful career with De Havillands and Hawker Siddeley Dynamics, he retired in 1986 and found his way back to his wartime friends through the Special Forces Club, of which he was chairman from 1989 to 1991.

He is survived by his wife Gay, who he had known since his school days and married in 1943 just as he joined SOE, and by two sons.

(He died on February 23, 2005, aged 83)

'Troff' Trofimov, MC
(Obituary *The Times* May 26, 2006)

'Troff' Trofimov, as he was known to his colleagues, was parachuted into the Mayenne *departement* of France on the night of July 8-9, 1944, with two Frenchmen: Captain André Duron and Lieutenant Roger Groult. They formed a team codenamed *Guy*, dropped, with another three man team, *Gavin*, ahead of the advancing Allied armies, to establish contact with such elements of the French Resistance as they could locate in the neighbouring *departement* to the west, Ille-et-Vilaine.

Teams *Guy* and *Gavin* were dropped into Mayenne because SOE had lost all contact with the French partisans in Ille-et-Vilaine, and suspected that SOE's *Parson* circuit working around Rennes had been penetrated by the Gestapo. Therefore the drop was made where it was reasonably certain that a French Resistance reception party would be waiting. The Mayenne partisans confirmed there was no contact with those around Rennes, but some cells were active elsewhere in Ille-et-Vilaine. They bought a car and the two teams prepared to move west accompanied by three partisans.

Disaster was only narrowly avoided as the car was being given a push-start; a German vehicle patrol appeared but was bluffed into doing nothing more than pushing the car aside to allow its own vehicle to pass. In the confusion, Trofimov and one of the partisans slipped away – probably deliberately as Trofimov had doubts about the viability of a group increased to nine. (He had a certain irascibility, which led to friction with those he did not particularly admire).

He spent the following three weeks wearing civilian clothes, gathering information on German positions around Gorron. Having made a thorough survey of them, he worked out an inadequately defended route into the town, then went forward to meet an American reconnaissance unit and led it to the central square. The German defenders pulled out and the town was taken virtually without a fight.

On August 7 Trofimov and his guide rejoined the two Jedburgh teams at Combourg, east of Dinan, where advance elements of the US 1st Army had arrived six days earlier. Working with the Americans, the two teams brought the partisan groups in Côtes du Nord into co-operation. Some 1,400 German prisoners were taken and the partisans established a force to screen off Saint-Malo, which the enemy continued to hold. On August 17, the two Jedburgh teams reported to Headquarters British 2nd Army and were returned to England. Trofimov was awarded the *Croix de Guerre* for his part in the capture of Gorron and mentioned in dispatches.

The liberation of Paris in August brought the work of the Jedburgh teams in northern France virtually to an end. Some were sent to work with partisans in Italy, but Trofimov and others volunteered for service against the Japanese in South-East Asia. He went to Burma, where the principal partisan groups were the Burma National Army (BNA) under General Aung San, father of the leader of the National League for Democracy in modern Burma, Aung San Suu Kyi, and the Anti-Fascist Organisation (AFO), which was seriously harassing the Japanese.

By then a major, Trofimov was parachuted into the Karen Hills in charge of a Jedburgh team codenamed *Mongoose*. This was one of a number working under the direction of the SOE's Force 136, which launched two major operations in support of General Sir William Slim's 14th Army in early 1945. The first, Operation *Nation*, comprising Jedburgh teams almost exclusively, dropped in the Pegu Yomas range between the Irrawaddy and Sittang valleys. The second, Operation *Character*, which included Trofimov's team, was primarily intended to raise the Karen tribesmen who had remained steadfastly in support of British interests throughout the Japanese occupation.

After the 14th Army had taken Meiktila in early March 1945, it was clear the Japanese planned their next stand astride Toungoo 125 miles to the south. Six Jedburgh teams were dropped in a line running southwards with the aim of leading Karen guerrilla attacks against the road and railway to prevent the enemy reinforcing Toungoo. This proved effective as ambushes, road blocks and derailments inflicted serious delays on movement, and Toungoo fell to the 5th Indian Division on April 22 before the Japanese could concentrate enough troops to hold it.

Trofimov was awarded the Military Cross for his vigorous leadership of his Karen guerrillas south of Toungoo and, with the work of the Jedburghs virtually complete in Burma as the 14th Army drove hard for Rangoon, he exchanged his operational role for an administrative one in a transit camp in Manipur. On demobilisation in 1946, he returned to the School of Architecture at Manchester University, where he had been studying before the war.

Aubrey Alwyn Edgar Trofimov (he disliked his given names

and always used 'Troff') attended the *College du Sacre Coeur*, Menton, on the Cote d'Azur, completing his schooling in England and going to Manchester University. He enlisted in the early months of the war and was commissioned into the Royal Artillery in 1943. On hearing volunteers were required by the SOE, he joined the other Jedburghs for training at Milton Hall, Peterborough, in April 1944.

He worked with an architectural practice in London from 1949, eventually becoming responsible for its work in north-east England, then set up in private practice in 1964. His work with a French developer on an estate at Le Touquet, which included golf courses and houses in a forest won him the accolade *Citoyen d'Honneur* of Le Touquet. Another development overlooking the Cherbourg peninsula was accomplished in co-operation with a former Resistance leader, Louis Petri.

He married Jean Helliwell, a freelance model, in 1949. She survives him with two sons.

(He died on May 6, 2006, aged 84)

Christopher Maude, MC
(Obituary *The Times* October 19, 2010)

Having won the Military Cross in France before the Dunkirk evacuation, served with the 1st Parachute Battalion in North Africa, in the invasion of Sicily and in Italy, Christopher Maude volunteered for SOE and was parachuted into occupied France in charge of a team to co-ordinate sabotage operations by the French Resistance.

John Christopher Clapham Maude as born in Manchester in 1920. He was educated at Haileybury and commissioned into the King's Shropshire Light Infantry in 1938. Called up on the outbreak of war, he was sent as a second lieutenant in charge of 43 men, most from the volunteer Militia force, to guard an airfield near Dieppe taken over by the RAF from the French. Shortly after the onset of the *Blitzkrieg* in the Low Countries and Northern France, the RAF squadron on the airfield was ordered home, and as the administrative staff in Dieppe prepared for evacuation Maude was given 50 Royal Engineer and Pioneer Corps reinforcements, extra light weapons and ordered to keep the airfield available for aircraft until further notice. He improvised anti-aircraft mountings for the Lewis guns, as twenty to thirty RAF aircraft landed each day requiring refuelling and food for the pilots. He had no other contact with the outside world until 2/7th Battalion The Duke of Wellington's Regiment passed the airfield en route for Dieppe. The commanding officer told him to wait for arrival of the 51st Highland Division, then to render the airfield unusable and withdraw with the Highlanders to St Valéry-en-Caux. Before leaving, Maude burnt 10,000 gallons of fuel, induced a farmer to plough the centre of the strip, covered the rest with carts and mined the entrances.

On withdrawal towards St Valéry, he was warned of the impossibility of the Navy taking troops off from there, so he made for the nearby cliffs, found a path down to the beach and called a ship by flashing a torch. Although wounded during the evacuation he got all his men away, except for several killed when a rope of rifle slings broke as they lowered themselves down the cliff. Most unusually, the citation for his Military Cross was initiated and signed only General Lord Gort, the C-in-C of the British Expeditionary Force.

After joining SOE, Maude trained as the leader of a Jedburgh team, codenamed *Nicholas*, comprising himself, Lieutenant Henri Penin and Sergeant Maurice Whittle. They were dropped on the night of September 10, 1944, in Haute-Saône. His objective was to contact the *Premier Régiment de France*, a Vichy unit reported to have joined the Resistance. The drop was accomplished but it was 50km from the last known location of the *Premier Régiment*. They lost their radio but recovered it with the help of the leader of the local *Maquis*, who guided Maude's team to a larger group at Magny-les-Jussey, some 20km away.

Almost immediately a German battalion began an operational sweep through the woods. Maude and Sergeant Whittle escaped with the radio while Penin kept in touch with the *Maquis*. The team were reunited the following afternoon, and hearing that German units were moving eastwards by every available road Maude reported this to London, with news that the enemy was preparing to concentrate at Luxeuil-les-Bains, 20km farther east. The *Premier Régiment de France* was not located, so Maude's team was instructed to return to England when they were overtaken by the advancing Allies.

Compared with other Jedburgh operations, many of

which achieved remarkable success, Maude did not rate his very highly. Even so, he had made resolute efforts in the face of significant danger and was awarded the *Croix de Guerre*.

In England his and other Jedburgh teams were briefed to parachute into German PoW camps, ahead of the Allied advance, and lead the prisoners to safety. The swift progress of the war rendered parachuting unnecessary and the teams were flown in by aircraft. Maude was mentioned in dispatches.

After the war he became a farmer and built up a herd of Friesians. He served for many years as divisional secretary of the Soldiers', Sailors' and Airmen's Association for Winslow, Buckinghamshire. With 13 other over 70-year-olds formerly of the Airborne Forces, he made a parachute jump into Studland Bay, Dorset, in 1990, raising £45,000 for military charities.

He married Diana Davenport, also a member of SOE, in 1945. She predeceased him, as did his second wife, Bridget Battersby, whom he married in 1973. He is survived by three daughters of his first marriage.

(He died on October 17, 2010, aged 90)

Many of the 'Jeds', as they called themselves kept in touch with each other over the years, their initial training for their exacting tasks having established friendships that endured their lifetimes. They were fortunate in that the duration of their operations were relatively brief and invariably exciting, thus not allowing for either boredom or tension between them to interfere with vigilance and consequently with security. Over the weekend of 12/13 June 2004, eighteen of the surviving British 'Jeds' met at Milton Hall near Peterborough, where they had trained, to mark the sixtieth anniversary of the start of Jedburgh operations in France in 1944.

A detailed account of each of the Jedburgh operations in France is contained in *Steel from the Sky* by Roger Ford (Weidenfeld & Nicolson 2004). While the Jedburgh team members sent to the Far East after the liberation of France served subsequently in Burma and Malaya, the American and French members, except for a few Americans in Burma, served in French Indo-China, modern Viet Nam, Cambodia and Laos.

10

Malaya and Indo-China

SOE had a Director in the Baker Street headquarters in charge of groups and missions in the Far East but, inevitably, men closer to the action had responsibility for planning operations and monitoring the agents in enemy territory. In the early days after Japan entered the war in December 1941, what was known as the India Mission ran four radio stations to agents on the ground: two in Calcutta to agents in Burma, Indo-China and Thailand, one in Colombo to agents in Malaya and Sumatra and one in Chungking for economic warfare activity and help for prisoner-of-war escape organizations. The headquarters was in Meerut, north-east of Delhi.

The man in charge of the Mission was Colin Mackenzie, a businessman and Old Etonian friend of the Viceroy, Lord Linlithgow. In March 1944 the Mission changed its title to 'Force 136' and in December moved to join SEAC (South East Asia Command) in Kandy, Ceylon.

Malaya

The history of SOE operations in Japanese-occupied Malaya, modern West Malaysia, differs from elsewhere in that it is dominated by a small number of dedicated, resourceful and resilient individuals, some of whom were already in the jungle and operating against the Japanese interest before Force 136 – the Far East arm of SOE responsible for Malaya – took over their control. Not all survived to have their exploits recorded by an obituary in *The Times* but their names occur in the stories of the others and occasionally in the accompanying text.

In the 1930s, as today, peninsula Malaya has a mixed population of Malays – a little over 50 percent, Straits Chinese – around 30 percent and a residual 20 percent of European, Indian and other stock. At the time of the Japanese invasion in December 1941, the British administration rested lightly on the nine states or sultanates, each of which had its own Malay ruler and individual treaty with Britain. The Malay population tended to look to their state rulers for administration, justice and order, while the Chinese were occupationally organized – mainly as rubber tappers, tin miners or businessmen – and provided the majority membership of the Malayan Communist Party.

The unprovoked Japanese invasion had come by sea onto the north-east coast of the peninsula and, having air superiority, had rolled back the British and Indian Army garrison units without much difficulty over a period of seven weeks to the causeway leading to Singapore. The island surrendered on 15 February 1942, despite the strength of Commonwealth troops assembled there greatly exceeding the attacking Japanese. The case for surrender was to avoid civilian casualties, principally from Japanese air attack, and because the island's water supply was already in enemy hands. That said, European prestige had suffered severely and few locals – whatever their ethnicity – anticipated a return of colonial rule.

Resentment and shortly loathing of the Japanese was quickly aroused, however, by the quite unnecessary brutality with which the conquerors dealt with the population, the Chinese workers in particular. This led to the formation of a resistance movement formed from the communist party with the title of 'The Malayan Peoples' Anti-Japanese Army'.

The only place from which resistance groups could both take refuge and begin any form of sabotage against the Japanese infra-structure was the dense jungle covering a great deal of the Malay peninsula. Inhabited on its edge where rubber plantations had been established and the rubber tappers – predominantly Chinese – worked, and in its dark interior by the primitive Sakai people, the jungle offered both cover and sustenance, just so long as the rubber tappers and Sakai remained amenable.

It was with these realizations in mind that a number of European stay-behind parties had taken to the jungle as the Japanese 25th Army had swept south. Although the idea of stay-behind parties had been rejected by the military authorities in Singapore, where the regional command was based, on the grounds that Europeans would be unable to operate in an enemy-occupied peninsula, the concept was revived just in time. In August 1941, five months before the Japanese invasion was launched, No. 101 Special Training School was set up in Singapore with a renowned author, mountaineer and arctic explorer in charge. This was the man whose name will always be the first to leap to mind in the history of wartime Malaya.

Lieutenant-Colonel Frederick Spencer Chapman, DSO and Bar
(Obituary *The Times* August 10, 1971)

Freddie Spencer Chapman, author, explorer, and a leader in jungle warfare was found dead on Sunday in the grounds of Reading University, where he was Warden of Wantage Hall. He was born on May 10, 1907; both his parents dying when he was very young, he was brought up by his guardian, an elderly clergyman, and his wife in a village on the edge of the Lake District. It was due to these surroundings that he acquired a love of the country and nature at an early age. At St John's, Cambridge, where he took an honours degree in history and English, he spent many happy hours with the mountaineer Geoffrey Winthrop Young, and suddenly found himself in a set where talk was all of belays, pitches and cornices.

Chapman became ski expert and naturalist to the British Arctic Air Route Expedition 1930-31. This was Gino Watkins's third expedition, the story of which was told by Chapman in his first book *Northern Lights* published in 1932. In 1933 Watkins returned to Greenland with three companions of the previous year, Chapman, John Rymill and Quintin Riley, but lost his life in a kayak (accident) 12 days after their return. Chapman's book *Watkins' Last Expedition* (1934) describes that party's activities.

For two years he taught at Aysgarth School, Bedale. Then in 1936 he was invited by Marco Pallis to join an expedition he was planning in the Himalayas to the Kangchenjunga district of Northern Sikkim. He could not miss the chance of visiting the highest peaks in the world, and so he arranged to take a term leave. While there he was asked by the Political Officer in Sikkim with whom he was staying, if he would be interested in talking a job in Tibet should the opportunity occur.

'I felt', he said, 'there was nothing I would rather do than spend the rest of my life in the practically unknown country of Tibet'. He joined the British Diplomatic Mission on July 31, 1936. The mission remained in Lhasa until the end of February, 1937. Chapman wrote of his impressions of the Holy City and of the journey through Tibet in *Lzasa: The Holy City*. On the way to and from Lhasa they had spent the night at Phari, on the most bleak and windswept part of the great Tibetan plateau from which the remarkable peak of Chomolhari (24,000ft) rises 10.000ft sheer from the dusty plain. It is even more sacred to the Tibetans than Everest but Chapman eventually secured permission from Lhasa to climb it and invited Charles Crawford, who was working for ICI in Calcutta to join him. With three porters Chapman and Crawford left Kalimpong for Gantok on May 7. Crawford had to leave the party and Chapman and Pasang made the attempt on the summit. Never before had two men attempted such a climb, an error of judgment on either side would have resulted in a fall of thousands of feet. Furthermore at this height the desire to succeed is almost negligible, and it is a continual mental fight. The heading of the account in *The Times* read: *The Ascent of Chomolhari. 24,000ft for £20*; and the leader compared this modest ascent of two men with the yak loads of luxuries which periodically march upon Everest.

Returning to England Chapman once again became a schoolmaster, this time as a housemaster at Gordonstoun. Early in 1940 he joined the 5th Battalion Scots Guards which had been formed as a ski battalion. In August 1941 Chapman was posted to Singapore and given command of a small school of guerilla warfare, the primary object of which was to organize and train 'stay behind' parties in various parts of the Far East which the Japanese might overrun. Early in January 1942 operations began behind and among the advancing Japanese, and were to continue for three years and four months. As an example, it was recorded that in one fortnight in 1942 with two companions he wrecked seven trains, cut the railway in about 60 places including the demolition of fifteen bridges, destroyed or damaged some 40 motor vehicles, and killed or wounded some hundreds of Japanese. One day he walked by accident into the middle of a Japanese camp and was immediately taken prisoner.

He escaped into the jungle during the night, survived sickness, malaria and other fevers, and made his exit by submarine to Ceylon in April 1945 after having been officially reported as missing, believed killed. Promoted to lieutenant-colonel Chapman managed to persuade the authorities that his return to Malaya was essential, and on August 26 he did his first parachute drop near Raub and joined Force 136 (the Far East code name for SOE) where he remained until the Japanese surrender. For his courage and fortitude, not on one day but on many days over the years, he was awarded the DSO and Bar.

The full story of his incredible adventures he told in *The Jungle is Neutral*. Demobilized in 1946 he became the first organizing secretary of the Outward Bound Trust until December 1947, when he once more became a schoolmaster at King Alfred School, Plon, Germany, where he was its first head.

He married in 1946 Faith Mary Townson and had three sons. After five years in South Africa as headmaster of St Andrews's College, Grahamstown, he was appointed in 1962 Warden of the Pestalozzi Village Settlement near Battle in Sussex, for displaced children, many of them Tibetans who he understood so well, could converse with, and was indeed a father to them. But four years in one place was long enough for Spencer Chapman, and in 1966 he became Warden of Wantage Hall, a post he enjoyed as much as all his previous occupations, with his outstanding satisfaction for the present and optimism for the future.

In addition to his DSO and bar. Chapman was awarded the Polar Medal (Arctic Clasp) 1931, the Gill Memorial Medal by the Royal Geographical Society, 1941, the Mungo Park Medal by the Royal Scottish Geographical Society, 1948, The Sunday Times Special Award and Gold Medal, 1949, and the Lawrence of Arabia Memorial Medal by the Royal Central Asian Society. He was a brilliant lecturer and photographer. His books speak for themselves. Freddie was all his life an incurable optimist. He based his philosophy on a saying of Gino Watkins who was perhaps his model hero – 'there's nothing good or bad but thinking makes it so'.

(He died on August 8, 1971 aged 64)

John Davis was another stalwart of the resistance against the Japanese and later against the communist guerillas who plagued the freed Federation of Malaya in the post-war years. He returned to wartime Malaya after avoiding capture and escaping to Sumatra. Despite his understanding of the aims of the Malayan Communist Party from his service with the Police Special Branch, that did not inhibit him from exploiting its potential.

John Davis, CBE, DSO
(Obituary *The Times* October 31, 2006)

At the time of the Japanese invasion of the Malay States in December 1941, John Davis was serving there with the police Special Branch, responsible for intelligence on the Malayan Communist Party (MCP). In anticipation of a Japanese attack, a plan had been devised by the Oriental Mission, Far Eastern office of the Ministry of Economic Warfare (based in Singapore), to harass the invaders with 'stay-behind' parties left in the jungle.

The MCP had agreed to co-operate with these, but the speed of the Japanese advance precluded Davis's participation at that stage. On the day after the surrender of Singapore on February 16, 1942, he and Richard Broome, of the Malayan Civil Service, crossed to Sumatra to seek news of the stay-behind parties there. Japanese activity forced their almost immediate return. Davis, Broome and others were then dispatched by the head of the Oriental Mission in a small vessel to Ceylon (modern Sri Lanka), where they arrived after 35 days without fresh food and a tiny amount of water.

Only a handful of 40 or so Europeans left behind in the Malayan jungle – who included Lieutenant-Colonel Freddie Spencer Chapman – avoided capture or death. Responsibility for them and for guerrilla action against the Japanese was transferred from the Oriental Mission to the Special Operations Executive's Far East office (later known as Force 136) headquarters in Ceylon. Plans were then put in hand to restore contact with the guerrilla forces in Malaya, to trace any survivors of the stay-behind parties and maintain contact by radio and submarine.

Davis, by now commissioned into the 6th Rajputana Rifles, landed from a submarine with a group of Chinese on the coast of the northern state of Kedah in May 1943. Having established these as agents with the local population, he withdrew to Ceylon by the next submarine.

Returning to Malaya by submarine in August 1943, Davis met Chin Peng, *nom de guerre* of the MCP guerrilla leader operating in Perak, south of Kedah. Chin Peng explained to Davis his opposition to the Japanese occupation and also the extent of the combined guerrilla and civilian organisation, the Anti-Japanese Union and Forces (AJUF) opposing it. They had heard that a European (whom they guessed was Spencer Chapman) had been training guerrillas in the AJUF camps for two years. Chin Peng arranged for the three men to meet on Christmas Day 1943. At a conference with the AJUF and MCP leadership on December 31, Davis signed an agreement on behalf of the Allied C-in-C South East Asia, Admiral Lord Louis Mounbatten, to provide arms, supplies and money in return for the guerrillas stirring up labour disputes and sabotaging Japanese shipping.

With radio contact with Ceylon broken for a long period, because of the loss of their sets, Davis and his party lived with the guerrillas in deep jungle. When contact with Colombo was restored in February 1945, he was appointed head of the Force 136 groups of agents in Malaya and promoted to colonel. A plan to co-ordinate operations against the Japanese in anticipation of Operation *Zipper*, the Allied landings in Malaya, was overtaken by the atomic bomb attacks on Hiroshima and Nagasaki in August 1945 and the Japanese surrender. Davis was awarded the DSO for his leadership in Malaya in 1942-44 and appointed CBE for his liaison work with the resistance from February 1945.

After the war he joined the Malayan Civil Service, but his association with Chin Peng was not over. At their first meeting in 1943, Chin Peng had made clear that as an avowed communist he was also opposed to British rule in Malaya. Even so, he co-operated loyally with the British against the Japanese in pursuit of the agreement Davis had signed in December 1943, and was appointed OBE for his services in 1946.

He now resumed his MCP activities, declaring the use of force against the British as a justified means of establishing a communist state. After a series of communist-inspired strikes in the tin mines and the murders of a number of European managers of rubber plantations, the MCP was proscribed. Chin Peng led about 5,000 of his followers into the jungle, where they dug up their wartime arms and, on June 16, 1948, 'declared war' on the British administration.

The 12-year Malayan Emergency began at that point, yet it might have been brought to a peaceful conclusion as early as 1956. By 1955 Chin Peng had recognised that his campaign of terror against the rural Chinese and Malays had failed. He sought talks with Tunku Abdul Rahman and David Marshall, the chief ministers of Malaya and Singapore respectively, but demanded a guarantee for his safety.

Davis, then a district officer, was asked, on the strength of his wartime friendship with Chin Peng, to be the guarantor. A delicately negotiated arrangement was made for Davis to meet the communist leader in a jungle clearing. There he greeted him with, 'Long time, no see' in Cantonese, and conducted him to the meeting, close to the border with Thailand. But despite the friendly atmosphere of the talks, agreement could not be reached with Chin Peng. He went back to the jungle and led his dwindling band of terrorists for a further six years.

Davis remained with the Malayan Civil Service until the Emergency ended in 1960, at which time he was deputy chairman of the war executive committee of Kedah province. His service to the country was recognised by the award of the JMN (Commander of the Order of the Defender of the Realm) in 1959 and the SMJ (Faithful to the Crown of Johore) in 1960.

On his return to England he became general-secretary of Kent Council Social Services (1961-74). He was subsequently to meet Chin Peng again during the latter's visit to England. During his call on Davis at his home in Sussex, Chin Peng conceded: 'I have great experience of struggle but not of how to build socialism.'

John Lewis Haycraft Davis was educated Aldro School, where he became a friend of Kim Philby, later to be notorious as a traitor, and at Tonbridge. He began his service with the Malayan Police in Pahang in 1931. He quickly mastered Malay and spent time in Canton and Macau learning Cantonese. This led him to intelligence work with Special Branch. He was a man of outstanding personality and complete self-assurance, yet modest about his own achievements to a degree that few could comprehend.

In 1946 he married Helen Ouin whom he had known since childhood. She survives him, with three sons and a daughter. Another daughter predeceased him.

(He died on October 27, 2006, aged 95).

Chin Peng, the faithful friend and collaborator with SOE in Malaya, does not yet have an obituary in *The Times*, as he is still alive at the time of publication of this book, aged – it is believed – 91. Born Wong Man Wa in Kampong Kohat in the west coast state of Perak in 1922, the son of an immigrant from China's Fujian province who set up as a bicycle dealer, he proved an outstanding student at the local Anglo-Chinese school and matriculated at the age of fifteen.

He joined the Perak branch of the communist party two years later and quickly became both the party's state secretary and a protégé of the national party leader, Lai Teck. The Japanese conquest of Malaya and fall of Singapore in February 1942 saw his appointment to the central standing committee of the Malayan Peoples' Anti-Japanese Army and he became a leading light in the guerilla group in Perak. It was in this role that he met Spencer Chapman serving with one of the stay-behind parties in March 1942 and set up food and supply lines for his support.

In January 1944, after Spencer Chapman had put Chin Peng in touch with John Davis as the leader of the stay-behind parties, Chin Peng met Davis to discuss co-operation with the Allied South East Asia Command.

In return for co-operation, the communist guerillas were to receive arms, supplies and training but strictly for the purpose of defeating the Japanese. No post-war commitment was given. After publication of the obituary for John Davis in October 2006, Chin Peng wrote the following to *The Times* from his place of exile in Thailand:

> Many people tend to believe that friendships cannot bridge the divisions of international conflict – particularly in situations where those with close bonds of trust and understanding find themselves in bitterly opposing camps. I would differ; and would even suggest that perhaps there might be a lesson for our troubled world today in the decades-long relationship that existed between myself and my friend John Davis.
>
> I first met John in September 1943 in Japanese-occupied

Malaya. He was there to establish links to the outlawed Communist Party of Malaya (CPM), the only active anti-Japanese resistance group then in existence in the country. John's credentials were signed by Admiral Louis Mountbatten, head of Britain's Ceylon-based South-East Asia Command, (SEAC.). I was representing the Perak state committee of the CPM.

That meeting forged an association that was expedient: we wanted to rid Malaya of a common enemy. But we both realised ultimately that the period of being allies in a common cause would eventually end. It did; but I can never forget my time with John in the Malayan jungle. He was an implacable leader in the most harrowing of circumstances. Once, John and I, with a band of CPM guerrillas, had gathered to recover a joint personnel and arms drop by the RAF. Things went terribly wrong.

Parachutes landed in wrong areas. We came under heavy Japanese machinegun fire. I was 20 at the time. John was in his early 30s. Perhaps for the first time in my life I knew the feeling of real fear. John appeared calm and in control. He was a man of principle and I recognised that very early on. I knew it when the CPM signed the Blantan agreement with SEAC in February 1945. This tied his cause and mine to an honourable agreement, albeit of limited duration.

I knew it when I saw him during the Malayan Emergency at the Baling peace talks in northern Malaya in 1955, which, sadly, failed. John had been deputized to look after me during the negotiations. He escorted me to and from each session. My one-time ally was now my enemy, something we both acknowledged; we differed on matters of politics and principle, but there was still great mutual respect that precluded personal enmity.

So when I visited the United Kingdom in 1998, I sought out my old friend. I wanted to show my deep gratitude for a man who, despite being vehemently opposed to my anti-British colonial struggle, always treated me fairly and decently. You cannot ask more of a man or a friend.

European farmers and rubber plantation managers provided an invaluable source of expertise and recruits for SOE operations in Malaya, not only for their knowledge of the country and one or more of its languages but also for their proven resilience to the climate and living conditions. One such man was Peter Dobrée.

Peter Dobrée, OBE
(Obituary *The Times* November 19, 2004)

At the time of the Japanese landings in north-east Malaya in December 1941, Peter Dobrée was dairy farming on land he had bought and cleared in the western state of Perak. He left to report for duty with the Singapore Volunteer Artillery, and when the British garrison surrendered on February 15, 1942, he joined a handful of resolute individuals who escaped from the island in small boats, eventually to reach Ceylon.

Commissioned into the 3rd Gurkha Rifles in 1942, he volunteered for special duties when posted to Dehra Dun in northern India. He had heard that some small stay-behind parties were still operating in Japanese-occupied Malaya and wished to put his knowledge of the country and languages to good use by joining them. His first attempt, by submarine in August 1944, failed owing to the outboard motors of their collapsible boats refusing to start due to the humidity inside the submarine.

A second attempt by submarine was cancelled when it was learnt that the operation had probably been compromised through the capture by the Japanese of another party which had been put ashore from a flying boat. Both these operations were under the auspices of Force 136, the section of the Special Operations Executive (SOE) operating in South-East Asia.

Dobrée's third attempt to get into Malaya, codenamed Operation *Hebrides*, was made by parachute in December 1944. Difficulties in pin-pointing suitable dropping zones using one-inch-to-the-mile scale maps had previously inhibited parachute operations, but Dobrée selected his DZ near the small town of Gerik in Perak. After an abortive attempt to drop by night, the party jumped at last light on December 16, and all landed safely. This was the first successful blind drop into Malaya during wartime and Dobrée and his party knew there would be no opportunity for them to be extracted before the liberation.

His task was to form an intelligence-gathering network and, should prospects be favourable, to establish a resistance movement in northern Malaya. Six days after landing he had set up a base camp and made radio contact with SOE headquarters in Ceylon. He then set about recruiting volunteers to gather intelligence on Japanese forces around Taiping and in Kedah across the inter-state border.

Both areas were suffering severe food shortages and, with rice at a horrendous price in the villages, volunteers came forward in greater numbers than he could handle or needed. By the end of March 1945, he had recruited, armed and trained 100 Malays and 80 Chinese volunteers.

In addition to organizing the air drop of weapons and supplies, he arranged the reception of four other parties of Force 136 who landed by parachute, providing them with guides and local contacts in the areas of their planned operations.

The enemy became aware of Dobrée's presence shortly after his arrival, but his jungle base remained secure until April 1945 when the Japanese located it and mounted a concerted attack. A series of protective ambush positions gave warning however, and, although Dobrée was wounded in the leg, and his volunteers were able to regroup in an alternative base camp deeper in the jungle. They also inflicted casualties on the attacking force, killing the local commander of the Kempetai, the Japanese security police. Despite this setback, Dobrée continued to extend his area of influence and had 300 volunteers working across north Malaya, gathering intelligence in anticipation of Operation *Zipper*, the Allied invasion scheduled for September 1945.

In the event, the atomic bombing of Hiroshima and Nagasaki, on August 6 and 9 respectively, brought about the Japanese surrender and changed the nature of the operation to one of occupation rather than invasion. Dobrée, who had been promoted to lieutenant-colonel during the course of his nine months in the jungle, was appointed OBE (Military Division) for his services with Force 136.

Peter George James Dobrée was born in Grays, Essex, the youngest of four children of Frank and Eliza Dobrée. He was educated at Westminster School before reading agriculture at Reading University, where he excelled at rowing. On graduation in 1935, he followed his two older brothers to the Far East and became an assistant rubber planter in Johore State, in southern Malaya.

Later he worked for the Malayan Colonial Service in Kuala Lumpur until establishing his own dairy farm. His book *Hot Rain Means Danger* describing his wartime experiences was published by the Malaysian University Press in 1994 and, in 1999, the State of Perak honoured him with the title of Datun for his services to the people of Malaysia.

He married Jill Rennie after the war, but the marriage was dissolved in 1963. In 1964, he married Mary Sumption, who survives him with two sons of his first marriage and a daughter and two stepsons of his second.

(He died on October 21, 2004, aged 91).

A policeman who returned to Japanese-Occupied Malaya to serve with SOE's Force 136 later became the head of Malaysia's Police.

Sir Claude Fenner, KBE, CMG
(Obituary *The Times* June 19, 1978)

Tan Sri Sir Claude Fenner, KBE, CMG, who was Inspector-General of the Malaysian Police Force from 1963 to 1966, died on May 15 at the age of 62. He had a distinguished war record against the Japanese and stayed in Malaya. Becoming the first and last Briton to head Malaysia's police force. Claude Harry Fenner was educated at Highgate School and joined the Federated Malay States Police as a cadet in 1936. With war coming to the Far East he fled from Singapore, escaping two days before it fell to the Japanese. He made his way to Australia via Indonesia and in 1942 joined the Nigerian Police.

Later he returned to South East Asia, volunteering for service against the Japanese in Malaya while he was serving with the British forces in India. As a member of the special force, Force 136, he gained experience of jungle warfare and was later parachuted into Malaya as a leader of guerrillas. At the end of the war he was a lieutenant-colonel.

He remained with the Colonial Police Force in Malaya after the war gaining the Colonial Police Medal in 1950 and the Queen's Police Medal in 1957. Following Malayan independence in 1957 he continued with the country's police force becoming successively, Commissioner of Police, Director of Police Affairs and in 1963, Inspector-General. This period was one of crisis for Malaysia owing to the state of confrontation with Indonesia and he was closely involved with the security of the area.

When he retired in 1966 he relinquished command of the police to its first Malaysian commander. But he continued to live in Malaysia and was Special Representative in Malaysia of the Rubber Growers Association.

He was appointed CMG in 1963, KBE in 1965 and had been honoured by the Federation of Malaya in 1961.

He married, in 1941. Joan Margaret, daughter of T. Fenner, of Queensland. They had one daughter.

(He died on May 15, 1978, aged 62)

While the interest of SOE in building up a resistance force in the jungle focused on the Chinese members of the Malayan Communist Party, effort was also made to involve the Malay element of the population. This was not easy: although many Malays gave their help and support on the ground, for the most part they shunned the communist party. There were, however, a number of Malay officers and soldiers who joined SOE, one eventually heading his country's armed services.

General Tun Ibrahim bin Ismail
(Obituary *The Times* March 4, 2011)

As the Japanese Army advanced down peninsular Malaya in 1942, British plans for establishing a resistance to the occupying power focused on the hitherto illegal Malayan Communist Party (MCP). To this end, eight British stay behind parties, later joined by a ninth, left the 101st Special Training School near Singapore for the jungle.

The MCP largely comprised Straits Chinese opposed to the British administration, but when the Soviet Union entered the war on the side of the Allies in 1941, they gave their support 'for the duration'. In the hope of counterbalancing this potentially subversive element, recruiters for the Special Operations Executive (SOE) welcomed indigenous Malays willing to be infiltrated back into their homeland. One such recruit was Lieutenant Ibrahim bin Ismail from the state of Johore, serving with the 19th Hyderabad Regiment of the Indian Army. In India, Ibrahim had met Major Tengku Mahmood Mahyideen, a fellow Malay attached to the staff of SOE's India Mission in Meerut.

On hearing of the requirement, Ibrahim volunteered for special service. After training in SOE techniques of sabotage and subversion, he was promoted captain to join a team of Malays led by Major (later lieutenant-colonel) Peter Dobrée of Force 136, as the India Mission became known when its headquarters moved to Kandy in Ceylon, modern Sri Lanka.

Dobrée's team was to be landed by submarine on the coast of the Malayan northwest state of Kedah in August 1944, but the operation was abandoned when the outboard motors of the folding boats to take the party ashore failed to start. Two months later, Ibrahim himself led a Malay team in an attempt to put ashore on the north-eastern state of Terengganu from a Catalina flying boat; this operation also had to be abandoned due to the presence of local fishing boats.

A second attempt a few days later involved his team being launched in kayaks from the Catalina but currents drove them ashore on one of the Perhentian islands south-east of Kota Bahru. The local headman provided a boat for the party to reach the mainland where, possibly alerted by the earlier Catalina sortie, the Japanese were ready and took them prisoner.

Under interrogation, Ibrahim adopted the practice he had been taught of inventing a story that, after he appeared to succumb to violence, might appear credible. He explained that the party was not fully trusted by the British and would prefer to work with the Japanese. To prove this, he undertook to operate his radio back to SOE's Kandy headquarters and did so, but omitting the security check. Kandy's response included a question that allowed him to let his masters know he was in enemy hands.

In consequence of his deception, the SOE was able to feed the Japanese with false information for the remaining ten months of the war in the Far East – in particular regarding the site of the intended Allied landing in Malaya. Hoping to draw more SOE agents into a trap, the Japanese instructed Ibrahim to request reinforcement. To maintain his credibility with them, Kandy arranged a parachute drop of supplies on a notified date, followed by a message saying the agent due to accompany them was taken ill during the 14 hours flight from Ceylon.

After the Japanese surrender in August 1945 Ibrahim and

his team were released. He was later appointed MBE for his services and resolution while in Japanese hands.

Ibrahim was the son of Dato 'Ismail bin Abu Bakar, a treasury official in the government of Johore. He first aspired to follow his father as an accountant, but decided on a military career and attended the Indian Military Academy at Dehra Dun. After the war he served in the Sultan of Johore's State Forces, transferring to the Malay (later Royal Malay) Regiment in 1951, at the height of the communist insurgency in Malaya.

He commanded the 6th Battalion in the late 1950s, was advanced to brigadier in 1962 to be the Director of Administration of the Federation's Army and then to command the 5th Infantry Brigade in Sabah during Indonesia's 'confrontation' and infiltration into East Malaysia. He was appointed commander of the 1st Infantry Division in 1966, became a member of the National Operations Council as a lieutenant-general after the interracial riots in Kuala Lumpur in 1969 and became Chief of the Defence Forces, as a four-star general in 1970, holding that appointment until retirement from the army in 1977.

He was the first Chief of the Defence Forces to be granted the honorific title 'Tun'. Subsequently he became chairman of the Malaysia Smelting Corporation and a director of the Straits Trading Company and Permodalal National. He is survived by his wife, Toh Puan Zakiah binti Ahmad, two sons and two daughters.

(He died on December 23, 2010, aged 88).

A letter to *The Times* shortly following publication of his obituary revealed more detail of Ibrahim's deception of his Japanese captors. Mr Ralph Erskine wrote:

'The obituary of Tun Ibrahim bin Ismail suggests that after the Japanese captured him, he omitted his security check to alert the Special Operaions Executive when radioing under duress. The full story reveals him being as quick-witted as he was courageous. Ibrahim's briefing officer wrote down the answer, 'Two Scotsmen left here two days ago', (letting SOE know he was safe) to his security question 'Have you met Mariam?' Having seized this, the Japanese would know SOE would not believe him unless he gave the correct answer.

Fortunately, he convinced the Japanese that the right answer would never have been written, and instead sent, 'Yes, I have met Miriam.' SOE then realized he had been captured and 'played' him as a triple agent for the rest of the war.

Indo-China

As may be seen from Chapter 9, when they had completed their duties in France, a number of the British 'Jedburghs' volunteered to serve in the Far East and were sent to Burma, where they achieved excellent results.

Under similar arrangements, some French and American Jedburgh team members volunteered for service in Indo-China, occupied by the Japanese. The situation there was more problematical than was generally expected as, although the Cambodian, Lao and Vietnamese populations had no love for the Japanese, who had occupied their countries without resistance from the forces of Vichy France who still had an armed presence there, they were unenthusiastic about return to colonial administration. One of the 'Jeds' who so volunteered received an obituary in *The Times* but it gave scant information about what happened after his arrival in Laos in 1945, concentrating instead on his involvement in the siege of Dien Bien Phu.

Colonel Jean Sassi
(Obituary *The Times* February 4, 2009)

Jean Sassi led what might be described as a forlorn-hope mission to relieve the pressure on the French troops besieged at Dien Bien Phu by the superior forces of Vietminh General Vo Nguyen Giap. A veteran of the 1940 German offensive through the Ardennes into northern France and later of the Allied 'Jedburgh' operations in France following the Normandy invasion, Sassi had the zeal and experience for such an enterprise but the odds were stacked too high against him.

The French plan to bring the Vietminh to a decisive battle at Dien Bien Phu in November 1953 succeeded but their intelligence had gravely underestimated the Vietminh strength, particularly in artillery, and their ability to concentrate around the French fortified camp. Some 10,000 French, French

Colonial and Foreign Legion troops had been parachuted or airlifted into the remote valley 180 miles west of Hanoi.

The first parachute assault battalion had to fight to clear the landing zone for the next drop but by the end of November the base was established with strong defended outposts; then, as Giap's artillery began its pounding, the weather reduced the delivery of air re-supply. The siege was to last more than five months and by mid-March the outlying strong points were beginning to fall as the ammunition and food stocks ran out.

Sassi was already working with the French special forces in nearby Laos with 200 Laotian pro-French Mèo partisans under his command. As part of an operation to attempt some relief, Sassi's Mèo detachment was parachuted in at a point from where it could attack the Vietminh artillery supply lines from China before fighting its way through to one of the remaining French positions on the Dien Bien Phu perimeter – codenamed *Elaine*.

They dropped on April 27, but *Elaine* fell to Vietminh attack on April 30 and the remaining French force ceased fighting a week later. Sassi and another force similar to his had made gallant attempts to intervene but time was against them.

Jean Henri Sassi was the son of Corsican parents living in Tunis but little is known of his early life. It appears that he fought in the French defensive battle in northern France in 1940 but it is unlikely that he was commissioned then, as he was only a second lieutenant when recruited in North Africa to join a force being raised and trained in England by the Special Operations Executive (SOE), known as the Jedburghs.

These were all parachutists and, unlike SOE agents already operating in German-occupied Europe, wore uniform and were to drop after D-Day (June 6, 1944). Their tasks were to call for arms and explosives to be parachuted to French Resistance groups and guide their subsequent acts of sabotage and attacks on German supply routes. Sassi was the junior member and radio operator of the three-man Jedburgh team codenamed *Chloroform* and led by Captain Jacques Martin that dropped east of Montélimar in the early hours of June 30, 1944. The team mission was to direct partisan attacks against the railway which ran north-westwards from Gap, in the Vercors, to Valence on the Rhône.

After a dispersed landing from 2,500 feet, the *Chloroform* team reassembled only to discover that the local Resistance was armed, well organised and had already put the Gap-Valence railway out of action.

Martin established a base further to the east and armed the local partisans by airdrop. Under his guidance, they cut the Gap-Briançon railway in mid-July and attacked German road traffic on the RN 94.

Through disregarding an order to move to the Drôme, the team avoided being caught up in the German attack by three divisions on French partisans on the Vercors plateau on July 18. They helped survivors of this attack before blowing the railway bridge over the River Savines on the eve of the Allied landings on the French Mediterranean coast on August 15.

Chloroform's operations were rated successful, and Sassi received his first *Croix de Guerre* for his part in them.

Together with other Jedburgh groups and individuals, he volunteered for service in the Far East with the SOE Force 136. This led to his introduction to Laos, where he served in 1945 before his return to France the following year to join the 11th (Shock) Battalion of the French parachute force as an instructor.

Four years later he went back to Laos to form the Mèo special force that he was to lead towards Dien Bien Phu in 1954. Subsequently, he returned to 11th (Shock) battalion for operations against the irregular forces of the *Front de Libération Nationale* (FLN) in Algeria.

When he retired, aged 54, in 1971, he was a colonel, a Commander of the Legion of Honour and held the *Croix de Guerre* with citations for Europe and also for South-East Asia.

(He died on January 9, 2009, aged 91)

11

Speculative Ventures

Winston Churchill's 1940 order to 'set Europe ablaze' was of course directed at the countries of continental Europe and Scandinavia recently invaded and occupied by Germany. He could not at that time foresee the Nazi scourge extending to the Balkans, although once it did he became an advocate of their liberation as a means of opening a front that would both distract German forces from North-West Europe and possibly deny Stalin easy access to them and the Mediterranean after the war. It was into the Balkan countries that SOE was to make its more speculative ventures.

As the foregoing chapters of obituaries have demonstrated, SOE needed no prompting to extend its reach into Greece and Albania, Italy – after the armistice of September 1943 had revealed the existence of guerilla bands in the those parts of the country where the *Wehrmacht* was still bitterly contesting every yard of territory – and Yugoslavia. Speculative ventures elsewhere came with a distinct change in the tide of the war, when it seemed possible that Hitler's allies of convenience – countries too weak to resist him who had reluctantly decided that it would be better to side with him than oppose him – might be ready to sabotage communications or other facilities on their territory serving the German war machine.

Although none of these ventures were to achieve lasting or spectacular success, the men who attempted them are perhaps the SOE heroes most deserving of praise. Not for them the certainty that at least a substantial proportion of the population of the country into which they were to be infiltrated had sympathy with their cause; at best there was rumour of the existence of political opposition, of partisans in rural areas, perhaps even names of rebel commanders and localities where they were active. Yet the other likelihood was that they would meet opposition born of fear of the still strong Nazi stranglehold, to be swiftly followed by betrayal.

Austria, Bulgaria, Hungary and Romania were all targeted. One gallant agent – Kurt Koenig, a German Army deserter – volunteered to carry out sabotage in his home country. He was parachuted in three times with a view to both sabotage and subversion. He returned twice through Spain after, according to his own account, sabotaging some railway lines. On the third occasion he was captured almost at once and executed.

Austria

German-speaking Austria had been incorporated into greater Germany by the *Anschluss* of March 1938, despite the union of Germany and Austria being specifically forbidden under the Treaty of Versailles. The event was engineered by the Austrian Nazi party which precipitated a *coup d'état* on the eve of a national referendum on the proposed union. The new regime invited Hitler to take over, and the country subsequently contributed a number of divisions to the German Army during the war. The centre of Austrian Nazism was in and around the second city of Graz; further west Carinthia – also facing Yugoslavia – was believed less enthusiastic. By August 1944, with the Italian campaign proceeding only slowly, the time seemed ripe for an investigation into southern Austria. The man who led it was a cavalry officer and fluent German-speaker.

George Fielding, DSO
(Obituary *The Times* April 12, 2005)

Having studied German at Freiburg University before the Second World War, George Fielding was well suited to lead an SOE mission into the Austrian provinces of East Tyrol and Carinthia, with the aim of stimulating acts of sabotage against German lines of communication into Italy. Given the Nazi grip on Austria as a whole, it might be thought that grave risks were being taken with the lives of brave men with only scant chance of their achieving worthwhile success.

When Fielding and his three companions were dropped by parachute into the Friuli district of north-eastern Italy on the night of August 12-13, 1944, the Allied armies advancing up the peninsula were still 200 miles to the south, facing the

German 10th Army on the Gothic Line. It was hoped that the SOE group would gain local support from Italian partisans, which proved to be the case with the Osoppo group intent on getting the Germans out of their country, but not the communist Garibaldi partisans, who were ill-disciplined and uncooperative.

Having based himself with the Osoppo at Forni Avoltri, 15 miles south of the Austrian border, Fielding dispatched one member of his team in civilian clothes and with false papers on a reconnaissance into Carinthia. He then found a dropping zone suitable for receiving resupply by parachute, and set about finding courier routes into Austria. All seemed set fair for making some useful contacts over the border, despite the known strong Gestapo network in the region, but the German Army got to hear of him and initiated an intensive search. So long as he and his party remained at Forni Avoltri they were entirely dependent on a 20-man strong partisan bodyguard for security. So, to ensure their commitment, Fielding promised to arm and supply them by air-drop. This undertaking was to give him as much concern as the German Army.

A combined American and British 'Balkan Air Force' had been formed that autumn with the purpose of supporting partisan groups fighting the German occupying forces in Yugoslavia and northern Italy. In the main, the pilots assigned to this work had appropriate experience, but the difficulties of finding dropping zones in mountainous regions susceptible to the onset of bad weather were seriously under-estimated. Fielding was not alone among SOE officers serving with partisans in Yugoslavia and Italy to have problems maintaining their credibility as they waited, night after night, for a resupply drop that never came or fell beyond reach.

Setbacks over air resupply, which were to leave his increasingly sceptical bodyguard ragged and barely capable of defending themselves, were offset by the safe return of the team member who had crossed into Austria. His report was far from encouraging, however, as he had found the local Carinthian population to be apathetic about Allied chances of defeating the *Wehrmacht*, and in great fear of the Gestapo. Fielding kept his party at Forni Avoltri for the next six weeks, hoping that his air resupply requests would be met, but to no avail. As the local skies were clear, he replied to radio excuses that bad weather precluded air drops with the message: 'More of the spirit of the Battle of Britain and less of the bottle of Bari.' This was later to earn him a rebuke.

Determined to see the local situation for himself, he crossed into Carinthia in early October, disguised as a peasant but with no papers. In two missions, he completed a reconnaissance of the Upper Gail valley, reaching the same negative conclusions as to the feasibility of forming Austrian sabotage groups as his colleague had done. Immediately on his return, his party was forced to withdraw into the hills by German patrols searching for them and, on October 14, two members of the team, Major Smallwood and his radio operator, were captured when the former slipped, breaking his arm and badly spraining his ankle.

On Fielding's return to Forni Avoltri to assess the possibility of further forays into Austria, he found the Italian partisans badly demoralised, because of failure of the promised air-drop, and he narrowly avoided capture when his hiding place was betrayed to the Germans, who had put an 800,000-lire reward on his head. Shortly afterwards, the passes were blocked by snow and he was ordered to march out to Slovenia, to be picked up by air. He set out with the survivors of another SOE group from a separate mission who had arrived at his base camp. The party was betrayed and ambushed en route, but escaped with loss of their mules and heavy equipment. Fielding was wounded in the arm in this skirmish but was able to continue the 300-mile march to Slovenia, from where they were flown to southern Italy.

Despite the lack of success in establishing pro-Allied partisan groups in Carinthia and South Tyrol, much valuable information was gathered and, so it was later assessed, some 6,000 German troops had been diverted in the efforts to capture him and his party. He was awarded the DSO for his outstanding leadership, resourcefulness and courage during his mission.

George Rudolf Hanbury Fielding was born in July 1915, a few weeks before his father was killed at Gallipoli. His mother took him to live in Switzerland, but he returned to England to be educated at Shrewsbury. After completing his studies at Freiburg, he worked for a year in Canada, running trap-lines on the edge of the Arctic Circle.

At the outbreak of war in September 1939 he was working as a cattle buyer in Chicago. He sailed for England and was commissioned into the 3rd King's Own Hussars, joining a squadron of his regiment which was diverted to Crete on its way to the Western Desert. When the island fell to the Germans, he marched with fellow wounded to a rendezvous with the Royal Navy and eventually rejoined his regiment in the desert. He was mentioned in dispatches and volunteered to serve with the SOE at the end of the North Africa campaign.

After the war, he farmed in the west of Ireland for several years, before returning to the Pays d'Enhaut in Switzerland, where he had lived as a boy. He participated in two commercial ventures there but spent as much time as he could on the ski slopes or painting.

In 1940 he married Georgina Pope, who predeceased him. He is survived by a son and daughter.

(He died on January 23, 2005, aged 89)

Bulgaria

Bulgaria was dragged into the war through Hitler's requirement to secure his southern flank during the invasion of the Soviet Union in June 1941. In consultation with King Boris of Bulgaria, he planned to pass through the country to occupy Greek Thrace, along the Mediterranean coast, a region he considered necessary to hold to forestall any Allied repetition of the Salonika campaign of the First World War that had heralded German defeat on that occasion. The attitude of the Bulgarian population seems to have counted for little in these deliberations as their Slavonic language links them with Russia rather than Germany.

Despite the absence of other encouraging indications, intelligence of a communist-inspired *coup d'état* in Bulgaria provided the stimulus for an early SOE venture into the country.

Kenneth Scott, DCM
(Obituary *The Times* November 13, 2008)

Kenneth Scott was a volunteer for an SOE group codenamed *Claridges* parachuted into Serbia in early 1944 to gain access to Bulgaria with the help of Marshal Tito's Yugoslav communist Partisans. Scott was the mission's sergeant radio operator.

Little was known of the effectiveness of resistance groups in Bulgaria. The pro-German Government had joined the Axis powers in early 1941, but Slav sentiment for Russia had held it back from joining Germany in the invasion of the Soviet Union in June 1941. An opposition leader, George Dimitrov, who had escaped to Palestine, held out hope for action by partisans located near Sofia. Therefore the SOE headquarters in Cairo decided an attempt should be made to establish contact. In January 1944 Major Frank Thompson was dropped into Serbia with a small SOE party to join one led by a Major Mostyn-Davies, who had made his way there from Albania.

In a preliminary expedition into Bulgaria, Mostyn-Davies was captured and shot, while Thompson only narrowly escaped. Accompanied by Scott as his radio operator Thompson then led, in a second expedition, a large group of Bulgarian partisans whom he had armed and trained in the mixed nationalities borderland after Hitler's move of the Bulgarian border westwards. The patriotic enthusiasm of the partisans appears to have persuaded Thompson to cross into Bulgaria proper before he was really satisfied with their level of training. His plan was to rendezvous with the Bulgarian partisan Chavdar Brigade based near Sofia, but contact was never established. Thompson's party was ambushed, many of the partisans killed on the spot and he and Scott were taken prisoner, Scott being wounded in the hand.

The two were interrogated by the Gestapo in the village of Litakovo. Thompson claimed prisoner-of-war status for both of them, but this was rejected on the ground that they had been captured with rebels moving against the 'legitimate' Bulgarian Government. Thompson was executed after a show trial, where he impressed his accusers by his composure. Scott had his wound attended to and on recovering the use of his hand was ordered by the Gestapo to open communication with SOE headquarters in Cairo.

Recognising that execution was the only alternative, Scott began transmitting, but in the first message omitted a security check and phrased the message to alert Cairo to his capture.

Either accidentally or because they were aware of the security check technique, his captors changed the text before despatch. Their hope was to gain information on future Allied strategic intentions from the SOE headquarters in Cairo, but they failed.

Scott was moved to Sofia at the beginning of September 1944 and housed in a Bulgarian jail. On the eve of the Red Army's declaration of war on Bulgaria on September 5, 1944, as its troops swept through Romania, Scott was informed that he would be shot. The arrival of the Russians under General Fyodor Tolbukhin came just in time to save him from execution. He was released, returned to England and received the Distinguished Conduct Medal for his service with SOE.

After demobilisation, Scott worked as an engineer. He returned to Bulgaria in 2000 to meet the few survivors of the 1944 foray into the country and visit the graves of Thompson and the partisans killed in the ambush. He was welcomed as a hero.

He is survived by his wife, Sonia, and their two daughters. (He died on September 30, 2008, aged 88)

Failure of the Mostyn-Davies and Thompson Missions to Bulgaria did not deter SOE headquarters in Cairo from trying again. Parachuting blind with virtually no information on the likely reception was discounted on this occasion; instead it was decided that entry should be from Bulgarian-occupied Greek Thrace, where SOE already had a man of the ground in the form of Major John Harington. Harington had earlier met with some success in establishing contact with Greek *Andarte* partisans in the Peloponnese, in 1943, and a year later was active with another *Andarte* group, hoping they would lead him to Bulgarian partisans over the frontier. An SOE agent keen to see some action was sent to join him.

Ian Macpherson, MC
(Obituary *The Times* January 25, 2011)

The Special Operations Executive (SOE) achieved significant successes in promoting sabotage and subversion in Axis-occupied countries during the Second World War. It also made more speculative efforts, principally to test the effectiveness and strength of the opposition movements, and

Ian Macpherson was one of the few SOE agents to undertake such a mission and survive to tell the tale.

He was commissioned into the Seaforth Highlanders in 1940 and made strenuous attempts to join a battalion in the Western Desert. He reached Cairo in 1942, having gained some priority through training in intelligence work and his language ability. He was sent first to Iraq, where the Rashid Ali coup had recently been overturned, and Persia (Iran) to glean intelligence for GHQ Cairo and the War Office.

On his return to Cairo he became a junior staff officer in the SOE office, directing and planning operations in south-eastern Europe. Eager for operational experience of some kind, he acquiesced in this, against an undertaking that he would be sent to join one of the SOE missions, 'if anything suitable comes up'. This turned out to be in Bulgaria. Bulgaria had accepted a German move through her territory to attack Greece in March 1941 and later declared war on Britain but not on the nearby Soviet Union. Macpherson spoke Russian and having consulted a primer, assessed Bulgarian as similar but with fewer grammatical complications.

Given two months to acquire a grasp of the language, learn parachuting and assimilate what was known of the opposition in Bulgaria, he was then flown to SOE's HQ in Bari to await an aircraft. The Bulgarians had taken advantage of the German invasion of Greece to occupy Thrace and as SOE already had Major John Harington there, leading a mission to the Greek *Andartes* (guerrillas), it was arranged that Macpherson should join him before they moved north over the frontier together. Accompanied by a corporal radio operator, Macpherson parachuted into Thrace in July 1944, linking up with Harington without difficulty.

Guided by the Greek *Andartes*, he and Harington crossed the Bulgarian frontier intending to separate later to try to contact the *Otechestven* (Fatherland Front), a loose affiliation of communists and other groups opposed to fascism. Brushes with the Bulgarian gendarmerie encouraged the two to stick together, and eventually they joined up with an *Otechestven* brigade near Plovdiv, 70 miles southeast of Sofia.

The partisans were eager to receive arms, and Macpherson arranged by radio with Bari for a substantial air drop to be prepared. Meanwhile events were moving swiftly elsewhere.

Russia declared war on Bulgaria at the end of August, and the communist elements of the *Otechestven* began to flex their muscles for a takeover.

Harington and Macpherson hastened to Plovdiv to make contact with the Russians to be met by polite explanations that their presence was now superfluous. Accepting the inevitable, they returned to Cairo via Turkey. In Macpherson's own words: 'It is unlikely that anything we did altered the course of events in that tip of Europe.' He was awarded the Military Cross for the coolness and skill with which he avoided the capture of his mission by the Bulgarian gendarmerie.

Ian Gibson Macpherson was born in Edinburgh in 1920 and educated at George Herriot School, from where he won a scholarship to *L'École Libre des Sciences Politiques* in Paris. After demobilization in 1946 he joined the Iraq Petroleum Company (IPC), which had been established in 1912 by the Armenian entrepreneur Calouste Gulbenkian in partnership with the Anglo-Persian Oil Company (a forerunner of BP) and other Western shareholders, to explore for oil in the Ottoman territories that became Iraq. The company's main find was at Kirkuk in Kurdish northern Iraq, where Macpherson was posted.

After serving as a representative for IPC's interest in Damascus and Beirut he returned to Kirkuk as general manager in 1957 just before Iraq's Hashemite dynasty was overthrown by the revolution of General Qasim the following year. He managed to steer the company through the difficulties caused by this revolution, notably fending off nationalisation.

He is survived by his wife, Antonia, a son and daughter.
(He died on December 1, 2010, aged 90)

Hungary

A predominantly compliant government in Budapest had taken Hungary into the war on the side of Germany at the time of Hitler's invasion of the Soviet Union in June 1941, having first allowed the passage of German troops to subdue Yugoslavia. A measure of independence had been maintained until the Red Army's advances in the spring of 1944 brought their forward echelons to the edge of the Carpathian mountains. In response to this threat to their virtually open south-eastern flank, the Germans occupied Hungary to begin construction of a defensive barrier to the expected Soviet offensive through the northern Balkan states.

Britain had been sympathetic towards Hungary's predicament from the early stages of the war and, despite the presence of Nazi supporters in and around the wartime government, it was judged that there might be sufficient latent opposition to merit SOE investigation. (A small group of potential saboteurs had been identified after Hungary's commitment to the Axis camp, but had been discovered and eliminated in early 1942.)

Long before then, however, a remarkable character who served SOE with distinction had done all he could to persuade the Hungarians to keep clear from what for them would prove to be a disastrous war.

Basil Davidson, MC
(Extract from *The Times* obituary of July 12, 2010)

Basil Davidson became one of the most authoritative writers on the 'wind of change' blowing through Africa and the often bloody aftermath. His 27 books about the continent, including the acclaimed *The Black Man's Burden* (1992), were full of sharp observations on the struggle for independence from imperial warlords and the internecine conflicts between ethnic groups to establish a nation state that often ensued. His passion for the continent also led him to research its ancient civilizations and he became a distinguished historian of Africa.

Davidson's impeccable left-wing credentials were underpinned by hid distinguished war record. He agitated for the resistance movement in wartime Hungary and later went behind enemy lines to aid Tito's partisans in the Balkans. He went on to become a journalist for *The Times* and The New Statesman before Africa became his dominating passion.

In October 1939 he was recruited into Section D of MI 6, soon to develop into the Special Operations Executive, and sent to Hungary the following January. He had two tasks in Budapest, first to establish and then run a news agency – which was legal and above-board – and second 'to promote resistance' which was neither.

While distributing British news to the Hungarian press and radio, he turned his attention to delaying, so far as appeared possible, Hungary's passage into the Nazi camp in a war which until then had gone all Hitler's way. Provided with funds which he deduced might be used for bribing local politicians, especially if sympathetic to his plan to have printed and circulated material likely to embarrass the Nazi-leaning regime and suggest an existence of a widespread ant-Fascist organization in the country.

The fall of France in June 1940 gave his London directors other things to think about and the long daily news summaries soon ceased. He persisted with both angles of his work, nevertheless, tapping informants for positive news and quoting prestigious names as sources for lines he wished to push. But by April 1941, it had become clear that Hungary was Hitler's next stop and it was time for Davidson and his non-indigenous staff to get out of Budapest. Belgrade was the most obvious haven but Yugoslavia was invaded three days later, so he and others headed for the Dalmatian coast.

Unfortunately, the two Sunderland flying boats sent from Athens to collect the British diplomats, journalists and sundry anti-Nazi friends from there had capacity for only ninety. Priority was rightly given to the wounded and foreigners certain to be shot on capture. Our Ambassador to Belgrade, Sir Ronald Campbell, stayed behind with the rest and, under pretence all were part of his staff, negotiated their transfer through Italy and the French Rivière to Spain, from where the military element went to Gibraltar.

(Basil Davidson died on July 9, 2010, aged 95)

The Hungarian Prime Minister at the time of the 1941 agreement with Germany, Count Paul Teleki, who opposed the agreement, had committed suicide when German troops crossed the Hungarian frontier on their way to Yugoslavia. He was replaced by Miklos Kallay, a man more attuned to German aspirations, but as it became clear in 1943 that Germany would eventually lose the war he let it known to the Western Allies that he was open to some form of negotiation that would, so he vainly hoped, avoid his country being overrun by the Red Army.

This hesitant, surreptitious encouragement from Hungary was suddenly given a strand of credibility by the appearance in Istanbul of one Veres Laszlo, who claimed to be a peace emissary on behalf of Kallay. This led to the dispatch of a series of SOE agents into Hungary during 1944, all of whom came to grief or were withdrawn. The only survivor of one such mission was the radio operator.

Robert Eden
(Obituary *The Times* May 1st, 2007)

Robert Eden was launched on one of the Special Operations Executive's more desperate missions, an attempt to stir up resistance against the Nazi-aligned Government in Hungary. Called up as a Territorial Army artillery officer and sent to the Middle East, after serving with the Libyan Arab Force of Bedouin operating in the desert under British officers to gather intelligence and conduct sabotage behind the Axis forward areas, he had transferred to the Cairo-controlled section of the SOE.

Training for operations in the Balkans, including crash courses in parachuting and Serbo-Croat, had followed. He and a small team of officers and radio operators were then dropped into Yugoslavia in early 1944, not to conduct clandestine operations there, but with a view to infiltrating agents across the River Drava into Hungary. The country was allied with Nazi Germany, and SOE was not sanguine about establishing a resistance movement there. But its Prime Minister, Miklos Kallay, had put out feelers to the Western Allies as an insurance policy against Soviet domination after the war, so attempts had to be made.

Agents were infiltrated by a variety of routes, but no successful contacts were made. So Eden turned his attention to guiding crashed Allied airman and escaped prisoners of war through Slovenia and Croatia to points from where they could be evacuated. He also reported on German aircraft activity in the region. In co-operation with Tito's partisans, his small group helped 150 aircrew and escaped prisoners towards safety.

On withdrawal from Yugoslavia, he was attached to 'Q' Patrol of the Special Boat Section for operations in Albania as 21st German Mountain Corps inserted after the Italian armistice in September 1943, was struggling to extract its troops from the country. After VE-Day he was sent to the Far East to help to repatriate Allied prisoners-of-war and internees formerly held by the Japanese.

This led him to Australia, from where he decided to take a

short spell of leave in New Zealand. Arriving in Auckland by flying boat, he was surprised to be ushered on to an aircraft to Wellington where he was greeted by the Prime Minister, Peter Fraser. A signal 'Eden arriving by flying boat' had led to the expectation of the imminent arrival of the British Foreign Secretary Anthony Eden, a distant cousin.

Robert John Pulleine Eden was the eldest son of Brigadier Henry Eden, who had been taken prisoner when the 51st Highland Division was obliged to surrender at St Valery-en-Caux in June 1940. He was educated at Rugby .On demobilization, he began a successful business career, while keeping up his military connections through membership of the Territorial Army SAS. He entered local government politics and became chairman of Essex County Council schools committee. Under his chairmanship, this was largely responsible for founding the Boarding Schools Association, still flourishing for independent and local education authority schools.

Just short of his 60th birthday, he bought a house on the fringe of Exmoor and took up hill farming and, as hobbies, training sheepdogs and bee-keeping. He also studied theology and became a lay reader and an assistant to the vicars of several of the more remote moorland parishes.

His marriage to the Hon Rosemary Vivian was dissolved in 1969. That year he married Elizabeth (Beth) Cleverly, who survives him, with a daughter of his first marriage and two daughters of his second.

(He died February 20, 2007, aged 87).

The fifth SOE Mission into Hungary, comprising a British officer – Major John Coates – and two Canadian-Hungarians, also met disaster, but thanks to their leader's stoicism, courage and negotiating skill all survived.

John Coates, DSO
(Obituary *The Times* March 9, 2007)

A conscientious objector on the outbreak of war, John Coates – who had read foreign languages at Cambridge – was selected after 13 months in the ranks for a commission in the Intelligence Corps. His skill and interest in languages led him, after volunteering for Combined Operations, to join No

10 (Inter-Allied) Commando as Intelligence Officer. This unit included men of nine different nationalities. Later, Coates transferred to No 30 Commando, with which he was to serve in Italy and Corsica.

Parachuted into Hungary by the SOE in September 1944, he was captured but escaped. Of all the German-occupied or satellite countries, Hungary was the least encouraging prospect for SOE-inspired subversion. The Nationalist Government was aligned to Axis interests until Miklos Kallay took over as Prime Minister in 1941. Although supporting Hitler, he had an eye to links with the Western Allies as an insurance against Soviet domination in the event of a German defeat.

In 1943 Hungary offered to surrender if the Allied armies could reach Hungary before the Soviet forces, and SOE thought it might be in with a chance. An initial, semi-diplomatic mission to Hungary, of which Coates was to have been a member, had to be abandoned after the German occupation of the country. It was consequently decided to send in a series of smaller parties to support resistance to the Germans by every means possible. Coates led one of these parties, following the reported success of another mission consisting only of a Canadian-Hungarian named Bódó. In fact, Bódó had been captured in July 1944.

Coates and two companions were dropped wide of their intended drop zone near Pécs, across the frontier with Yugoslavia, on September 13, 1944, but were captured during the next few days. He and his companions were brutally interrogated. Thanks to his stoicism and leadership over the ensuing months of imprisonment, none of them revealed the true nature of the mission, maintaining they had come to help Hungarian partisans. By sticking to their cover story and some skilful negotiation with their Hungarian captors, Coates managed to protect his men and to organize the escape of one of their group and of an SOE officer from another mission, before escaping himself in December 1944 together with his radio operator.

Coates sheltered with a Hungarian family on the outskirts of Budapest and later reported to an advance patrol of the Red Army. His bravery earned him a DSO. He returned to Hungary in 1945 to wind up SOE's commitments there and try to locate and recompense individuals who had helped the British in any way. His final posting was in Germany, where he eventually joined the Allied Control Commission.

He joined the Diplomatic Service in 1947, returning to Cambridge in 1949 to study Russian and subsequently served with the British embassies in The Hague, Vienna, Moscow and Helsinki. He took early retirement in 1962 to pursue an academic career. He held teaching appointments at the universities of Idaho and Cambridge and joined the secretariat of the Royal Society in 1964. In 1965 he was granted a research fellowship by Clare Hall, Cambridge, to complete his PhD thesis into the literature, especially the poetry, of the Komi people in the northeastern corner of European Russia. In 1968 he was appointed dean of students at the University of East Anglia and lecturer in Finno-Ugrian studies, which enabled him to continue his research interests.

His thesis on Komi poetry led to an invitation to spend two months of 1974 in the Komi autonomous republic of the Soviet Union. This visit, quite exceptional in Soviet times, marked him further as a leading authority on the language and literature of the Komi people.

Coates will be mourned by many friends, young and old, world-wide as a profoundly generous, loyal and imaginative man with an exceptional gift for languages – and who also was great fun.

He married Norma 'Bobbie' Bishop in 1946. She predeceased him, as did one of their sons. He is survived by a son and his partner of nearly thirty years, Frances Cooley.

(He died on December 25, 2006, aged 88)

Romania

Prior to Romania joining the Axis camp under Marshal Ion Antonescu in 1941, SOE had radio contact with the leader of the National Peasant Party – Luliu Maniu – who had given a half-promise of anti-German sabotage in return for financial subsidies. The possible target of principal interest to Britain was the supply to Germany from the Ploesti oilfields, but capture of the wireless transmitter brought negotiations to a halt. Subsequently, SOE's interest focused on re-establishing contact with known politically dissident groups in the country with a view to encouraging subversion. While from the strategic standpoint of the Western Allies, Romania was associated with the Russo-German Eastern Front, rather than the southern Europe campaigns, by 1943 it was judged that the Allied progress in the war merited an investigative venture.

The first led by a Captain David Russell in the spring of 1943 ended abruptly when Russell was murdered and robbed by unknown assailants. A second comprising Colonel Gardyne de Chastelain, one British and one Bulgarian officer began disastrously but eventually turned out well. Parachuted into Romania ten miles from their intended dropping zone in December 1943, the party was captured virtually at once.

De Chastelain nevertheless maintained his composure and, after being taken to Bucharest, assumed the role of negotiator on behalf of the Allies for a separate peace. With typical Romanian subtlety, he was kept on ice until the Red Army broke through the Moldavian front in August 1944 when a coup was engineered against Antonescu and de Chastelain was flown to Cairo to request Allied air support against impending German attack.

Colonel de Chastelain died in Canada and received no obituary in *The Times*. (His son, the Canadian General John de Chastelain, was a member of the international commission, comprising former President Martti Ahtisaari of Finland, the US Senator George Mitchell and himself, charged with overseeing the de-commissioning of IRA weapons in the early stages of negotiations that led up to the Good Friday Agreement of 1998).

(Colonel A G G de Chastelain, DSO, OBE died in 1974)

Two officers whose entire lives might be described as speculative ventures served SOE in a variety of roles and countries. This book would be impoverished without inclusion of their obituaries.

Colonel Andrew Croft, DSO, OBE
(Obituary *The Times* July 3, 1998)

The title of Andrew Croft's autobiography, *A Talent for Adventure* published in 1991, was something of an understatement of his remarkable life. In the 1930s he was a pioneering Arctic explorer who was able to put his experience to good use in hazardous Special Operations Executive work in Scandinavia during the Second World War. Next, he was sent to the Mediterranean where he conducted commando operations against the coasts of Axis-held France and Italy.

After the war his knowledge of cold weather fighting was a great asset in devising tactics to combat the Soviet threat on Nato's northern flank. Then, in the bitter winters experienced during the Korean War, the tests he had conducted on cold weather kit in Canada proved invaluable to Commonwealth troops. After leaving the Army he commanded the Metropolitan Police Cadet Corps.

It was the first Headmaster of Stowe, J. F. Roxburgh, who spotted Croft's potential when he chose him and two other Lancing College boys to go with him as seniors to help to found the new school in 1923. To his acknowledged qualities of leadership Croft added a sense of responsibility and – what was not so usual in schools then – an understanding of those boys who were insecure or downright vulnerable. These qualities he derived in part from his home background: his father was vicar of Kelvedon and later rural dean of Chelmsford.

From Stowe he went to Christ Church, Oxford, and from there to Germany to learn the language. He happened to be in Berlin early on the morning of February 28, 1933, and witnessed the Reichstag fire. Although, as he later recalled, the building was surrounded by Nazi Brownshirts 'I remember noting that there was no fire brigade – no one was trying to put the fire out'.

He then had a brief spell teaching at a Sussex prep school, but in the autumn of 1933 he was invited to join Martin Lindsay's three-man expedition to cross Greenland. A venture at first regarded with scepticism by the pundits, it was an outstanding success, and led to the longest self-supporting dog sledge journey ever made. In it, Croft's skill with the huskies was a major element, and he did most of the driving.

Croft spent the year 1934-35 in India as ADC to the young Maharajah of Cooch Behar, but was back in the far North in the following year, this time with an Oxford University expedition organised by Sandy (now Sir Alexander) Glen to Nordauslandet, the northernmost of the islands of Svalbard, 600 miles from the North Pole. He next had three years at Cambridge, working with Louis Clarke, the director of the Fitzwilliam Museum, and spent a winter on secondment to an expedition to Swedish Lapland where he researched into reindeer.

When war broke out in 1939 his knowledge of Arctic conditions was put to good use as a British Army liaison officer trying to organise aid via Norway to the Finnish Army in its desperate defence against the invading Soviet Union in the Winter War of 1939-40. When the Germans invaded Norway in April 1940 he eluded their clutches in Bergen and made his way over trackless mountain country to join Allied forces at Aalesund. He was evacuated to England only to be returned to Norway late in April 1940. But by that time the campaign was going badly, and all British and French forces were evacuated by early June.

In 1941 Croft was sent to Stockholm as assistant military attaché – in reality an SOE intelligence-gathering job. In neutral Sweden he rubbed shoulders with many of the German military. One of his favourite stories was how on one occasion he and the German attaché were sharing a sauna. As the temperature and humidity mounted it became a matter of pride not to be the first to quit. Eventually the German was forced to give up and as he burst from the cubicle the Swedes outside broke into a cheer. Emerging second, Croft was puzzled at this applause from the Swedes until one of their number told him they had had a bet between them that the first of the two men to be forced to leave the sauna would be regarded as the representative of the nation that was going to lose the war.

From Sweden Croft went in March 1942 to the Shetland Islands, from where, with Glen in a Catalina flown by a pilot of Coastal Command, he conducted an aerial survey of the limits of sea edge ice in the Arctic Ocean. The information gained from a series of long and hazardous flights over trackless wastes and hostile seas was vital for the routing of convoys to the Russian ports.

In 1943 Croft was sent to the Mediterranean where he launched a number of commando raids on the coasts of Italy and the South of France from bases first in North Africa and then in Corsica. Later, after the surrender of Italy, he conducted SOE operations in support of the landings on the French Riviera. These buccaneering small missions, executed without interference from the top brass, were absolutely his forte, and he was awarded the DSO.

After the war Croft was recognised internationally as a leading authority on special operations as a whole and on Arctic warfare in particular. As the Cold War developed this became of increasing significance and his War Office duties embraced attachments with the Canadian Forces for Operation *Musk Ox* in 1945-46, an operation conducted in Canada's hostile northern wastes, to test equipment and vehicles in conditions of low temperature. This was invaluable when the Korean War suddenly burst on the war-weary Western Allies in 1950, and United Nations troops found themselves battling with icy winter conditions.

In the 1950s Croft commanded successively the Junior Leaders at Plymouth and the Army Apprentices School at Harrogate. Both these appointments were highly congenial to a man who had many years before at Stowe demonstrated his ability to inspire the young.

Retiring from the Army in 1960, Croft became Commandant of the newly-formed Metropolitan Police Cadet Corps, a command he held for ten years until his final retirement in 1971 to a beautiful house at Strand on the Green, on the Thames near Kew Bridge, where he and his wife gave a warm welcome to visitors. He had been appointed OBE for his work with young soldiers in 1970.

Croft's wife Rosalind died two years ago. He is survived by three daughters.

(He died on July 3, 1998, aged 91)

It would be hardly correct to characterize the second man as a typical agent of SOE, achieving results by careful planning with close attention to their security. Peter Kemp did not live like that.

Peter Kemp, DSO, MC
(Obituary *The Times* November 6, 1993)

Peter Kemp was in many ways a throwback to an earlier era. He followed the career of what used to be called 'a soldier of fortune' if latterly under the convenient disguise of a war reporter but, in fact, he was a deeply committed reactionary who believed in bringing his convictions to the life of action. He made an early start at that when at the age of 21 he joined the Franco side in the Spanish Civil War.

He first saw fighting on the outskirts of Madrid, taking

part in street battles against Republican troops who were only a few yards away, before a chance meeting with General Millan Astray the 'Father' of the Spanish Foreign Legion led to his being offered command of his own platoon in that elite corps (an unusual distinction for a non-Spaniard). Having been several times wounded, he was put out of action in the summer of 1938 by a mortar bomb which shattered his jaw.

Back in London, he ran into an old acquaintance from Spain, Douglas Dodds-Parker (later Conservative MP for Banbury – see Chapter 5). This led to his being recruited into MI(R) a forerunner of the Special Operations Executive under whose aegis he again was allowed to assume the mantle of a military adventurer.

During the second world war he took part in a variety of cloak-and-dagger enterprises leading raids on German-held lighthouses and signal-stations around the Channel Islands, parachuting into Albania (where he found himself giving military aid to Enver Hoxha, the communist leader) vainly trying to save Poland for the West and finally intervening on behalf of the French in Indochina and of the Dutch in Indonesia. He was awarded the MC in 1941 and the DSO in 1945.

Peter Mant McIntyre Kemp was born with a conventional enough background as a son of the Empire. His early years were spent in India where his father was judge of the High Court of Bombay and not, as Kemp himself used to like to claim, the Chief Justice. Sent back to England to be educated at an early age as all children of the Raj were he went first to a prep school in Sussex, then to Wellington and finally to Trinity College, Cambridge, where he gloried in what he called his 'unfashionable Tory faith'. His original intention had been to follow in his father's footsteps by reading for the Bar but the outbreak of the Spanish Civil War in July 1936 diverted him from that path for ever.

Permitted to follow his own inclinations, Kemp would certainly have elected to stay in the Army after the war but the tuberculosis that he had contracted in the Far East led to his being invalided out. His health never quite recovered and he was forced to find work selling insurance for Imperial Life, only retiring in 1980. The company was unusually tolerant of his wanderlust and, provided he brought them in business over the course of a year, made no objections to his various forays.

So it was that, unable to fight, Kemp built up a parallel career as a war reporter and trouble-shooter. He went to Hungary in 1956 to cover the Soviet invasion, nominally as *The Tablet*'s correspondent, and in 1965 was sent by the *News of the World* to Southeast Asia write a series of articles on the theme of communist subversion in the region. He also made more than tourist's visits to Central and South America, Rhodesia and the Congo and towards the end of his life returned to Albania for *The Sunday Telegraph*. He wrote a number of vivid books about his exploits and experiences: *Mine Were of Trouble* (1957), *No Colours or Crest* (1958), *Alms for Oblivion* (1961) and his autobiography, *The Thorns of Memory* (1990).

He was twice married and twice divorced.
(He died on October 30, 1993 aged 88)

There were other speculative ventures by courageous and resourceful men and women for whom, for one reason or another, no obituary appeared in *The Times*. One very speculative venture was pursued by Captain D. J. 'Don' Stott of SOE who conducted a one-man campaign in Athens in the autumn of 1944.

A New Zealand officer of SOE, Stott had taken part in the destruction of the Asopos railway viaduct in June 1943 (see Chapter 6) and returned by parachute at the end of September together with Captain Harry McIntyre. Their mission was to examine the chances of destroying German aircraft on airfields around Athens, destroying the Asopos viaduct again, as the Germans had repaired it, and preventing the destruction of the Marathon dam in the event of a precipitate German withdrawal, as it controlled the water supply to the Greek capital.

Having decided after detailed and hazardous reconnaissance that attack on the airfields was impractical and the Germans were giving no signs of withdrawal – precipitate or otherwise – he decided to open negotiations with right-wing political leaders in Athens with a view to gaining their agreement to co-operation with British Forces when German evacuation came. This move was motivated by his deep distrust of the communist-controlled Greek National Liberation Front that was planning to seize power when the Germans left.

The full and complex story of Stott's negotiations and contacts with Greek and German representatives is admirably told in Richard Clogg's chapter on the subject in Mark Seaman's collection of SOE ventures *Special Operations Executive; A New Instrument of War* (2006). Stott was not successful in his negotiations but could not be faulted for sheer audacity and determination. He returned safely to SOE headquarters in Cairo but was captured and executed by the Japanese after landing in North Borneo for investigations on SOE's behalf in March 1945.

Mention has already been made of the venture by Philip Worrall into German prisoner-of-war camps holding British troops (Chapter 6) but surely the most intrepid venture of all was made by Mrs Olga Jackson.

Belgian but married to an Englishman, she was parachuted into Belgium at the moment when Montgomery's 21st Army Group was poised to sweep into the country from France. Although she spoke no German, her task was to make contact with as many senior German officers as possible and undermine their morale by pointing out that their war was already lost, as it certainly was; she achieved no recorded result but survived.

12

Appraisal

SOE reached its maximum strength in the late summer of 1944 with a complement of just under 13,000. Of this total, 450 were drawn from the women's Auxiliary Territorial Service (ATS), 60 from the Women's Auxiliary Air Force and 1,500 from the FANY; 1,200 were civilians. Many of the 1,362 of officer status of both sexes were of outstanding quality, as borne out by the selection of obituaries in this book. That many achieved success in their subsequent private lives offers support for the selection process, although those responsible for recruitment were obliged to draw from a restricted field. The Special Operations Executive retained its reputation for enthusiastic amateurism until its disbandment in 1946, but the heroism and initiative displayed by many of its agents ensured that reputation won both admiration and respect.

This summary and tribute should not be allowed to obscure faults in the system and human frailties that impaired the smooth and successful running of the organization from time to time. Anyone who has ever had charge of an outstation – civilian or military – will be familiar with the suspicion that those 'back at headquarters' have lost their judgement, if not their minds. Confidence in the Baker Street headquarters at regional headquarters overseas and that of agents in the field seldom wavered once Major-General Colin Gubbins had taken over responsibility as Executive Director in 1943. Agents directed by the regional staffs in Cairo and later in Algiers and then Bari – for the southern Europe and the Mediterranean theatre – and by Meerut in India and later Kandy in Ceylon, for South East Asia Command, occasionally had reason to question their instructions.

There were two principal reasons for this: first, lack of understanding at headquarters of conditions on the ground and second, a tendency by headquarters staff to try to over-control missions or agents in the field. The most frustrating problem for those working with or among Resistance groups was the long delay and sometimes failure to deliver requested air-drops of weapons and explosives, leading to loss of partisan confidence in the undertakings made to them by SOE agents urging them into action against Axis forces.

It would be invidious to mark out individuals for apparent failure in these respects but one short extract from one obituary and two others in full may give a flavour of individual performance.

Lord Glenconner

(Extract from *The Times* obituary of October 6, 1983)
Lord Glenconner, who has died in Corfu at the age of 84, had throughout his life been occupied chiefly with the considerable industrial and commercial interest which he had inherited and with others which he had acquired. But he was also devoted to the fine arts, and to literature, and practically throughout his life was an extensive traveller.

During the Second World War he was head of the Cairo office of the Special Operations Executive from 1942 to 1943. As such he was responsible for SOE activities in the Balkans at a critical time, as well as in the Middle East and Turkey.
(He died on October 4, 1983, aged 84)

The brevity of mention of his work during the war rather suggests that Glenconner may not have been a success as director of SOE operations in the Balkans. The truth is that, having been responsible for the south-east Europe section in Baker Street for some time, he was posted to Cairo to try to sort out problems within the staff there, and then leave senior army officers responsible for one or more countries to get on with the detailed planning and direction. He appears to have been successful in that role. He was replaced in Cairo by a soldier:

Major-General W. A. M. Stawell, CB, CBE, MC

(Obituary *The Times* June 20, 1987)
Stawell, an intelligence staff officer who organized much of the secret war against the Nazis behind their lines and then

helped in the rehabilitation of post-war Europe, has died aged 92.

William Arthur Macdonald Stawell was born in British India on January 22, 1895. His father was in the Indian Civil Service – that it is to say, was one of the thousand-odd British civilians who governed the sub-continent.

He went from Clifton to Woolwich, and was commissioned into the Royal Engineers on the outbreak of the Great War in 1914. By the end of it he had fought in Macedonia, Serbia, Bulgaria and Turkey as well as in France and received the MC for gallantry. Like many Engineers, Billy Stawell had an orderly mind. From 1931 he served almost continuously for 17 years on the Staff, at the War Office, at Aldershot, in India and in England again.

In 1940 he was back at the War Office, as a brigadier, to be assistant director of military intelligence. He then had a short spell commanding 148 Infantry Brigade. Fearsome staff quarrels in Cairo, nothing to do with him, created a vacancy there for an officer of his standing to take charge of the Special Operations Executive's work in the Near East. The post in question had changed hands six times in three years. Stawell at least knew something about intelligence; he seemed fit for the job.

He found out at once that he was in charge of a subversive force, not an intelligence organization; and realized also that the type of command he could exercise was quite unlike a normal soldier's role. SOE's tasks were so intricate, so diverse, and so secret that its high command could play only a small and remote part in them. This sort of work needs many years preparation, which SOE, not formed till July 1940, did not have. Stawell fought SOE's corner as nimbly as he could, at an exalted level – with his friend Field Marshal Alexander and other Allied commanders in the Mediterranean – and did not try to interfere with agents' work in the field.

By December 1944 the strain had become too much for him, and he returned to England on sick leave. He recovered enough to take up in November 1945, another administrative post as deputy chief of operations for UNRRA, the United Nations relief body which was wrestling with Europe's hordes of refugees. He then spent two years as deputy chief of intellignece for the Control Commission in Germany.

The Army by this time was much shrunk in size; the Cold War had replaced the hot; he had turned 50, and retired. He had been appointed CBE in 1944 and CB in 1945 in recognition of his work for SOE.

He settled near Lowestoft, to sail and to play golf, with his wife. In 1926 he had married Amy Bowring, a New Yorker, who died last year. They had one son.

(He died on June 11, 1987, aged 92)

The headquarters and base at Guyotvile a little to the west of Algiers, codenamed *Massingham* and set up after the Allied invasion of French North Africa in December 1942, to direct SOE operations in the western Mediterranean theatre, including southern France and Italy, was criticized for careless packing of the parachutes dropping arms and supplies to partisans. Francis Cammaerts (see Chapter 8) sent a furious signal to Baker Street complaining of this problem and an expert was sent posthaste to Algiers to improve matters.

After Colonel Douglas Dodds-Parker (see Chapter 5) arrived to take charge of *Massingham* in January 1943 the headquarters functioned well; although arrangements for holding agents in Algiers before despatch on their respective missions remained primitive, leading to many complaints.

The SOE headquarters and base for what had been *Massingham*'s area of responsibility moved to Bari in early 1944. This led to two complaints from agents, notably in Albania and northern Italy. The first centred on a perception that the headquarters staff had taken on the euphoria of victory – possibly fuelled by the bucolic atmosphere of the Adriatic port – and were neglecting their duties. Having not received long-promised arms and supplies by parachute, George Fielding (see Chapter 11) signalled testily from Forni Avoltri in northern Italy: 'More of the spirit of the Battle of Britain and less of the bottle of Bari.' Some effort was made to tighten things up in Bari but a more sinister complaint was shortly to emerge.

Dating back to the time when British support to Mihailovic and his Chetniks was switched to Tito and his Partisans, which of course occurred while operations in Yugoslavia were directed from Cairo, suspicions began to arise in the minds of agents in the field that some SOE staff officers were of communist inclination. This concern took serious hold after the move from Algiers to Bari, even to conjecture that some of the staff officers were agents of the Soviet NKVD.

These hypotheses partly owed their origin in the Foreign Office policy that it would be unethical to supply arms to contesting guerilla groups if there was the slightest possibility that they would use them to fight each other, rather than the Germans. Such fears were certainly justified in Albania, northern Italy and Yugoslavia – with some serious reservations in France concerning the political motivations of the communist *Francs-tireurs et partisans*, as distinct from the Gaullist *Forces françaises de l'intérieur*.

While investigations into complaints about the political leanings of the staff at Bari revealed some of moderate left-wing views, the suggestion that they were communist or communist-controlled was proved to be fanciful. The communist conspiracy theory generated by SOE agents in Albania is examined in detail by Roderick Bailey in his book, *The Wildest Province* (2008), and comprehensively disproved.

In summary, while the early concepts of SOE operations in Europe and Scandinavia may certainly be faulted for their planning and occasional political insensitivity, not to mention naivety in the case of Holland, and a failure to pass lessons learned by one Baker Street section to another, the introduction of more experienced Directors showed much improvement.

The situation in South East Asia, where information gathering and then operations were directed by the India Mission in Meerut, then from Kandy under the mantle of Force 136, benefited from sound direction from the outset. The key figure in this was Colin Hercules Mackenzie.

Colin H. Mackenzie, CMG

(Obituary *The Times* December 23, 1986)

Colin Hercules Mackenzie was born on October 5, 1898, and educated at Eton and King's College, Cambridge, where he was senior scholar, got a first in Economics, and won the Chancellor's Medal for English Verse. During the First World War he served with the Scots Guards in France and suffered a serious wound, resulting in amputation of his left leg from the hip.

His business career was with the Glasgow cotton firm of J & P Coats, which he joined as their first graduate trainee. By his early twenties he was on the board, where his outstanding intelligence made him effective in debate, and where he also showed a capacity for taking decisions. In his wide travels for the company – with which he remained, apart from war service, until his retirement in 1958 – he became convinced that world markets could not be supplied satisfactorily from Britain alone. His greatest business achievement was to bring a sometimes reluctant board to share his belief, and the Coats mills overseas, particularly those in Asia and South America, are a lasting tribute to his flair.

His record during the Second World War, though very little known, was of real importance. When SOE decided that a separate operational unit should be set up in India, the Viceroy, Lord Linlithgow, who had been a fellow director on the Coats board, suggested that Mackenzie should be given command. The new unit, called Force 136, (from December 1944) developed rapidly as it established political, economic and military missions in the five countries of South-East Asia Command.

Its contribution in the Burma campaign was, in one instance, vital. In the Sittang valley the lives of about 2,000 men were saved by the action of Force 136 guerrillas in preventing the Japanese from reaching Toungoo before the British 14th Army. Mackenzie was the mainspring of that preventive action, for without his efforts the guerrilla force would never have existed.

The Colonial government-in-exile had managed to persuade General Oliver Leese, commander of all land forces in SEAC, to ban the issue of arms to anyone associated with the Burmese nationalist movement. Mackenzie would not accept the order. The unarmed Karens had suffered murderous reprisals by the Japanese the previous year for helping Force 136 agents, and Mackenzie told Mountbatten, the supreme commander, that to deny arms, even for self-defence, to the Burmese partisans was to condemn them to death.

Mountbatten overruled Leese's order, men and arms were dropped, and the ensuing operation held the Japanese 15th Division for ten days while British troops captured Toungoo for the loss of some 60 men, though Mountbatten had thought the price of its capture might be 3,000 lives.

After his retirement from Coats, Mackenzie was chairman of the Scottish committee of the Arts Council from 1962 to 1970. In this post he used his business acumen and diplomatic skill to win for Scotland a proper share of the national allocation of funds for the arts. On his personal initiative the Western Theatre Ballet was brought to Scotland to become the now highly successful Scottish Ballet Company. During his chairmanship the Scottish arts committee was reconstituted as the Scottish Arts Council – further evidence of his success in raising the profile of the arts in Scotland. In 1970 he was awarded an Hon LLD by St Andrews.

(He died on December 21, 1986, aged 88).

A more critical view of the accomplishments of the India Mission/ Force 136 and its direction is made by Dr Charles Cruickshank in his *SOE in the Far East* (1983). His book is authoritative and thoroughly researched, providing detailed accounts of operations in the Far East, but his critique in the final chapter arouses controversy.

His principal criticism is that political direction from London, including that from Winston Churchill, revealed a fundamental misunderstanding of conditions in the Far East and, in consequence, opportunities for sabotage were neglected. Further, he attributes this failing in the direction of the SOE Missions and agents in the Far East to control being in civilian hands, i.e. those of Colin Mackenzie, rather than in military hands. Emphasizing this point, he suggests if Mountbatten, as C-in-C South East Asia Command, had placed the SOE missions entirely under military control the war in the Far East would have been significantly shortened.

The argument in support of Cruickshank's case for sabotage has support in the final analysis of Operation *Longcloth*: the 'Chindit' Long Range Penetration Group plan to disrupt Japanese supply lines to their divisions in Northern Burma facing the Chinese under the American General Stilwell in early 1943. Despite the conclusion of the Official History that 'The operation had no strategic value,' post-war investigation revealed that the Japanese deployed three first-class divisions to try to intercept and destroy the Chindits and the whole campaign plan of General Mutaguchi – who later commanded the Japanese 15th Army – was changed in light of damage the Chindits had inflicted on Japanese lines of communication. Against this, however, account must be taken of the airlift required to supply 3,000 men advancing in eight columns through the jungle, and that the Chindits suffered 30 percent casualties, and many of those who returned were never fit to fight again.

Although Dr Cruickshank credits Colin Mackenzie with trying to keep London off his (Mackenzie's) back – and consequently off the backs of his agents – by stalling in response to demands that SOE operations should be directed towards sabotage rather than subversion or the building-up of guerilla forces, he still implies that a switch of tactics to sabotage would have been beneficially decisive to the Allied cause. Such sabotage as was achieved against the Japanese by SOE does not support this assertion.

Attitudes of the native population, other than that of the Burmese hill tribes who were steadfast in their support, were not as naturally in support of 'liberation' as were the peoples of German-occupied Europe. This was in part due to Asian 'fatalism' and part to the uncertainty of what reversion to colonial rule would bring.

The Times obituary for Dr Cruickshank, published on February 23, 1989, included mention of his history of SOE in the Far East without comment. The reference to his history of the Greek and Crete campaigns in 1941 contained the following extract:

> 'He blamed Eden and Wavell for allowing wrong decisions to be made and contended that the British should never have set foot on the Greek mainland; instead they should have concentrated on making Crete impregnable'.
> (Dr Cruickshank died on February 19, 1989, aged 74)

It is always risky for a professional of one discipline to comment on the ability or intellectual processes of those of a different discipline. Dr Cruickshank's propositions regarding the benefits of sabotage in the Far East and the strategic significance of Crete – quite aside from making the island impregnable when it was impossible to provide it with more than brief and spasmodic air cover from Egypt – do suggest that he was regarding each of these situations from an academic rather than a practical standpoint.

SOE had many critics both during and after the Second World War. Some of the criticism was certainly valid but imagine the chorus of complaint that would have arisen if nothing had been done to plan or foster sabotage and subversion in territories held by the enemy. 'Why on earth has no one thought of blowing the bridge

at so-and-so or arming the partisans in somewhere or other......'
and so on. That so much was achieved was due to the imagination
and administrative attention of the planners and the immense
courage and resolution of the men and women who put their lives
at risk – and who in many instances lost them – in order to carry
the war to the enemy.

Select Bibliography

Books

Bailey, Roderick (2008), *The Wildest Province, SOE in the Land of the Eagle*, Jonathan Cape.

Bailey, Roderick (2009), *Forgotten Voices of the Secret War*, CPI Cox & Wyman, Reading.

Binney, Marcus (2002), *The Women Who Lived For Danger*, Hodder & Stoughton, London.

Cruickshank, Dr Charles (1983), *Special Operations Executive in the Far East*, Oxford University Press.

Foot, Professor M. R. D. (2001), *SOE in the Low Countries*, St Ermin's Press in association with Little, Brown and Company (UK), London.

Foot, Professor M. R. D. (2004), *History of the Second World War; SOE in France*, Frank Cass, London.

Foot, Professor M. R. D. and Langley, J. M, (1979), *MI 9: Escape and Evasion 1939-1945*, Book Club Associates by arrangement with Bodley Head.

Ford, Roger (2004), *Steel From The Sky: The Jedburgh Raiders, France 1944*, Weidenfeld & Nicolson, London.

Liddell Hart, Sir Basil H., (1970), *History of the Second World War*, Book Club Associates, London.

Mackenzie, Professor William (2000), *The Secret History of SOE, The Special; Operations Executive 1940-1945*, St Ermin's Press, London.

Seaman, Mark (2006), Edited, *Special Operations Executive: A New Instrument of War*, Routledge Taylor and Francis Group, London and New York.

Spencer Chapman, F. (1949), *The Jungle is Neutral*, Chatto and Windus, London.

Stafford, David (2000), *Secret Agent: The True Story of the Special Operations Executive*, BBC WorldWide Limited, Woodlands.

Articles: from Mark Seaman's *Special Operations Executive: A New Instrument of War*, (2006) Routledge Taylor and Francis Group, London and New York.

Bailey, Roderick, (2006), *SOE in Albania: the 'conspiracy theory' reassessed.*

Clogg, Richard, (2006), *'Negotiations of a complicated character' Don Stott's 'adventures' in Athens, October–November 1943.*

Foot, Professor M. R. D. (2006), *SOE in the Low Countries.*

Kraglund, Ivor (2006), *SOE and Milorg: 'Thieves in the same market'.*

Jespersen, Knud J. V., (2006). *SOE in Denmark.*

Pearton, Maurice, (2006), *SOE in Romania.*

Woods, Christopher, (2006), *SOE in Italy.*

Index

Page references in bold refer to pages in the plate section